A Basic Introduction to the New Testament

# A Basic Introduction to the

# New Testament

*Edited by Robert C. Walton*

SCM PRESS LTD · LONDON

First published as Parts One and Four of
*A Source Book of the Bible for Teachers*,
edited by Robert C. Walton, SCM Press Ltd 1970

334 00073 4

First published in this edition 1980 by SCM Press Ltd,
58 Bloomsbury Street, London WC1

Photoset by Granada Graphics Ltd
and printed in Great Britain by
Fletcher and Son Ltd, Norwich

# CONTENTS

# INTRODUCTION

Straightforward, matter-of-fact information about the Bible is not always easy to come by. On closer inspection, books with promising titles often prove too superficial or too complex, presuppose specialist knowledge or engage in special pleading.

This *Basic Introduction to the New Testament*, and its companion volume on the Old Testament, set out to present enough information to make the reader feel at home in the way modern scholars understand the Bible and to provide a basis for exploring the results of their work further without losing sight of the main contours of the landscape. After short discussions of the nature of the Bible and the way in which modern scholars approach it, a series of articles covers the historical, social, cultural and religious setting of the New Testament. Against this background there are sections on the nature of the gospels, the message and ministry of Jesus, the life and thought of St Paul and the early church. A list of books for further reading gives some guidance as to where more detailed information can be found.

The articles were originally commissioned for *A Source Book of the Bible for Teachers*, first published by SCM Press in 1970 and still available. Because the *Source Book* contains a good deal of material relevant only to teachers it seemed worth while to reissue separately the sections specifically on the Bible so that they could be used by students (who will find these books particularly useful in studying or revising for examinations), clergy and any other interested readers.

# ILLUSTRATIONS

# 1 What is the Bible?

'The book of books, the storehouse and magazine of life and comfort, the holy scriptures.' This is George Herbert's answer to the question which is the title of this article. He was a seventeenth-century parson and poet, a man of deep and sensitive faith, a Christian of mature understanding. Such an answer, however, is not enough for the twentieth-century. In a secular age, to say that the Bible is 'the word of God' or that it enshrines 'divine revelation' is to use phrases which have lost their meaning. They are vague and imprecise and belong to a different world from that of a present-day audience.

What, then, is the Bible? It is not, from a literary point of view, a book, though it is normally bound between two covers, often of funereal black. Between these covers are two Testaments, the Old and the New. The Old Testament is a selection of the literature of the Israelite people over a thousand years of their history, roughly comparable to the English literature which has survived from the Anglo-Saxon Chronicle to the writings of Sir Winston Churchill. The comparison is, of course, inexact. There is a far greater volume of English literature, partly because the English suffered no foreign invasion since the Norman Conquest; still more, because since the fifteenth century books have been printed, not inscribed by hand. The New Testament is a selection of the literature of a new religion – Christianity – in the first hundred years of its existence. These selections are to some extent arbitrary, depending partly upon what chanced to escape destruction, but also upon the needs of the communities which preserved the writings. There was the wastage of the years but also deliberate acceptance and rejection.

This literature is not all 'religious' in the narrow sense of that word. In the Old Testament there are tales of long ago which, like the Norse sagas or the story of King Arthur and the Knights of the Round Table, tell of the nation's origins and reveal the inward, intuitive interpretation which the people of Israel put upon the realities of their national life. There are many historical narratives, and like any shelf of history books these vary both in accuracy and in literary quality. There are codes of law; reporting of events which today we should call 'current affairs'; protests against social injustice; poetry and songs both sacred and secular and a special kind of literature which has preserved the spoken and written message of the prophets. The New Testament begins with four brief records of the life of Jesus and the first three of these – the Gospels of Mark, Matthew and Luke – are linked together in a particular literary relationship. Some events in the early history of the Christian church are recorded in the Acts of the Apostles, and there is a selection of letters written by Paul of Tarsus and by others to warn, encourage and instruct individuals or the members of young churches, in places like Corinth, Ephesus, Philippi or Rome.

In the varied literature of the Old Testament we can read about the fluctuating fortunes of the people of Israel. They began as nomadic tribesmen, some of whom had escaped from slavery in Egypt, who slowly infiltrated into the land of Canaan until at last they possessed it. Then they changed their way of life, ceasing to be 'wandering Arameans' and settling down in fortified villages and walled towns. About 1000 BC they were welded into a single nation by a remarkable king named David, under whose leadership, and that of his son Solomon, Israel became an empire with influence and prestige in Middle-East politics. After Solomon's death the nation split into two separate kingdoms; Israel in the north and Judah in the south. The dreams of empire and world power declined and both nations were overwhelmed by more powerful neighbours. When the Old Testament ends and the New Testament begins, Israel is an unimportant outpost of the Roman empire. The ministry of Jesus was exercised, the Christian church took root, in a world dominated by Roman power.

## The arrangement of the Bible

By modern standards, the books of the Bible are arranged in a most arbitrary and confusing way. The thirty-nine books of the Old Testament are not printed in the order in which they were written, which would enable us to trace more easily the development of Israelite thought and experience. Moreover, many of the books consist of different strands of writing by different authors which, at a later stage, have been woven together by an editor. Two examples may be given. The book of Genesis, which is printed first in the Bible, consists of at least three separate strands of writing by different authors which, at a later time, were amalgamated by someone else. The earliest of these strands was probably written down about the time of David (c.1000 BC), though it tells of events which belong to a much earlier period. Another strand of tradition was later woven in with this, and Genesis was finally edited in its present form by members of the priestly class round about 400 BC.

The second example is the book of Isaiah. It consists of three separate collections of writings. Chapters 1–39 refer mostly to events which occurred in the lifetime of the prophet Isaiah (c.740–701 BC), though there are insertions of a later date. Chapters 40–55 consist of prophecies by an unknown author living towards the end of the exile (c.542–538 BC), while chapters 55–66 contain oracles by unknown men living in Palestine about 450 BC.

## The truth of the Bible

The Bible is more than 'a slab of ancient history in archaic language'. It contains many different kinds of truth. It is, in part, a source book for the history and social life of Israel, and without this information the nation's religion cannot be understood. It reflects the nation's way of life, reveals its developing standards and values, and bears witness to the head waters which nourished and sustained its soul. It is also the record of the spiritual wrestlings, questionings and affirmations of a deeply religious people, and traces their progress and their decline in thought and action towards a deeper understanding of God's purpose. It contains, in the New Testament, documents which preserve in rather fragmentary form recollections of the life and ministry, the death and resurrection of Jesus of Nazareth, interpretations of those events, and information about the early formative years of the Christian church.

At first sight it may seem that there is little of

religious value in narratives which tell of kings crowned and buried or deposed and assassinated, and of armies defending frontiers or extending a nation's territory by conquest; little to stimulate man's spiritual quest in the enunciation of laws which one finds in the books of Exodus and Deuteronomy; little to help a man to worship in the often unbridled denunciations of the prophets. Let us be honest and admit that there is nickel among the gold. Yet – and it is this which makes the Bible relevant in every age and gives it unity – all these activities by which a nation lives are declared to be the direct concern of God. When a historian or chronicler records victory or defeat in battle, he sees behind the event the overruling purposes of God. When a lawyer codifies a set of laws, and includes one about safety precautions for houses with flat roofs (Deut.22.8), he is writing down 'the commandments, the statutes and the judgments of the Lord'. When a prophet denounces greed and exploitation he prefaces his stern warning with the phrase, 'Thus saith the Lord', and when he speaks of people abiding 'in a peaceful habitation, in secure dwellings and in quiet resting places' (Isa.32.18), he is transmitting to sorely battered men and women a promise of God. This unity is the reason why the biblical library may properly be bound up as one book. Every part of this corpus of literature, whether poetry, law, or prophecy; whether recollections of the deeds and words of Jesus, or letters to young churches, speaks of the will of God, the acts of God, the purpose of God.

ROBERT C. WALTON

ΜΑΤΑΚΑΙΓΡΑϨΟΝ
ΟΓΔΟΗΚΟΝΤΑΚΑΙ
ΕΠΗΝΕΣΕΝΟΚ͞Ϲ͞
ΟΙΚΟΝΟΜΟΝΤΗϹ
ΑΔΙΚΙΑϹΟΤΙϷΡΟ
ΝΙΜΩϹΕΠΟΙΗϹΕ
ΟΤΙϷΡΟΝΙΜΩΤΕ
ΡΟΙΟΙΥΙΟΙΤΟΥΑΙ͞Ϣ͞
ΝΟϹΤΟΥΤΟΥΥΠΕΡ
ΤΟΥϹΥΙΟΥϹΤΟΥϷϢ͞
ΤΟϹΕΙϹΤΗΝΓΕΝΕ
ΑΝΤΑΥΤΗΝΕΑΥΤΩ
ΕΙϹΙΝΚΑΙΕΓΩΥΜΙΝ
ΛΕΓΩΕΑΥΤΟΙϹΠΟΙ
ΗϹΑΤΕϷΙΛΟΥϹΕΚ
ΤΟΥΜΑΜΩΝΑΤΗϹ
ΑΔΙΚΙΑϹΙΝΑΟΤΑΝ
ΕΚΛΙΠΗΔΕΞΩΝ
ΤΑΙΥΜΑϹΕΙϹΤΑϹ
ΩΝΙ
ΟΠΙϹ
ΧΙϹΤⲰ
ΛΩΠΙϹ
ΚΑΙΟΕΝΕΛΑΧΙϹ
ΑΔΙΚΟϹΚΑΙΕΠϷΛ
ΛΩΑΔΙΚΟϹΕϹΤΙΝ
ΕΙΟΥΝΕΝΤΩΑΔΙ
ΚΩΜΑΜΩΝΑΠΙ
ϹΤΟΙΟΥΚΕΓΕΝΕϹⲰⲚ
ΤΟΑΛΗΘΙΝΟΝΤΙϹ
ΥΜΙΝΠΙϹΤΕΥϹΕΙ
ΚΑΙΕΙΕΝΤΩΑΛΛΟ

ΠΑΝΤΑϷΙΛΑΡΓΥΡΙ
ΥΠΑΡΧΟΝΤΕϹΚΑΙ
ΕΞΕΜΥΚΤΗΡΙΖΟΝ
ΑΥΤΟΝ
ΚΑΙΕΙΠΕΝΑΥΤΟΙϹΥ
ΜΕΙϹΕϹΤΕΟΙΔΙΚΑΙ
ΟΥΝΤΕϹΕΑΥΤΟΥϹ
ΝⲰΠΙΟΝΤⲰΝΑΝ
ΘΡⲰΠⲰΝΟΔΕΘ͞Ϲ͞
ΓΙΝⲰϹΚΕΙΤΑϹΚΑΡ
ΔΙΑϹΥΜⲰΝΟΤΙΤ
ΕΝΑΝΘΡⲰΠΟΙϹΥϮ
ΛΟΝΒΔΕΛΥΓΜΑΕΝ
ΠΙΟΝΤΟΥΘ͞Υ͞
ΟΝΟΜΟϹΚΑΙΟΙΠΡ
ϷΗΤΑΙΜΕΧΡΙΙⲰΑΝ
ΝΟΥΑΠΟΤΟΤΕΗΒ͞ι͞
ΛΕΙΑΤΟΥΘ͞Υ͞ΕΥΝΓΓΕ
ΛΙΖΕΤΑΙ
ΟΥΝΟΜΟΥΜΙΑΝ
ΚΑΙΡΕΑΝΠΕϹΙΝ
ΠΑϹΟΑΠΟΛΥⲰΝΤΗ
ΓΥΝΑΙΚΑΑΥΤΟΥΚΑΙ
ΓΑΜⲰΝΕΤΕΡΑΝΜΟΙ
ΧΕΥΕΙΚΑΙΠΑϹΟΑΠ
ΛΕΛΥΜΕΝΗΝΑΠΟ
ΑΝΔΡΟϹΓΑΜⲰΝΜΟΙ
ΧΕΥΕΙ
ΑΝΘΡⲰΠΟϹΔΕΤΙϹΗ

# 2 The Biblical Scholar and his Tools

What is the Bible? The previous section compared a seventeenth-century answer with one which might be given today. But for the same contrast, we might choose a period even nearer home. In the Bible, 'every scientific statement is infallibly accurate, all its history and narrations of every kind are without any inaccuracy'. That verdict comes from mid-Victorian England, from a popular manual much used by potential clergy, at a time when the church had a virtual monopoly on education. Doubts might be stirring, particularly as science began to raise serious problems, but a similar view was shared by the vast majority of Christians. To challenge it publicly in England was to invite personal abuse, dismissal, even legal action. *Essays and Reviews*, a collection of essays by Oxford scholars, was condemned after a petition signed by 11,000 clergy and over 150,000 laity, when its most provocative essay merely urged that the Bible should be approached like any other book.

The change to a more modest assessment of the Bible has happened in just over a century, not a long time alongside its whole history. It came about because questions were asked quite unlike any others in the past. These questions were prompted by a revolution which has affected not only the Bible, but the entire modern world.

### The beginnings of modern biblical scholarship

At the end of the eighteenth century, an old world was showing signs of strain. A political and social revolution was under way, and with it came another in the realm of ideas, with new philosophical questioning and the slow development of the scientific method. Its consequence was that nothing was accepted any more simply because it was old, honoured, accepted; it all had to be tested, for the new principle was 'begin from doubt and build up knowledge on well-established foundations'. Even the Bible was not exempt.

The traditional claim was that the Bible was the word of God. The question now was: if that is so, how is it so? Is the Bible really different from other books? Is it true? Is it an accurate record? The only way to find out was to look and see, and so modern scholarship began. The chief questioners were not outsiders, but were themselves Christians, who did not hesitate to apply the strictest tests to their beliefs. This is not always recognized, but it is a tribute to the integrity of the first pioneers.

### What is 'criticism'?

Professional study of the Bible by scholars is usually called 'criticism'. What is meant by the word, however, is not always clear, and it can give a misleading impression, because it has two different senses. In everyday talk, we use 'criticism' in an unfavourable sense, to mean passing a negative judgment on, finding fault with. But 'criticism' also has a more specialist sense, as when we talk about artistic, literary or musical criticism. Here the word describes a method of interpretation which draws out the qualities of a work in a systematic way, and it need have no unfavourable overtones. After all, critics often write good reviews.

Now, because of the way in which biblical criticism had to begin, challenging accepted and often dearly cherished views, and because of the sometimes unwelcome conclusions that it had to come to, it was taken very much as criticism in the unfavourable sense, and this association still clings to it. But the aim and ideal of scholarly investigation is criticism in the second sense: a systematic attempt at *understanding*, by examining and explaining the form, content and background of the Bible in the light of all available and relevant knowledge.

If he is going to understand, the critic needs to ask the right questions, those that will help him to express his subject in an undistorted way. With the Bible, finding the right questions was not easy at first, and there were some false starts before the proper approach was found.

### Asking the right questions

As we saw, the first kind of question to appear concerned the Bible as authoritative and holy Scripture: 'Is this true ?', 'Did that happen ?', 'Is there a possible explanation for this ?' There were great arguments about whether Genesis could be reconciled with science or whether the Israelites could have crossed the Red Sea with dry feet, or whether Moses could have written the books which bear his name, or whether Jesus could have turned water into wine. Each of these questions was discussed as though the whole fate of the Bible depended on the answer.

At the same time, however, such discussions came in the way of seeing what the Bible might be if it were allowed to speak for itself. They showed too much eagerness to make the Bible measure up to a particular set of standards. They tended to involve only a few incidents in the Bible at the expense of the rest. They were often about a principle rather than what the Bible actually contained. Above all, they ignored one all-important fact: the writers of the books of the Bible were different from us in many ways. Their world was different, their way of thinking was different, the questions they asked were different. Another approach was needed.

As they gained experience, scholars learnt to match their own questioning to that of the *world* they were investigating. They learnt that they had to do more than look at a book by itself; they had to recreate its world. It might be Palestine in the tenth century BC or Babylon in the sixth or Corinth in the first century AD; only when there was better knowledge of how people in these places and times lived and thought and spoke would the relevant parts of the Bible take their place in the new picture.

A useful illustration of this development has been given by Dr Leonard Hodgson; he comments that:

> modern zoology began when, instead of relying on Aristotelian and heraldic representations of animals in traditional bestiaries, men based their research on the observation of the actual nature and behaviour of living creatures . . . As a result of this last century's biblical studies, we are at a similar turning point in the history of Christian theology . . . A hundred years ago our forefathers looked to the Bible in the same way that mediaeval zoologists looked to Aristotle and heraldic bestiaries. To their successors' substituting of observation of actual animals corresponds our

attention to the historical provenance of the biblical writings.

This meant cultivating a historical sense. That, too, has been developed only over the last century. But now if affects almost any arts subject, from music to languages, and even some of the sciences. We begin to understand a thing by looking at its origins and discovering how it came to be so.

Biblical criticism had been in progress some time before this point became clear. And in any case, it was originally in no position to reconstruct past worlds. It did not have sufficient material to do so. But this does not mean that useful and lasting work could not be done on more limited, though still important matters. Even before archaeology made its impressive contribution towards understanding the Bible, a great deal was learnt about the text of the Old and New Testaments and the literary character of the various books.

### Can we trust the text that we read ?

Editions of the Bible can be bought today in many languages; the Bible is probably the easiest book in the world to get. But there is a gap of more than 1800 years between the time when its last book was finished and the present. What has happened to the Bible down the ages ? How can we be sure that what we read now corresponds to what was originally written ? Printing by movable type was only invented in the fifteenth century; for a thousand and more years before that manuscripts had to be laboriously copied by hand, either through one scribe making a single copy from a manuscript in front of him, or through a scriptorium, where a lector dictated a manuscript to a small group. Ancient manuscripts

were written with no space between words and with abbreviations for many common words; unintentional mistakes must have been easy. In addition, manuscripts must often have been altered deliberately, perhaps by scribes who thought that they were correcting mistakes (and whose insight was not always as good as their intentions).

The task of reaching a text as close as possible to the original and of explaining how this text was handed down is known as *textual criticism*. It is a highly complicated business and applies not only to the Bible but also to any ancient manuscript.

### The New Testament

To see how strong the textual evidence for the New Testament is, it is only necessary to compare it with what the classical textual critic often has to work on. The 'bible' of the ancient Greeks, Homer's *Iliad*, is preserved in about 650 manuscripts of various kinds; the best-attested Greek tragedian, Euripides, in about 330; at the other end of the scale, the first six books of the *Annals* of Tacitus, the late first-century Roman historian, survive in only one manuscript, dating from the ninth century. On the other hand, there are over 5000 extant manuscripts of the New Testament, though many of these contain only part of it, and their age varies.

### 1. Manuscripts

(a) *Dating*. Dating manuscripts is done by examining closely the context in which they were found, their format, the material used and the style of writing. The palaeographer, as the specialist in this kind of work is called, develops a 'feel' for dating, in the same way as the expert in antiques, but he has one independent test to help him. This is a scientific test known as the Carbon 14 process (for more details, see below). When classified, manuscripts are assigned a letter or number for easy reference.

(b) *Papyri.* The earliest text of any passage from the New Testament that we have is a papyrus fragment from the Fourth Gospel, probably dating from early in the second century. This fragment contains only a few verses, but there are more extensive papyri, covering the greater part of the New Testament, from the third century to the seventh. These are about eighty in number.

(c) *Uncials.* Parchment manuscripts are much more numerous, because they are more durable. Pride of place among them goes to the great 'uncial' manuscripts dating from the fourth century to about the tenth. They are named after the type of letters in which they are written, rather like our capitals. The two most famous of these, Codex Vaticanus and Codex Sinaiticus, only became available for detailed study in the late nineteenth century, in quite dramatic circumstances. Originally they contained all the Old Testament as well. There are 250 uncial manuscripts now extant.

(d) *Minuscules.* In the ninth century, a new style of writing was invented, of smaller letters in a running (cursive) hand, which enabled books to be written more quickly and more cheaply. This writing is called 'minuscule'. From this time onwards we have a wealth of material: over 2500 manuscripts in all.

(e) *Other sources.* In addition, there are almost 2000 Greek New Testament lectionaries, selections to be read on particular days of the year. Translations of the New Testament made at an early date into Syriac, Coptic, Latin, Georgian, Armenian, Gothic, Ethiopic and Old Slavonic can be used for comparison. Finally, there are New Testament quotations in the writings of Christian theologians from the second century onwards which indicate something of the text they knew.

In view of the complex variety of evidence which goes back almost to the beginning, it is unlikely that any large-scale interference with the text has gone undetected. But the complicated manuscript tradition has produced a mass of minor variants which need to be resolved. Furthermore, there may have been slight changes between the time of the originals and the dates of the earliest manuscripts we possess.

### 2. *Making a decision*

It has been said that 'to teach another how to become a textual critic is like teaching another how to become a poet'. A full account is impossible, but here are some indications of how decisions are made.

First, manuscripts can be organized into groups or 'families', i.e., the critic can see which manuscript was copied from which. This becomes evident if, for example, an obvious error occurs at the same point in the text of two different manuscripts. Assuming that each was copied from only one manuscript, a common descent can be assumed. (The process is similar to that used in detecting forms of cheating in schools !) Later manuscripts in families, great-great-grandchildren and the like, can often be disregarded completely. This clears the air.

Four major groups are recognized and classified by geographical area:

(a) the *Syrian* (the Byzantine Empire: used for European Protestant translations up to the Revised Version);

(b) the *Western* (an early group, much given to paraphrasing);

21

(c) the *Alexandrian* (influenced by one of the great ancient literary centres);

(d) the *Neutral* (Codex Vaticanus and Codex Sinaiticus; so-called because this group is thought to be nearest to the originals).

After this classification, further decisions are still necessary. Mistakes are possible in the best manuscripts, and generally inferior ones sometimes preserve the truth. So decisions have to be made on individual readings, drawing on past experience of possible causes of error, and knowledge of the author and subject-matter of the writing in question. Two obvious examples are:

(a) The more difficult reading is to be preferred. The tendency among scribes was to make a text more understandable, and unless an obvious error has been made, the reading which is harder to make sense of is usually more likely to be original.

(b) Assimilation. Where, as in the first three Gospels, passages are similar, the scribe might alter, e.g., a less familiar wording in Luke to one he knew well from Matthew. Here the divergent reading is more likely to be original.

In this way, grounds for a decision are gradually built up. Time has given rise to a large and sophisticated literature about textual criticism which takes experts years to master; but it has also brought us to a position when we can be more certain about the text of the New Testament we use than ever before.

### 3. *Some examples*

What difference does it make ? A comparison of the Authorized (King James) Version with any of the newer translations will often show obvious changes. A few examples may be mentioned in passing.

(a) The last twelve verses of the Gospel of Mark were not originally part of the Gospel; they were added later, and the Gospel originally ended, or is irretrievably lost, after Mark 16.8 (see RSV).

(b) John 7.53–8.11, the story of the Woman Taken in Adultery, is an intrusion into the Fourth Gospel, though it may well be authentic material from elsewhere.

(c) I John 5.7 f. in the AV (KJV) is a late addition to the text, probably a reader's comment that was once written in the margin.

But there are not many 'spectaculars' like this; the majority of decisions are over much smaller questions, e.g., the description of Stephen in Acts 6.8: AV 'faith and power' becomes 'grace and power' in RSV. This is a difference in the text chosen, not in translation. Sometimes the choice is very finely balanced; do we read 'we have peace' (RSV) or 'let us have peace' (RV) in Rom.5.1 ?

### *Who wrote the books ?*

Having established that he has a reasonably accurate text to work from, the critic's next concern is with the origin and background of the books of the Bible. Who wrote them, where and when? He has two ways of answering his questions. First he can see what information has been handed down about authorship and circumstances by earlier authors: this is known as *external evidence*. Secondly, he can examine the books carefully and see what their content suggests: this is known as *internal evidence*. Unfortunately the two often disagree.

### 1. *External evidence*

Numerous remarks about authorship, etc., can be found in Jewish and Christian commentators. They vary from the plausible (that the Gospel of Mark was written by John Mark and contains reminiscences of the apostle Peter) to the implausible (that the text of the 'Five Books of Moses' was dictated by Ezra, through inspiration, when they had been lost at the Fall of Jerusalem). Often apparent fact and apparent fancy are combined, as when, for example, at one moment the second-century theologian Irenaeus remarks that Luke was a follower of Paul and wrote down the gospel he preached, and at the next that there must be no more and no less than four Gospels because there are four zones of the world, four winds, and four faces to the cherubim.

In particular, we have to remember the temptation there was to embellish claims about the Bible to show what a marvellous book it was, and the pressure in the case of the New Testament to demonstrate that a book was written by, or had connections with, an apostle, to qualify it for inclusion in the church's official collection (canon). If all this sounds dangerously near to forgery, we must remember the historical background; ancient literary conventions were rather different from ours.

In any case, the ancients were often quite in the dark about the origin of books which after all were not first written to be Holy Scripture. Sometimes they seem to have made their own guesses from internal evidence. In that case their external evidence is internal evidence in disguise. (Irenaeus seems to have come to his conclusion about Luke and Acts on internal evidence.) Because of this, the critic approaches external evidence suspiciously; he checks each argument carefully, and because he has better facilities for investigation than the ancients, he usually prefers to trust what he can discover from a book itself.

*2. Internal evidence*

As he studies some of the biblical books, the critic may begin to doubt what tradition says about them. The 'Five Books of Moses' do not in fact seem to have come from him. Not only do they record his death, but they contain material apparently from a much later time. The German scholar Wellhausen described how difficult it was to read the 'historical books' of the Old Testament on the assumption that, say, Saul and David knew Leviticus; everything fell into place when he tried the theory that the Law, rather than coming from Moses, belongs to a period later than that of I Samuel–II Kings. His approach is typical of the modern scholar: he tries to construct the kind of sequence which fits the known facts and shows how one thing grows out of another.

Some conclusions from internal evidence are:

(a) Careful reading of the book attributed to Isaiah shows that it seems to come from three different periods spread over more than two hundred years. Of course, there are loose ends, but the assignment of material to two writers in addition to Isaiah makes better sense.

(b) All the letters attributed to Paul do not come from his hand. The headings of the Authorized Version assign him fourteen letters, but some are problematical. The Epistle to the Hebrews has a very different style and subject-matter from the rest (and even the external evidence is doubtful). The Epistles to Timothy and Titus also suggest a different historical setting, later than Paul's time. These are therefore usually attributed to other authors. Over Ephesians, Colossians and II Thessalonians the debate is fiercer. Some claim that these were written by disciples or imitators of Paul, others that Paul himself wrote them.

Here, however, the differences are less important precisely because they are slighter; a decision either way makes little difference to our reconstruction of first-century Christianity.

Usually, however, dating and finding an appropriate background are vitally important. The way in which the biblical literature is arranged will make all the difference to our picture of the world of the Bible. And as we saw earlier, this is the critic's final aim.

### How were the books written ?

When he has reached the probable circumstances in which a book was written, the critic tries to go further back, for it is only rarely that an author wrote as it were 'out of his head'. This happens, for example, with some of the letters of Paul, but even they refer to or draw on other material. I Corinthians is a reply to an earlier letter written to Paul from Corinth, and before that came a still earlier letter from him which is now lost. Clearly I Corinthians will mean much more if something of the file of earlier correspondence can be reconstructed. Other biblical books incorporate chunks of earlier material. Where this happens is not always easy to detect; just as the ancient world had different conventions about authorship, so too it had different conventions about quotation. Borrowings were not documented and acknowledged in footnotes as they are today; in fact, imitation was thought to be a form of flattery.

One vivid illustration of this comes from the book of Proverbs. When a document from ancient Egypt, the *Sayings of Amenemopet*, came to light in 1922, it became clear that this was the source for several chapters of Proverbs, which reproduced it almost word for word.

Investigating the sources on which authors drew is one way of finding out more about their works. The process is known as *source criticism*.

Source criticism is easier in some places than in others. As soon as the first three Gospels are set out in parallel columns it is plain that they are in some way related. Exactly what this relationship is may be more difficult to define, but the material for a solution which explains which Gospel came first and how the others made use of it is there to hand. Similarly, I and II Chronicles draws on much of I Samuel–II Kings; what the Chronicler leaves out of the latter can be seen by a careful comparison and sheds much light on his views. In these instances, as with Proverbs and *Amenemopet*, both the 'source' and the book in which it is used still survive.

Where a book uses sources without too much alteration, it is possible to detect them even if they do not survive in their original form. In the first five books of the Bible, the Pentateuch, for example, an analysis of style and vocabulary makes it possible to detect different strands of material, each of which can be followed for some length. Within the prophetic books, it is often possible to distinguish sayings which go back to the prophet himself from the comments and additions made at later times, and even to see alternative ways in which his prophecies were first combined.

The difficulty arises when the final book is a more polished literary work in which earlier sources have been worked over and given a new form. Did the evangelist John know the Synoptic Gospels, or only a form of the tradition on which they also drew ? Did he make use of other sources ? It is very hard to tell. What sources did the author of Acts have ? There must have been some, but his style is so good and his literary skill so great that discovering the material on which he drew is about as easy as returning a well-baked cake to its original ingredients !

Source criticism can penetrate behind a book to an earlier stage. But its aim is not just to get back as far as possible. It seeks to illuminate the whole process of the literary composition of a book: the middle and end as well as the beginning. Later material added to the original can tell us much, say, about the way in which the prophets were regarded by their followers, just as insertions discovered by textual critics can tell us a bit about what earlier generations thought as they read the Bible. Here, too, is one way of discovering the personality of a writer, as well as the tradition on which he drew.

## *Before writing*

Source criticism is essnetially a literary process. It deals with the relationship of one document to another. But there are more ways of handing on tradition than by writing it down. Literature is usually preceded and accompanied by an oral stage in which stories, poems, hymns, proverbs, even laws, are passed on by word of mouth. Even modern civilization has its oral tradition, e.g., anecdotes and sayings, which only occasionally find their way into writing. Biblical literature begins from an oral tradition and is fed by it at numerous stages on the way.

As with the transmission of books by copying, so too with oral tradition some general principles can be established, this time by comparison with similar cultures and parallel situations. In this way the critic can see what is likely to happen to oral material.

At the oral stage, the individual is a much less prominent figure (for how many, e.g., 'shaggy dog stories' do you know an author ?). Much more influential is the life of the community and the activities in which it engages. These shape spoken material and produce distinctive forms. Hence study of the oral stage of tradition has come to be known as *form criticism*.

What a 'form' is can be illustrated from the modern world; we can recognize the difference between a joke and a limerick, a hymn and a ballad, a testimonial and a legal charge. All these are forms. Form, content and purpose even now are closely connected; a testimonial will not normally be written as a limerick nor a legal charge as a ballad (though see Gilbert and Sullivan's *Trial by Jury* !). But our society is a complex and relatively sophisticated one and so few conclusions can be drawn from forms. In a less highly developed, more structured community it is a different matter.

In the ancient Near East, forms are closely related to the life of the community. Once it is accepted that a particular form will have been determined by its place in the life of the community, we can argue back from the form (which we have) to the community life (which has passed away). This method is not an abstract one, as a check on conclusions reached is often possible from relevant archaeological evidence.

Here are some illustrations:

### 1. *The Old Testament*

(a) *The Pentateuch*. Here it is possible to identify by their forms riddles, work-songs, hymns, legends, prescriptions for worship and codes of law of various kinds (e.g., 'apodeictic law': 'Thou shalt (not) . . .' has a different form from 'casuistic law': 'If a man . . . then'). Like all forms, these are usually fairly brief. This helps us to see something of earliest Israelite interests and concerns.

(b) *The Prophetic Books*. Prophetic oracles assumed particular forms, and when we have recognized these it is possible to use the knowledge to distinguish what the prophet originally said from what has been added later.

(c) *The Psalms*. These differ in form: compare a hymn like Ps. 100 with a lament (Ps. 44) or a thanksgiving (Ps. 124). This helps us to reconstruct the pattern of Israelite worship.

(d) *Proverbs*. Even the collections of proverbs can be analysed by forms, which help to indicate their background and origin.

### 2. *The New Testament*

(a) *The Gospels*. The stories about Jesus assumed different forms depending on their use in the early church. Compare, for example, the shape of the 'controversy stories' in Mark 2.1–3.6 with that of the 'miracle stories' in 4.35–5.43. Here, too, we can argue from the form to the use of these stories in the church.

(b) *The Epistles*. An epistle is itself a form, and by recognizing the characteristics of an epistle it is possible to distinguish real epistles (e.g., of Paul) from books like Hebrews or I John, which though named epistles are much more like sermons. Were they ever sent as letters ? Within the epistles, early Christian confessions, hymns, etc., may be detected (perhaps Phil.2.5–11; I Cor.15.3 ff.).

Form criticism is inevitably a less precise approach than source criticism, but its uses have been proved.

It can also help in clarifying the character and purpose of the writers in whose work the 'forms' are included. Arrangements of individual units may be the only way in which a writer who is faithful to the tradition he has received may make his point. For example, is the order in the Gospel of Mark purely historical, or are units sometimes arranged on a different principle to put over a theological point ?

When the method of form criticism is extended in an attempt to discover the intentions of the final author or editor, it is known as *redaction criticism*. (This rather ugly name comes from the term used for the author/editor, 'redactor', which indicates that he is half-way between the one and the other.) As an approach, it tends to be very subjective, because of the complicated questions it has to ask, but it, too, is a promising development.

## Archaeology and the world of the Bible

The methods we have looked at help the critic to understand the *Bible*; they are used hand in hand with his more general work, as a historian, in understanding the biblical *world*. Here archaeology is his chief tool.

The amazing discoveries at Qumran are the most publicized achievements of modern archaeology, but there are many more besides. Specific details will be found in the sections which follow. Numerous important sites have produced material of various kinds, bringing to life a whole new world of Palestinian, Egyptian and Mesopotamian culture. New Testament studies have been helped, too. Discoveries of second-century writings by Gnostics (a deviant form of Christianity) have been made at Nag Hammadi, in Egypt; these help us to see what happened in the obscure period between the end of the New Testament and the first 'Fathers'.

The amount of new information provided by archaeology is enormous, but it is important to see just what its limitations are. Here, too, mistakes were made at the start because this had not been realized. A comparison will show the right way and the wrong way:

1. In his excavations at Ur in the 1920s, Sir Leonard Woolley found a stratum of mud some ten feet thick and on the basis of this confidently concluded that here was evidence of Noah's flood. He was not slow to publicize this. But why should the mud be a relic of *Noah's* flood ? It has no label to say so, and other explanations are far more likely. This is a hangover of the mistake mentioned earlier, the concern to *prove* the Bible right. (Werner Keller's book, *The Bible as History*, is a thorough-going representative of this concern.) But the Bible is not there to be vindicated; it and its world are to be understood.

2. A better illustration of the uses of archaeology is the study of Megiddo, a vital fortress in Lower Galilee from Canaanite times to the days of the Maccabees, which has been described as the most important archaeological site in Palestine. No sensational conclusions can be drawn from here to particular biblical events, but simply trying to understand what Megiddo was like at various periods deepens our knowledge of the biblical world.

Responsible archaeologists are only too anxious to point out the limitations of their work. Its contribution is usually of this latter general and indirect kind: to bring to life past cultures and their conditions. Discoveries need to be interpreted, and there is as much room for disagreement and alternative explanations here as with any complex study. Exaggerated claims ought therefore to be treated with care. Even when new written documents are found, the chances that they relate directly to the biblical narrative are slight. But once this has been said, there is much that archaeology can and has done.

### Technological tools

From what has been said so far, it will have become clear that the critic's most important tools are his own acuteness, sympathy, imagination and insight. Like the historian and the literary critic, he must have many of the qualities of the artist. But the scientist, too, has produced aids which he can gratefully use.

Photography has transformed the study of texts. Not only is it easy to copy precious manuscripts, but photographic techniques can make difficult manuscripts more legible and even detect what lay under erasures. The Carbon 14 Process, mentioned earlier, can date accurately the age of materials by measuring the rate of emission of the rare isotope whose name it bears. Impressive resources can be marshalled for a particular project, e.g., opening the great Copper Scroll of Qumran.

Computers can be used in problems that require analysis of statistics, as in classifying manuscripts or enumerating characteristics of style. Striking conclusions have already been published, but it should be emphasized that this kind of work is very much in its infancy, and that in any case the amount of material available for the computer to work on is often too small to be significant.

### Assured results ?

All these critical activities are still being actively carried on. Of course, no individual scholar would consider that he has mastered more than a very limited aspect of them; he is conscious how much the drawing of a wider picture is a co-operative effort. Unfortunately, however, there is a problem here. When individual results are put together there are often considerable disagreements. Indeed, the first thing that strikes and dismays many students is the extent to which authorities disagree. Where two scholars differ radically in their conclusions, each producing a mass of individual facts, which is the non-specialist to choose ?

First, it should be remembered that the openness of biblical scholarship, the way in which it follows the same pattern as other studies, is an important guarantee of its genuineness. There is little room for biased argument and special pleading. Biblical criticism is not a 'closed shop'. In other subjects, history, philosophy, languages, even science, similar disagreements are not uncommon. So biblical scholarship does not stand entirely apart.

Where it differs is in the importance attached to its conclusions. So much has in the past been based on the Bible that changes in understanding are felt to have very far-reaching significance. But if, as is so often the case, there is just not enough evidence to come to any definite conclusion, then living with questions is the only answer. And we shall have to get used to it.

But in that case, can we be sure of anything ?

It might be misleading to single out a set of assured results and present them by saying 'of this much, at least, we may be certain'. All results are only probable, though some are more probable than others, and many 'assured results' of the past have since been overturned. The reader has to make up his mind for himself; first, perhaps, as a result of the impression made by this book. Many different writers have contributed to it, by no means all of the same background or viewpoint. Is their approach convincing ? Does the book as a whole add up to the beginnings of a picture which seems capable of being developed into a coherent shape ? Or is it a ramshackle assemblage of doubtful ideas with little to support them ?

A good deal of tension will go out of the question 'Of what can we be sure ?' once the distinction drawn earlier between 'understanding' and 'proving' has been made. The Bible bears witness to God through the whole life of a particular people and the way in which it looked at the world – and life has many aspects. Begin to see that, and a great deal will fall into place of its own accord.

JOHN BOWDEN

3 Jewish Religious Life in the First Century AD

## Background and sources

The Jewish scene in the New Testament period was a continually changing one. This is hardly surprising, in view of the earth-shaking events which took place between AD 1 and AD 100. In AD 70 the temple, the central symbol and focal point of Judaism, was destroyed, with many far-reaching consequences. During the first century the foundations of a new form of Judaism began to be laid with the emergence of the Rabbis, their codification of the tradition and their approval of an authorized canon of Jewish Scripture. There was constant conflict with Rome, to the point of a series of savage battles; and, no less important, there was an increasing conflict with Christianity, which arose from the heart of Judaism and with its growing success posed a great many urgent questions.

The Judaism that emerged from this turbulence was as unified as it had ever been. A council of rabbinic teachers, meeting at Jamnia about AD 90, managed successfully to reorganize the chaos with which they were confronted. Their measures led to the eventual elimination of a number of competing forms of Judaism and the predominance of a single version, Rabbinic Judaism, the Judaism of today. During the first century, however, these competitors were very much in evidence, so that as well as reckoning with a changing historical situation, we have to keep in mind that there were variations in Judaism from group to group and from place to place.

First, a distinction has to be made between Palestinian Judaism and the Judaism throughout the Roman Empire (the Judaism of the Dispersion), with its greater contact with the Hellenistic Greek atmosphere of the Mediterranean world. The distinction is by no means a clear-cut one, for Palestine, too, had been strongly influenced by Greek culture, but living in a foreign country, being at a considerable distance from the temple, and approaching the Torah in Greek and not Hebrew (to give only a few examples) all had their effect upon the Jews of the Dispersion.

Secondly, within these two broad categories there were more specific groupings. In Palestinian Judaism there were Pharisees, Sadducees, Essenes and Zealots, to mention the best known; and the obvious, though often neglected, split between the educated and the uneducated, those who could read and those who could not. Similar differences will certainly have existed in Hellenistic Judaism, with Hellenistic philosophy and religion exercising their attractions even perhaps to the degree where Judaism turned into gnosticism, but they are very hard to trace.

It is, in fact, difficult to document any of the groupings or to describe them in any great detail, even where we know that they existed. Our problem is the old one – lack of information. So thoroughly did Rabbinic Judaism carry out its work of unification that it is often almost impossible to see the views of the movements it replaced, particularly those with which it did not agree. A list of the sources of our information with their particular characteristics may give some idea of the problem:

1. The *Rabbinic writings* fall, roughly speaking, into four main groups. (*a*) the *Mishna* is a compilation of legal requirements, written down about the end of the second century AD, in the form of legal opinions; (*b*) the *Gemara* is a discussion of the Mishna. The two together form the *Talmud*, of which there are two versions, Babylonian and Palestinian, completed at the end of the fourth century AD. (*c*) The *Tosefta* collects sayings which failed to be included in the Mishna (individual verses are known as *baraita*). (*d*) *Midrash* is a term used to describe commentary on the Scriptures; sometimes it is legal, but it can also be elaboration of the biblical text.

As material for historical reconstruction these writings are almost useless. They have no interest in historical sequence or relationships, nor do they offer any chronological detail. They certainly contain early material, handed down orally, but because they were compiled later than the council of Jamnia, their view of the past is selective, hazy and either partisan or idealistic. For example, there is nothing in them to suggest the Maccabaean revolt or the destruction of the temple. What clues they do offer are in the realm of Jewish religious thought and institutions.

2. For our knowledge of the history of the period we depend on the Jewish historian *Josephus*. Josephus lived between AD 37 and 100, and his two major works, the *History of the Jewish War* and the *Jewish Antiquities*, present a unique picture of developments in the first three-quarters of the century. These books do, however, have their drawbacks. Josephus was a client of the Flavian emperors and had to be tactful in his presentation of Judaism; he also had to come to terms inwardly with his own position, which other Jews regarded as treacherous. We therefore have to allow for some bias. Furthermore, Josephus is silent about Judaism after the end of the war of AD 66 and so leaves us completely in the dark about the developments which led to the council of Jamnia.

3. For much of our knowledge of first-century Judaism we are indebted, directly or indirectly, to Christianity. This is especially true of our knowledge of Hellenistic Judaism. It was the Christian church that preserved the writings of Josephus and of Philo of Alexandria (born *c*.20 BC). Otherwise they would have remained unknown, as would the Jewish books which go to form the Apocrypha. Christianity also preserved the apocalyptic literature between the testaments; the Rabbinic writings are essentially non-eschatological. This, of course, raises the question how widespread apocalyptic hopes for the future were during the first century. Was it a popular way of thinking, or was it confined to minority groups ? Because we know so little about the authorship of the Pseudepigrapha, as this literature is called, the answer is not obvious.

4. Christian sources themselves tell us much about Judaism, and chief among them is the New Testament itself. Often it alone offers evidence for first-century Jewish practice and for some details of Roman administration. But historical reliability is difficult to decide. The pictures of Judaism in the second half of Acts are usually accepted as reliable, but the first half is more of a problem. In the Gospels, we have to allow both for bias, and for lack of information. For example, the portrait of the Pharisees in Matthew is certainly conditioned by later opposition between Jews and Christians

towards the end of the century. Similarly, it would be difficult to tell what the temple was like merely from the references to it in the Gospels and their accounts of Jesus' cleansing of it; one notable Jewish scholar has even remarked: 'It is difficult to believe the evangelists had ever seen the temple or had any clear understanding of what it was.' In the letters of Paul we have first-hand evidence of the mind of a first-century Jew – but what kind of a Jew was he ?

5. Finally, and most vivid among all our sources, is Palestinian archaeology and its two most spectacular finds: the site of the Qumran community and its literature, and the citadel of Masada. Qumran and the Dead Sea scrolls have given us an extensive view of the life of a sect previously known only from occasional references. Masada illustrates two greatly contrasting times, the luxury of the desert palace of Herod at the beginning of the century and the tragedy of the last stand of the Zealots in AD 73; it has also provided the lost original Hebrew text of the book of Ecclesiasticus (preserved beforehand, by Christianity, only in Greek) and a fragment from the Dead Sea scroll literature.

Here again we come to a problem. How far can we assume a connection between these two sites which by chance we know particularly well ? Are there consequences for the wider picture of first-century Judaism ? As one area is highlighted, the amount that we do not know about the rest stands out all the more.

## The temple

Until it was destroyed by the Romans in AD 70, the temple at Jerusalem was the official centre of Jewish worship, a great place of pilgrimage and an immensely powerful symbol. Although Jewish theology had increasingly stressed the transcendence and otherness of God, the temple was still regarded as being in a special way a divine dwelling place: the scenes reported by Josephus immediately before its fall suggest a confidence, even then, that God would not allow it to be harmed.

The temple standing in the first century was in fact the third to be built, following Solomon's temple destroyed in 587 BC and the one that replaced it after the return from Babylon. Herod the Great began work in 20/19 BC on the same site but according to a different ground plan, in the prevailing Roman-Hellenistic style of architecture. Construction went on for a very long time: certainly until AD 64, and it may be that the temple was still unfinished at its destruction.

Nothing remains of the temple proper today, apart from the great platform now surmounted by the Moslem Dome of the Rock and the sub-structure of the massive surrounding walls. For an idea of what it was originally like we depend on two descriptions, one in Josephus and the other in the Mishna tractate Middoth; they do not always agree, but provide enough information for a general picture.

The site of the temple was on a hill in the south-eastern part of the present Old City. A great paved court was laid on the temple platform, surrounded by magnificent colonnades against the outside walls. This court was accessible to people of any race or faith, Gentiles included, and was by no means reserved for purely religious activities. In common with other ancient temples, the Jerusalem temple was used as a safe-deposit for valuables, and other quasi-commercial transactions were carried on there.

Within the court was an enclosure surrounded by an embankment, with steps going up to a wall with nine gates. Inscriptions, the Greek text of one of which has been found, warned Gentiles against going further:

No foreigner may enter inside the barrier and embankment. Whoever is caught doing so will have himself to blame for his ensuing death.

On the east side of the inner area was the Court of the Women, the regular place of assembly for public worship. Women were accommodated in a gallery round the court, which contained trumpet-shaped boxes to receive offerings. Fifteen semi-circular steps led up to a broad gate which gave on to the west side, divided into the Court of Israel and the Court of Priests, where the regular sacrifices were offered.

Finally, at the heart of the temple itself lay the Holy Place, again elevated by twelve steps. Within was a vestibule which gave on to the main doorway of the temple sanctuary. Here were the sacred objects in gold, the seven-branched lampstand, the table for the shewbread and the altar of incense: a curtain screened the Holy of Holies, containing no furniture whatever, which only the high priest might enter, once a year, on the Day of Atonement.

Thus the elevation of the temple and its holiness increased progressively towards the centre, as did the elaborateness of its ornamentation. Built of great blocks of gleaming white stone and decorated with all possible splendour, it must have been a breath-taking sight. Josephus' praise is lavish; he remarks that the outside of the building was covered with so much gold that the onlooker could scarcely look directly at it in bright sunlight. He adds that after the sack of Jerusalem the market of gold for the whole province of Syria was completely glutted, so that the standard of gold was depreciated to half its value. Even allowing for exaggeration, we, too, can be impressed.

### Temple worship

The foundation of the worship offered at the temple was the daily sacrifice, offered morning and evening on behalf of the people. So fundamental was it that it was never interrupted once during the rebuilding of the temple. A positive understanding of the joy taken in the ritual sacrifice of animals and the significance attached to it is perhaps the hardest thing for modern Westerners coming to grips with the Bible to achieve, but there is abundant evidence of that joy and of the belief that sacrifice could bring forgiveness. The system was at its height in the last days of the temple, when probably more care and money was lavished on it than at any other time.

Public sacrifice was accompanied by a lengthy ceremonial and was followed by private sacrifices, both sin-offerings and votive offerings. The whole of Palestine was divided into twenty-four divisions, each of which was on duty in turn for one week (see Luke 1.8 f.). Priests and Levites from the course on duty were responsible for offering the sacrifices, and lay representatives were deputized to be witnesses on behalf of the whole people. A yearling lamb was killed and then followed a service of prayer; incense was offered and the lamb solemnly burnt; the priests pronounced a benediction and the choir of Levites sang the appointed psalm, the ceremony being accompanied by the blowing of trumpets.

More numerous sacrifices were offered on

33

the sabbath and on major festivals. The most important of the latter were the Feast of Weeks (Pentecost), the Feast of Tabernacles (Succoth) following the Day of Atonement, and the Feast of Passover. Of great antiquity, these feasts had accumulated many overtones of meaning. The Feast of Weeks was a thanksgiving for the grain harvest, but also commemorated the giving of the Law on Mount Sinai; the Feast of Tabernacles, or Booths, recalled the time when the Israelites were wandering in the desert and lived in tents, but also contained an ancient prayer-ceremony for rain; the Passover, while commemorating the deliverance from Egypt, was also associated with the Feast of Unleavened Bread, which originally also had an agricultural significance.

Pilgrims came to all these festivals, often covering vast distances to be present. Passover was the annual peak; one estimate gives the total number of pilgrims likely at that time as about 125,000, compared with the approximately 55,000 permanent residents of Jerusalem. The Passover meal was eaten in domestic surroundings, in table-fellowships of between ten and twenty; pilgrims had by law to stay that night within the limits of Jerusalem itself, as they were ritually interpreted. Despite the flexibility of this interpretation, the crush must have been immense.

## *The temple staff*

Just as the temple embodied in itself the aspirations of Jewish worship, the high priest stood as chief representative and symbol of the Jewish people. On paper, so to speak, he was a lofty and almost superhuman figure, set apart from his people and standing above them. His descent, his marriage, his whole way of life were to be of the utmost purity. Invested for life with the sacred garments, he alone could enter the Holy of Holies, on the Day of Atonement, as we have seen. Whenever he appeared, to take part in sacrifice or other ritual, as he willed or as custom prescribed, he was accompanied in state and accorded all due reverence.

In reality things were rather different. The Jewish people were not their own masters. Making theological prescriptions was one thing – keeping to them was another. Both Herod and the occupying Roman forces appointed and dismissed high priests quite arbitrarily, for political reasons. Nor was the failure entirely external. Simony, nepotism and rivalry between priests was all too common, and belonging as they so often did to the richest families, high priests could be harsh and politically self-seeking.

But the pendulum must not be allowed to swing too far in this direction. As sacred mediator between God and the people and representative of the people, the high priest was a supremely important figure. There was a long and sacred tradition behind him to counterbalance any personal failings, and his position gave him unique influence – religiously towards his people and politically even towards Rome. Even deposed high priests retained considerable authority.

(One problem connected with the high priest is that first-century documents, including the Gospels and Acts, regularly talk about 'the high priests' in the plural, although only one was in office at any time. Possible explanations for this are either that the references are to members of the high-priestly families, or that they denote a group of the chief priests of the temple who formed a well-defined body, including some of the officials to be mentioned below. Perhaps the latter suggestion is more plausible.)

Under the high priest there was an extensive temple staff, some of whom were permanently in residence, while others came to Jerusalem as their duty required. Chief among the permanent staff was the captain of the temple, who had overall responsibility for the routine worship of the temple and was principal assistant to the high priest. He was chief of the temple police force, with power to arrest on temple property. A group of overseers (no less than seven) was responsible for the organization of the temple, and a group of treasurers (no less than three) administered its considerable income.

As has been said, the ritual was carried out by twenty-four courses of priests and the same number of courses of Levites, who were not in permanent residence. It has been estimated that there will have been some 7200 priests involved, and a rather larger number of Levites. Specific duties were assigned to individual priests in turn; the climax of a priest's life came when he went into the sanctuary alone to make the incense offering. The Levites functioned as singers and musicians, servants and guards.

### The Law

The temple and its priesthood may have been the most striking symbol of Judaism, but had they been its exclusive centre, Judaism would never have survived their fall. The way in which it adjusted to the situation after AD 70 shows that there were other strengths; these strengths had as their common basis the Law, and to a considerable degree the history of the different parties within Judaism is the history of different interpretations of the Law. Even while the temple still stood, even within Judaea itself, there seems to have been an increasing pre-occupation with the scriptures and their implications, and this preoccupation will have been even more characteristic of the Jews of the Dispersion. A movement like that found at Aumran is unthinkable without this development, which comes to full effect in Rabbinic Judaism.

The beginnings of the trend are to be found in the Babylonian exile and the period after the return. During this period the Pentateuch took final form and was accorded its place of honour as the *Torah, the* Law; the Prophets had taken a place beside it by the beginning of the second century BC and the Writings were recognized during the first century AD.

'Law' gives a wrong idea of this written basis of Judaism; the Hebrew, Torah, does not have quite the same significance. The word means 'instruction' or 'doctrine' rather than 'law', and of course the Pentateuch, to which it is applied, is by no means only a law-book. Nevertheless, that is what it became as it was made the object of more and more intensive study. The methods which were used sometimes seem bizarre in the extreme and the discussions over finer points interminable in their casuistry; but, as with sacrifice, it is essential to try to see the positive elements which such study was believed to bring and the enjoyment with which it was carried out.

Here, as well as in considering the parties within Judaism, it needs to be remembered once again that the Gospels – and Paul – present only one side of the picture; the other side also needs to be looked at sympathetically.

### The Sadducees

Party lines within Judaism began to be laid down at the beginning of the second century

BC. By the first century AD they were well established, though again too rigid a classification is dangerous. We know there were differences within particular groups, and familiarity with the make-up of modern church denominations ought to put us on our guard against supposing that groups were too uniform.

The Sadducees probably take their name from Zadok, the high priest in the time of David, but that is no more than a guess. They were the priestly, aristocratic party, whose interests centred on the temple. They were opposed to the new developments represented by the Pharisees, and with the destruction of the temple and its consequences became the losing party and faded away. As a result, we are more than usual in the dark about them, as our information comes from their opponents and gives an essentially negative account of their characteristics.

The high priest was usually a Sadducee, but this does not mean that all Sadducees were priests. It seems likely that the Sadducean party also included the Jewish lay nobility, landowners with considerable resources. By virtue of the character of its membership, the party was drawn from a select social background; for the same reason, it was essentially conservative in its outlook. The make up of the party and the conditions under which they lived kept them out of touch with developments in popular thought and their necessary involvement in the politics of their time will not have helped their standing with the people.

Sadducean interpretation of Scripture was literal in contrast to that of the Pharisees, whose oral tradition they rejected. From this basic position will stem their well-known denials of resurrection, future rewards and punishments, angels and spirits, and providence. These facts are recorded by Josephus, Matt.22.23 and Acts 23.8 – the way in which they are recorded is too terse for us to be able to generalize usefully from them. Perhaps they are less useful than they look; it may be that, like aristocrats and prominent church leaders of all times, the Sadducees were not particularly interested in theology.

## The Sanhedrin

The supreme Jewish council was the Sanhedrin; the word is a version of an Aramaic transliteration of the Greek *synedrion*, assembly. It consisted of seventy-one members. It is not easy to see just who belonged to it because of the way in which it is portrayed in the sources: Josephus and the New Testament present a political side and the Rabbinic literature a religious side. This led some scholars to suppose that there were two Sanhedrins, one political and one religious. Such a solution, however, is rather drastic, and it is much more likely that the Rabbinic sources are reinterpreting the Sanhedrin and reading back into it features which it took on after the fall of the temple. The very nature of Judaism meant that political and religious questions were inextricably intertwined.

In the earlier post-exilic period the Sanhedrin will have consisted of senior priests and representatives from the aristocracy; later, Pharisees gained representation in it and increased their influence. The effective power it had varied considerably, depending on the regime of the time; the question becomes important in connection with the trial of Jesus. No firm conclusion can be drawn from the evidence, as is clear from the arguments which still continue.

## The scribes

The scribes were a new rising upper class, which increasingly replaced the old hereditary aristocracy in influential positions. Their power grew with the influence of the Law and the importance of its interpretation, and was based on the knowledge they had acquired through their study. To become a scribe required a long period of training both in methods of interpretation and in the material of the tradition. The aim of this training was for the scribe to be able to make his own personal decision on religious and judicial questions. Official recognition came with 'ordination', for which there was a minimum age limit. Later sources give this as forty years of age; this may be an exaggeration, but it shows the seriousness with which training was regarded.

The recognized scribe had an unrivalled reputation, as Ecclus.39.1–11 shows. He could hold key positions in the administration of justice, in government and in education; the Pharisaic representatives in the Sanhedrin will have been scribes. On the other hand, being a scribe was not necessarily a remunerative occupation; it seems that many of the scribes were quite poor and had to support themselves by working at a trade.

Scribe is the name of a qualification, not that of a party. Although the question is a confused one, it is unlikely that the scribes should be completely identified with the Pharisees; the Sadducees had their own traditions and their own scribes. Obviously, however, the Pharisee scribes would be the more predominant. (Here once more the terminology in the Gospels needs to be used with care.)

## The Pharisees

If on the whole the scribes regularly appear in association with the Pharisees, there is of course a difference between the two. Not all Pharisees had a scribal education, for the Pharisees were a lay movement which set out ideally to embrace the whole of the Jewish people. The meaning of the name is again uncertain, but is probably best understood as 'the separated ones'; like the title 'Christian', it may first have been given them by their opponents. The Pharisees developed out of the earlier movement of the Hasidim; we can only guess at how organized a movement they formed and what changes took place between the Maccabaean period and the first century AD.

If we wanted to contrast scribe and Pharisee, it could be said that the scribe was essentially concerned with a theological emphasis whereas the Pharisee was preoccupied with ritual matters. Being a 'separated one' meant striving to be separated from impurity of all kinds. But of course a contrast like that will not do. For the Law and the understanding of the Law was the means of avoiding impurity, so that the work of the scribe was indispensable. The leaders of the movement will have been scribes. By 70 BC they seem to have gained entry to the Sanhedrin, and from then on they never altogether lost power, though they had many serious setbacks.

The Pharisaic movement was probably an association of closed groups with particular specified rules of conduct. Would-be Pharisees will have had to accept certain regulations before being admitted and then to serve a probationary period before being granted full membership. The Pharisees were engaged in a struggle on two fronts: on the one hand they had to fight to preserve the purity of Judaism in the face of the 'people of the land', those who sat lightly to the ritual laws – it was this fight that led to the rules and regulations of which the Gospels present so hostile and negative a picture. On the other hand, and at a different level, they opposed the Sadducees in the struggle for the leadership of the people.

As we saw, the Sadducees were essentially conservative and inflexible in their approach to the Law; as a result they were unable to cope adequately with new needs and changing situations. The Pharisees tended in the other direction. The essence of their position was a distinction between the written Law and the oral tradition. The written Law had to be understood and interpreted, to meet changing times and situations, in the light of the oral tradition. The tradition served to safeguard the Law by 'putting a fence' round it; the ten commandments became six hundred and thirteen; directives were worked out for all possible eventualities.

That is the negative way of looking at it. More positively, we might say that the Pharisees saw that if the Law was to continue as the living basis of Judaism it had to be interpreted in a flexible way; otherwise the time would come when it could no longer speak to the present. The danger here was that with their more flexible method of interpretation the basic material and intent of the Law would be submerged by its interpretation – and that is what tended to happen. With flexibility, too, came the inevitable consequence that disputes arose over variant interpretations. The later Rabbinic literature is full of this kind of discussion; the most famous arguments from an earlier period are those between the schools of Hillel and Shammai, teachers who flourished at the very beginning of the Christian era.

Shammai was proverbially strict, conservative and irascible; Hillel patient, gentle and liberal. The most famous anecdote about him is typical of the best in the Pharisaic tradition. A proselyte wanted to learn the whole Torah while standing on one foot. After Shammai rebuffed him, the proselyte came to Hillel. 'Do not do to your neighbour what you would not want to be done to you,' Hillel told him, 'that is the Torah, the rest is commentary. Now go and learn it.'

## *Rabbinic Judaism*

After the council of Jamnia, Judaism became known as Rabbinic Judaism, not Pharisaic Judaism, though the two are directly connected. Where Pharisaism ends and Rabbinism begins is almost impossible to say, and the question is more a modern one than one that a first-century Jew would ask. The change in name is connected with the use of the word 'Rabbi'.

At the beginning of the century, Rabbi was not a formal title, but a mode of address, 'My master', used as a mark of respect. It is used a number of times in this way in the Fourth Gospel, in remarks to Jesus (e.g., 1.49; 6.25). By the end of the first century, however, it had taken on formal significance, as is indicated by Matt.23.7 f., a passage which dates from the time of the early church rather than that of Jesus. In the second century it was firmly established, and that is the way in which it is used in the Rabbinic literature.

It was the Pharisaic/Rabbinic development which shaped the future of Judaism; the heightened prominence of the Law after the fall of the temple was accompanied by an institution which had been increasing in importance for some time before AD 70, the synagogue and its worship.

## The synagogue

The Greek word *synagoge*, from which the synagogue takes its name, is used in the Greek Old Testament to translate the Hebrew word *'eda*, 'congregation'. In such cases it does not, of course, refer to a building at all. So when we investigate the beginnings of the synagogue we have in effect two separate questions to answer: first, when did groups of people begin to meet together for prayer and the study of Scripture; secondly, when did these meetings begin to take place in a building specially designed for the purpose ?

There is unlikely to be any clear-cut beginning for the first process, which will have happened gradually from the exile onwards. Jewish sources, of course, trace the institution of the synagogue, like everything else, to Moses; the earliest beginning, however, is likely to be the movement with which Ezra was connected, and there will have been other contributory factors in different places. In Alexandria, Jews will have come across Greek religious associations, which met regularly once a week; in many places Jews may well have had regular meetings as part of municipal life. It is even possible that there may be some connection between the synagogue and the meetings of members of the course on duty at the Jerusalem temple – those who did not go to Jerusalem are thought to have met together at home for prayer when the sacrifice was being offered in the temple. The difficulty with this last suggestion is knowing when the practice to which it refers actually began. At any rate, by the first century there was certainly a strong

tradition of regular meetings for prayer and study of the Scriptures – and probably there were also special buildings in which these meetings took place.

Archaeological exploration has revealed only one possible synagogue from the first century – spectacularly enough, on the site of Herod's palace at Masada. Strong reasons were found for supposing that one of the rooms there had been converted and used as a synagogue by the Zealots who occupied it for their last stand. Otherwise there are no remains of synagogues earlier than the second century AD. On the other hand, there is written evidence to suggest that even in the first century, synagogues were widespread. There may be some question whether the scene in the synagogue in Luke 4.16–30 is historical, but it is difficult to write off the many references in Acts to synagogues throughout the Mediterranean world (e.g. 9.2; 13.5; 13.14; 14.1; 16.13; 17.1). These references cover Syria, Cyprus, Asia Minor and Greece; Josephus makes special mention of synagogues in Caesarea and Tiberias; and Acts and Rabbinic writings both mention synagogues in Jerusalem itself.

One can no more speak of the typical synagogue than one can speak of the typical church. The ground plans of those which have been unearthed vary considerably, and no sequence of architectural development can be established. Under the influence of the Jerusalem temple, sometimes there will have been elaborate external decoration; in Babylon, attention was chiefly lavished on the interior.

The synagogue was more than a place of worship; it was also something of a social centre with secular uses, a place for judicial and political, as well as religious, gatherings. Some scholars even believe that the synagogue was used as a place where hospitality could be offered to travellers. It was certainly a centre for education, where children may have received elementary instruction and where teaching was given to adults who wanted help in reading the Scriptures. Above all, in the Dispersion the synagogue was an important factor in unifying the Jews who lived in a place.

There was no permanent 'minister' of a synagogue, as there usually is in a Christian church. The principal official was the 'head of the synagogue' (*archisynagogos*), who played a chief part in all synagogue functions, was ultimately responsible for the conduct of services, and at some stage may have chosen the lessons. He was assisted by the *hazzan*, an official the meaning of whose title is obscure: it is interpreted as anything from 'sexton' to 'overseer'. The *hazzan* seems to have performed most of the practical duties of the head of the synagogue and was responsible for much of its administration; the traditional idea that he was a kind of village schoolmaster seems to be incorrect. The synagogue also had its council of elders; in predominantly Jewish areas these will also have been civic officials.

Despite the variety of purposes it could serve, the synagogue was primarily a place of worship, and services were held on sabbaths and feast days. The central act of worship was the reading of Scripture, and the interior furnishing of the synagogue was directed towards this purpose. A special shrine contained rolls of the Torah (and also, perhaps, of the Prophets), which were treated with solemn reverence. Even when worn out they would be respected: a storeroom (*geniza*) in a Cairo synagogue containing worn-out scrolls provided some exciting discoveries, including a document also found at Qumran, at the beginning of this century. Near the shrine would be the dais from which lessons were read and sermons given. The main lesson was from the Torah, and was followed by one from the Prophets; it is thought that by the first century a triennial cycle of readings in the Torah had been established, but this is a matter of some dispute. In Palestine, the reading would be in Hebrew, sometimes accompanied by an Aramaic translation; in the Dispersion the Greek translation was read out. When a competent person was present, the reading of the lessons was followed by a sermon expounding them; there seems to have been a custom of inviting any visiting teacher who happened to be present to deliver this address (Acts 13.14). The service opened with the *Shema* ('Hear, O Israel'), and the reading and interpretation of the Scriptures will have been preceded and followed by prayer.

It is difficult to tell whether women were separated from men in synagogue services in the first century. Only Philo gives any explicit information, suggesting that women occupied a gallery in the synagogue at Alexandria; Rabbinic writings are silent, and architecture is little help. On the whole it seems likely that in view of the position of women in society at this time, silence is not to be interpreted in a positive way: women will either have been segregated or excluded.

## Judaism in the Dispersion

During the first century, there were more Jews living outside Palestine than within it. Estimates vary, but a rough guess would be that there were rather more than two million Jews in Judaea and about four million elsewhere. The Dispersion (Greek *diaspora*) had taken place gradually and for a number of reasons; there were, of course, the forced deportations to Babylon, where about a million Jews lived, but trade took Jews elsewhere round the Mediterranean almost from the beginning. There were particularly close connections with Egypt, where Alexandria had a great Jewish community; there were also Jews in North Africa, Syria, Asia Minor, Greece and Italy.

These Jews had to preserve their identity in a culture which was predominantly Greek. They were therefore organized into communities, living in separate quarters of a city and having the power of self-government to a considerable degree. Both the Hellenistic states and the Roman government allowed a great deal of freedom to religious associations, but the privileges of the Jews went well beyond this. They were on the whole in an excellent position towards the state, but had to pay for it by suffering the constant ill-feeling of their neighbours, which on occasion damaged official relations.

Although the language of the Dispersion was Greek, these Jews still looked to the temple while it stood, and paid a great deal of money to support it. The synagogue, however, will have been a far more regular influence in their day-to-day life. The problem of knowing how far Greek culture affected Jewish beliefs has already been mentioned; we do not have enough evidence. The two writers from whom we have extensive works are very different in character, although they are almost contemporaries; Philo from Alexandria and Paul from Asia Minor.

Paul's life and thought is described in detail elsewhere; in contrast, Philo seems calmer, more cultured, more philosophical – very much the traditional university don. His writings comprise some historical works, a set of questions and answers, almost in commentary form, on Genesis and Exodus, and a great number of essays on particular subjects in the Pentateuch. His principal tool is allegory, and he uses it to commend the Jewish Law to the Greek world. By reading the ideas of Plato and the Stoics back into the Old Testament in this way, Philo is able to present Moses as the great philosopher, whose ideas have been borrowed by the Greeks. He is helped by the Greek translation of Torah; the word *nomos*, law, already had many philosophical and scientific overtones. We do not know what sort of an audience Philo reached in his own time, but his works had considerable influence on early Christian writers.

If Pharisaic Judaism culminated in the Rabbinic tradition, Hellenistic Judaism gave way to Christianity. It had no future in the context of Judaism, just as Jewish Christianity had no future in the context of the church. A modern Jewish comment is apt: Jewish Christianity withered since it lacked survival power; Hellenistic Judaism withered since it lacked survival value.

## Qumran

In one respect, the movement of which the community at Qumran formed a part may be seen as an extreme development of Pharisaism, which took the principle of separatism to new heights; it probably originated during the Maccabaean period.

The people of Qumran are almost certainly Essenes, a group mentioned by Philo, Josephus and the Roman naturalist Pliny the Elder, though the title is never used in the Dead Sea scrolls. There are some discrepancies between the ancient accounts and what we know at first hand, but the similarities are close enough to be convincing. Details of the life of the community are provided by the site itself and two documents containing regulations: the Community Rule, formerly called the Manual of Discipline, and the Damascus Rule, so called because it describes a group which migrated to Damascus and entered into a new covenant. The latter document was found in a Cairo *geniza*, but fragments have also turned up at Qumran; it probably represents a different stage of development from the Community Rule, as there are again some dissimilarities.

The larger movement of which the Qumran community was a part did not all live in isolation in the desert. It had representatives in communities in villages and towns all over Palestine who had closer contacts with day to day social life. The Qumran community represents the greatest degree of separation; the remains of its buildings show that it was virtually self-sufficient. Wherever they lived, members shared the same beliefs and hopes; they regarded themselves as the remnant of the true Israel, and they looked for a messianic age to come. Their beliefs were reflected in their organization, into clergy and laity and into twelve tribes and smaller subsidiary units.

The priests had ultimate authority, though there was a community assembly and a council of twelve laymen and three priests to show that the laity also had their share in decisions. The two chief officials seem to have been the Priest and the Guardian (or Inspector), responsible for ritual and community life; there is much dispute over the precise nature of their work.

Once their suitability had been established, new members entered into the 'new covenant' in the presence of the whole community. What happened after this is disputed. There is evidence of a progressive training: a two year probationary period, during the first year of which the candidate took no part in the more sacred activities and retained his possessions, followed by a second when his property was kept by the community until his training was complete, and when he was admitted to some sacred functions; finally, full membership was granted, possessions were renounced and he took a full part in meals and worship. The question is whether this sequence applied to all members, or only to a select inner group; the second alternative seems more likely. In that case there will have been a superior council within the community. Marriage was not forbidden, even to the inner group, and some female skeletons have been found at Qumran, but those looking for ultimate perfection are likely to have chosen celibacy.

Like other Jewish groups, the people of Qumran studied the Scriptures avidly, but their biblical commentaries show that they had their own special method of interpretation. They applied the texts of the prophetic books to their own history and future, using an approach not dissimilar to that found in apocalyptic and parts of the New Testament. The Commentary on Habakkuk is the best example of their work. From their reading of Scripture they expected two Messiahs, a priestly Messiah of Aaron and a Messiah of Israel (and also the Teacher of Righteousness, a mysterious figure who also played a part in their history ?; here again the texts are puzzling and there is much argument). The War Rule describes the final battle between the spirits of light and the spirits of darkness which would be paralleled by a similar battle on earth before the final victory was won.

These future expectations helped to condition the day-to-day life of the sect and were an important reason for their continued purity.

Their negative attitude to the rest of Judaism around them led to a rejection of the traditional calendar and a rejection of temple worship. Their own worship centred on the common meal, which probably represented the eschatological feast that would be celebrated in the last days.

The discovery of the Dead Sea scrolls and their contents at first led to some exaggerated ideas about the significance of the Qumran sect in relation to Christianity. In fact, very few direct connections between Qumran and the early church can be demonstrated, and none on matters of central importance. A reading of the scrolls alone will make it quite clear that their main importance is in the light that they shed on the different forms of Judaism to be found at the beginning of the Christian era.

(The most convenient introduction to the Dead Sea scrolls and translation of the texts is to be found in Geza Vermes, *The Dead Sea Scrolls in English* published by Penguin Books.)

## The Zealots

Politically, the Pharisees were quietists; they were advocates of non-vioence in relationship with Rome. The chief characteristic of the Zealots, who had much in common with the Pharisees, was their approval of violence in defence of their faith.

There are probably connections between the Zealot movement and the Maccabees, but its beginning is usually taken to be a revolt against the census of Quirinius in AD 6. Judas, the leader of the revolt, was a Galilean, the son of an Eleazar who was executed by Herod; his son led the last stand of the Zealots at Masada. The Zealots refused to pay Roman taxes; they take their name from their zeal for the temple and the Law, which is amply illustrated in the writings of Josephus. Josephus writes very disapprovingly of them and labels them *sicarii* ('assassins'); he could hardly do otherwise in his position.

Luke's list of apostles includes Simon, called 'the Zealot' (Luke 6.15; Acts 1.13); the parallel passages in Mark (3.18) and Matthew (10.4) have 'the Cananaean', which is the Aramaic form of the same word. The presence of a Zealot among Jesus' followers, coupled with recorded actions of Jesus like the cleansing of the temple and the fact that he was crucified by the Romans on a quasi-political charge has prompted elaborate theories about the connection between Jesus and the Zealots. It can only be said that there is just not enough evidence to make out a case – either way.

## The Samaritans

Had it been prophesied around AD 30 that the only movements to survive the next two thousand years would be the successors of the Pharisees, the followers of Jesus and the Samaritans, the forecast would have been considered too ridiculous to be worth a second thought. Yet this is what has happened. A group of the despised Samaritans still lives and worships near Mount Gerizim, despite all the troubled history of Palestine.

The Samaritans were the inhabitants of what was once the northern kingdom of Israel. In New Testament times it is clear from both Jewish and Christian sources that there was hatred and hostility between them and the Jews. Unfortunately, beyond the recognition of this enmity there is much that is blurred and indistinct.

The Samaritans regard themselves as the

true Israel, which was split off from the rest of the people when the latter were tainted by the sin of Eli, priest at Shiloh in the time of Samuel. Though they were deported at the fall of the northern kingdom in 722 BC, they returned forty-five years later. The Jews, on the other hand, regarded the Samaritans as the descendants of the colonists who repopulated the northern kingdom after the Assyrian conquest. Because of this, they felt Samaritan religious observances to be fatally tainted.

The Samaritan view cannot be right, but the Jewish view is also exaggerated in the opposite direction. What the truth was has now been lost. Developments after the Jewish return from exile, with their new concerns, seem to have led to constant rivalry between Jews and Samaritans. How it began is obscure, but it reached its climax when the Samaritans built a temple of their own on Mount Gerizim. The date of its building is unknown; it was, however, there by the early second century BC, and does not seem to have been new then.

In 129 BC, John Hyrcanus destroyed the temple on Gerizim, adding to Samaritan hatred. Herod married a Samaritan woman, so relations may have become slightly easier during his reign; it is even possible that for a time Samaritans had access to the Jerusalem temple. However, Josephus reports that a new act of defilement, the scattering by Samaritans of human bones in the temple grounds, stirred up the old hostility again. The first century was a bad period: Jews on pilgrimage from Galilee, passing through Samaria, were set on and attacked; in the end Samaritans were treated by Jews as Gentiles.

Earlier references to the Samaritans contain a number of vivid sayings about their impurity; John 4.9 has an old comment about the practice of Jews and Samaritans not using the same vessels for this reason. Yet the Samaritans shared the same Torah with the Jews (without the Prophets and Writings, which they did not accept). These were the people whom Jesus chose to illustrate gratitude and love.

JOHN BOWDEN

4 Rome and the Middle East

*The chief scource for this period is the Jewish historian, Josephus, who was born in* AD*37 and lived until at least* AD *100. A modern translation of his* History of the Jewish War, *which records Jewish history from 167* BC *to* AD*73, is available in the Penguin Classics series.*

## Rome and Israel

By 63 BC Rome had acquired thirteen provinces, from Spain in the west to Cilicia in the east. In that year the Roman general Pompey, who had been campaigning in Asia Minor, created the new provinces of Bithynia with Pontus and Syria. From Syria, Pompey planned a campaign against the rich kingdom of the Nabataean Arabs, with its capital at Petra, but before he could embark on this he was led to intervene in Jewish affairs. Since 67 there had been civil war in Judaea between Hyrcanus and Aristobulus, the two sons of the late king and high priest, Alexander Jannaeus. The history of the Jews under the leadership of this family, the Hasmoneans, had been expansionist; in particular, the kingdom of Judaea now included Idumaea to the south and Galilee to the north, and the inhabitants of these areas were compelled to adopt the Jewish faith. Now, Hyrcanus, the elder brother, was high priest and was to become king when his mother Queen Alexandra died. Aristobulus, however, who was the more forceful character, had seized most of the country and was challenging this settlement. The matter was brought to Pompey's attention at Damascus, and he condemned Aritobulus and confirmed the settlement.

Aristobulus prepared for war and, after once agreeing to surrender but breaking his promise, was besieged in the temple at Jerusalem. This first Roman siege of Jerusalem lasted three months, and, when it ended, the Gentile Pompey entered the Holy of Holies in triumph, but from religious scruples did not touch the vast treasures of the temple. He again confirmed Hyrcanus in the office of high priest, but did not make him king.

The general shape of Pompey's settlement of the East was dictated by two factors, the presence on the Euphrates frontier of the growing power of Parthia and a typically Roman reluctance to extend direct control further than was necessary. Syria was thus the only area under direct Roman rule, though even within this province there were self-governing enclaves, such as the league of ten cities known as the Decapolis. Dependent upon Syria, however, were a number of client kingdoms, areas still under the control of their native rulers, who were obliged as allies of Rome to assist in the defence of the frontier. To the south of Syria there were three such kingdoms, the Nabataean, the Ituraean, and the Jewish, which was greatly reduced in size by the loss of certain areas, such as Joppa, Jamnia, and Samaria, which had been Jewish for many generations.

## Herod the Great

The man responsible for Pompey's supporting Hyrcanus was Antipater, the father of Herod the Great. He was an Arab, though Jewish by faith, being a member of the leading family among the Idumaeans (or Edomites). Like his father, he served as governor of Idumaea within the Jewish kingdom, but, more important, he was the power behind Hyrcanus' throne. He already enjoyed friendly relations with the Banataeans and had married a princess from their country. Now, however, he realized that, with the establishment of Roman control over Syria, the conditions of political life in the Near East were totally changed: from now on it was only through co-operation with Rome that Judaea could hope to preserve any freedom of action; opposition to Rome would lead to utter ruin. This pro-Roman policy was to be the basis of his own success and that of his son Herod.

It was not an easy policy. There were elements in Judaea opposed to it, to whom the various member of Aristobulus' family would seem natural leaders. There was the possibility of a clash between his Nabataean sympathies and his pro-Roman policy. Above all, there was the fact that Rome did not speak with one voice, for this was the beginning of the period of anarchy and civil war at Rome that was to last for some thirty years. Antipater dealt successfully with all these difficulties.

In 49 BC, when war broke out between Pompey and Caesar, Antipater naturally supported the former, whose defeat and death a year later faced him with a major crisis. Luckily for him, Caesar found himself in considerable difficulties in Alexandria, where he had intervened in civil war on behalf of Cleopatra; both in the military and in the diplomatic field Antipater rendered him valuable service and was duly rewarded. Caesar confirmed Hyrcanus' position as high priest and as ethnarch (President of the Jewish nation – the title king was in abeyance). Antipater received Roman citizenship and was appointed procurator of Judaea, thus becoming the official representative of Roman power in the kingdom and its

effective ruler, as Hyrcanus was now little more than a figurehead. To assist in running the state, Antipater made his eldest son, Phasael, prefect of Jerusalem and his second son, Herod, governor of Galilee.

Herod was now twenty-six; he was tall and handsome in appearance, an able speaker, and according to Josephus, 'overflowing with energy'; moreover, he already had considerable experience both of Romans – ten years earlier he had rapidly struck up a friendship with Mark Antony – and of the Arabs and Jews among whom he had been brought up. He seized the opportunity now offered him in his first official appointment with typical vigour by hunting down a group of bandits who were infesting the border-land between Syria and Galilee. As a mark of his gratitude the governor of Syria added Samaria and parts of Syria to the area under Herod's control.

The murder of Caesar in 44 brought Antipater and his family into peril once again. Faced with opposition in Rome, the chief assassins, Brutus and Cassius, left Italy to enlist support in the east for their war against Mark Antony and Octavian. Cassius demanded seven hundred talents from the Jews, and, although this was more than they could afford, Antipater persuaded them to agree and divided the sum between the various regions of Judaea. The first to secure his quota was Herod, who thus won the favour of Cassius, and soon after Cassius gave him temporary command of all Syria 'as they hoped for valuable assistance from him'.

The defeat of Brutus and Cassius at Philippi in 42 thus necessitated another display of political dexterity by Herod and Phasael; the situation was the more difficult as Antipater had been murdered a year before, and the legal position of his sons was unclear. It says much for Herod's personality that he was able to confront the victorious Antony in the presence of a large hostile delegation and to recover his firm friendship; a few months later he and Phasael were appointed tetrarchs of Judaea. (The word 'tetrach' is familiar to readers of the New Testament. It originally meant the ruler of a fourth part, but then came to indicate the ruler of any area, though usually one who did not enjoy full sovereignty.) Hyrcanus remained high priest and ethnarch, but effective power lay with the brothers, who would co-operate closely with the Romans.

One reason for Antony's ready support for Herod and Phasael was the continuing Parthian threat. In 53 the Roman general Crassus had attacked Parthia but had suffered a crushing defeat at Carrhae. Antony now planned a second expedition, but in 40, before he could act, the Parthians invaded Syria. With them came Antigonus, the son of Aristobulus and pretender to the Hasmonean throne. He attracted strong support from the Jews, and within a short time Judaea was in revolt. Hyrcanus and Phasael were captured, and the latter killed himself. Herod was forced to leave Jerusalem secretly. He left his family in the strong fortress of Masada and fled to Petra; failing to win support there, he eventually made his way by Egypt and Rhodes to Rome, where he appealed to Antony. Antony, 'recalling Antipater's hospitality and filled with admiration for the heroic character before him, decided on the spot that the man he had once made tetrarch should now be king of the Jews'. However, it was not until 37 that Herod was able to enter Jerusalem, escorted to his capital by a force of Roman legionaries.

In 31 Octavian defeated Antony at the battle of Actium; this marked the end of the period of civil wars in Rome and is usually considered the starting-point of the Roman Empire. Herod, who had, of course, backed Antony, was lucky not have been present at the battle; due to some intrigues on the part of Cleopatra, who envied his influence with Antony, he was campaigning against the Nabataeans at the time. Even so, his meeting with Octavian after the battle cannot have been easy and demonstrates once again the combination of daring and flexibility that enabled him to survive so long. He admitted his friendship with Antony, but, in Josephus' words, asked Octavian to consider 'not whose friend, but what a good friend I was'. Octavian confirmed him in his position and restored to Judaea certain territories which Antony had given to Cleopatra. Shortly afterwards, Herod also made the acquaintance of Octavian's chief minister, Agrippa; the two became firm friends, and it is after him that the later members of the family, mentioned in the Acts of the Apostles, were named.

Externally, Herod now found the situation easier; he based his policy on his friendship with Augustus (as Octavian now became known) and Agrippa, and they did not let him down. Thus, when Augustus visited Syria in 20 BC, he dismissed certain complaints against Herod – and so effectively that the complainants committed suicide –, increased his territory, made him one of the procurators of Syria, and appointed his brother, Pheroras, tetrarch of the area east of the Jordan. In 15 BC Agrippa, who had now become Augustus' junior partner in ruling the Empire, with particular responsibility for the east, paid a very successful visit to Judaea, and in the next year Herod travelled a thousand miles to join Agrippa in a naval campaign in the Black Sea. On their return together to Asia Minor, Herod was able to secure Agrippa's support for the Jews of the Dispersion, some of whom were being unfairly treated by the Greeks in whose cities they lived. At this stage, as Josephus puts it, 'In Augustus' affections Herod was second only to Agrippa, and in Agrippa's second only to Augustus.'

Herod never enjoyed the same success in his relations with the Jews. He was an Idumaean and, therefore, could not combine the offices of king and high priest, as the Hasmoneans had done; the separation of the two offices served as a permanent reminder to his subjects of the fact that he was a usurper and the nominee of a foreign power and was, moreover, a lasting contradiction of what Josephus called the 'theocratic' tradition of the Jews. Nevertheless, his achievements, particularly on the material level, were far from negligible. He developed the economic resources of his kingdom, rebuilt the temple in Jerusalem, and founded two new cities – the port of Caesarea, which was on such a scale that it took twelve years to complete, and the city of Sebaste (the word is the Greek equivalent of Augustus) in Samaria. When severe famine struck Judaea in 25 BC, he acted promptly and vigorously, selling the gold and silver furniture from his palace to buy corn from the Roman governor of Egypt; he, of course, was a personal friend.

Furthermore, he took an active interest in the welfare of the Jews of the Dispersion, intervening, as we have seen, to secure for them free enjoyment of certain rights previously conceded by the Romans; notable among these were the right to contribute to the treasury of the temple in Jerusalem and the right of exemption from military service, which would have involved infringement of the strict laws governing the sabbath.

It is difficult to recognize in this vital and capable ruler the tyrannical monster who, in the story told in Matt.2.16 f., ordered the massacre of the innocents. This story is not recorded anywhere apart from the Gospel of Matthew. Herod was under severe pressure by reason of his chaotic family situation. He married ten wives and had fourteen children, nine of them male, but the struggle for the succession centred at first on the sons born to him by his first two wives.

Before Herod became king, he had married Doris, a commoner and, like himself, an Idumaean; their son, Antipater, was Herod's eldest child. Even before the Parthian invasion of 40 BC, Herod had realized that this marriage brought him no diplomatic advantage. The success of Antigonus on that occasion brought the matter home to him, and in 37 he married Mariamne I. Doris and Antipater were banished from the court. The new match seemed ideal. Not only was the bride strikingly beautiful, but she united in herself the two rival branches of the Hasmonean family, being the grand-daughter of both Hyrcanus and Aristobulus; Herod might reasonably hope that this marriage would seem in a sense to legitimize his position and thus bring peace and security to the kingdom. His hopes were soon disappointed, for Mariamne detested him from the start and constantly schemed against him for the benefit of her own family. Her chief rival at court was Herod's sister, Salome, who found natural allies in Doris and Antipater. In eight years these intrigues led through the murders of Mariamne's brother, Aristobulus, who had become high priest, of Herod's uncle, Joseph, and of several minor figures to that of Mariamne herself.

Nevertheless, Herod treated her children

with great kindness, sending the two sons, Alexander and Aristobulus, to be educated in Rome. There they moved in the highest society and became well-known to the imperial family. In 18 BC, when Herod visited Rome, they returned to Judaea with him, were clearly marked out for the succession, and became very popular. The intrigues between the two families continued, and Salome took advantage of Herod's visit to Agrippa in 14 BC to suggest on his return that the young men were plotting against him. The charge seemed plausible, and Herod reacted by recalling Antipater to court and, a year later, by making him his heir. Augustus effected a reconciliation between Herod and the sons of Mariamne in 12 BC, but explicitly recognized Herod's right to dispose of his kingdom, whole or divided, as he pleased, provided that he retained sole control until his death. (This was, perhaps, not the concession it seemed. Augustus did not want to become involved in Herod's family affairs, and, for the rest, he was permitting Herod only the right to make what will he pleased, without in any way guaranteeing its enforcement. The brusque removal of Archelaus in AD 6 bears this out.) The reconciliation was short-lived, and, in an atmosphere of increasing tension, of plot and counter-plot, the scheming continued, until, in 7 BC, Alexander and Aristobulus were tried *in absentia* before the governor of Syria. Given no chance to defend themselves, they were convicted and executed.

Antipater's position must now have seemed secure and was recognized in a second will, but he was not content to remain crown-prince for long and was soon scheming against his father. On this occasion the plot also involved Herod's brother Pheroras and another of his wives, Mariamne II. It was the death of Pheroras in 5 BC that occasioned its detection. Antipater was recalled from Rome, where he had been spreading rumours against his half-brothers, Archelaus and Philip, was accused in private before Varus, the governor of Syria, and was condemned and imprisoned. Only the need to inform the Emperor of certain matters which had come to light during the trial delayed his execution.

By now Herod was seriously ill, both physically and mentally, and it was clear that he could not live much longer. (One diagnosis of his illness, based upon the description given by Josephus, is that it was arterio-sclerosis, among the symptoms of which are rapid changes of mood and delusions of persecution.) In 4 BC, amid mounting opposition from the Pharisees and only a few days before his own death, Herod had Antipater executed and issued his fourth, and final, will.

Under its terms the kingdom he had built up was to be divided between three of his sons, the eldest of whom was only eighteen. Archelaus was to be king of Judaea proper, of Idumaea, and of Samaria; his brother, Antipas, tetrarch of Galilee and Transjordan; their half-brother, Philip, tetrarch of Gaulonitis, Trachonitis, and Paneas, the areas in the north-east of the kingdom. To his sister, Salome, whose intrigues had done so much to darken his last years, Herod left large estates and a huge sum of money. An even larger sum was bequeathed to Augustus and other members of the imperial family. Archelaus was ordered to carry his father's ring and all state papers to Augustus and to request his confirmation of the will.

### Tetrarchs and procurators

#### 1. Archelaus

The vigorous action of Salome ensured that

Archelaus' succession was not contested, but he soon showed that he had little of his father's political flair. An unwise speech of his just before the Passover led to rioting in the temple, and his attempts to check it veered from untimely concessions to unnecessary force; eventually he sent in the army, and three thousand worshippers were killed. Shortly after, he left for Rome to seek confirmation of his father's will, which was disputed by his brother Antipas.

During his absence there were further disturbances in Judaea. These were occasioned by the rapacity of Sabinus, the procurator of Syria (and so, the emperor's chief financial agent in the area), in attempting to take over Herod's property before knowing Augustus' decision as to the succession, and led through bitter fighting between Romans and Jews around the temple to full-scale rebellion directed as much against Archelaus as against the Romans. (Significantly enough, the only elements to remain loyal were the troops whom Herod had recruited from among the Greek population of his kingdom.) The governor of Syria was compelled to intervene in strength and after a brief but bloody campaign – 2000 of the rebel leaders were crucified – order was restored.

This news cannot have made Augustus' decision in Rome any easier, and it was further complicated by the arrival of a deputation from Jerusalem – backed, we are told, by the large Jewish colony in Rome – requesting him to abolish the Herodian kingdom and either bring the area under direct Roman rule or leave it autonomous. Despite all this, Augustus largely confirmed Herod's will, only withholding from Archelaus the title of king; for the time being, at least, he was to be only ethnarch.

Back in Judaea he showed little interest in the welfare of his kingdom, and soon earned a reputation for cruelty, which is reflected in the statement that Joseph was reluctant to pass through Judaea on his return to Nazareth (Matt.2.22). Finally, in AD 6 Jews and Samaritans combined to denounce Archelaus to Augustus for marrying his dead brother's wife – forbidden by Jewish law – and for his treatment of his subjects. Augustus exiled him to France and decided to make a province of Judaea.

The complexity of the following years, during which Judaea itself was a province while Antipas and Philip continued to rule their tetrarchies, can be seen in Luke's painstaking attempt to date the start of John the Baptist's ministry:

> Now in the fifteenth year of the reign of Tiberius Caesar, Pontius Pilate being governor of Judaea, and Herod being tetrarch of Galilee, and his brother Philip tetrarch of Ituraea and of the region of Trachonitis, and Lysanias the tetrarch of Abilene, Annas and Caiaphas being the high priests, the word of God came unto John . . . (Luke 3.1 f.).

Two points here call for elucidation: the reference to Antipas as Herod and the mention of two high priests. On Herod's death, Archelaus and, on his banishment, Antipas assumed the name Herod, and, except in Matt.2.1–22 and Luke 1.5, all references to Herod in the Gospels are in fact to Antipas. The Romans had deposed Annas from office, appointing his son Caiaphas in his place, but according to the Law a high priest remained until his death, and many Jews refused to recognize the change.

## 2. *Philip and Antipas*

Philip continued to rule over his tetrarchy

until his death in AD 34, when for three years it became part of the province of Syria. Most of his subjects were Gentiles, and his task was probably easier than that of Archelaus. He seems to have made an efficient and conscientious ruler.

Antipas, who also remained in power until his death (AD 39), is better known, from the references to him in the Gospels and perhaps particularly as the man responsible for the death of John the Baptist; moreover, his tetrarchy, of Galilee and Transjordan, was the scene of much of Jesus' ministry. On the death of Augustus in AD 14 Antipas did all he could to win the approval of his successor, Tiberius, and it may have been his scheming to this end that lies behind Jesus' reference to him as 'that fox' (Luke 13.32). One example of this policy was his foundation of a new capital city on the Sea of Galilee, which he named Tiberias in honour of the emperor.

On a visit to Rome he fell in love with Herodias, the wife of his half-brother, Herod-Philip. This presented a serious problem. First, Antipas was already married to a daughter of the king of the Nabataeans, and any move that jeopardized the security of the eastern frontier would be unpopular in Rome. Secondly, if he obtained Herodias by divorce, he would be infringing Jewish law. Nevertheless, Herodias and Antipas were determined to marry, and Antipas' wife returned secretly to Petra, her rejection reviving the dormant hostility between the Nabataeans and the family of Herod. It was for this marriage that John the Baptist denounced Antipas, a course which led to his death and the dramatic story of Herodias' daughter, Salome (Mark 6.14–29).

An incident showing Antipas in rather better light occurred during Pilate's governorship of Judaea. According to the Jewish writer Philo, Pilate wished to dedicate some golden shields, carrying the emperor's name, in the temple. A deputation consisting of Antipas, three of his brothers and the leaders of the Sanhedrin protested unsuccessfully to Pilate, but a letter to Tiberius secured a more favourable reply: the shields should be dedicated in the temple of Augustus at Caesarea, where they would give less offence.

In AD 37 Tiberius died, and with him Antipas' fortunes. The new emperor, Caligula, made his friend, Herod Agrippa I, the grandson of Herod the Great, king of Philip's former tetrarchy. Herodias, angry at what she considered a slight to her husband, set off with him to Rome to complain, but an accusation by Agrippa that Antipas was in league with the Parthians sealed his doom. Antipas was banished, and his tetrarchy and revenues given to Agrippa (AD 39).

Meanwhile, Archelaus' region had been a Roman province for thirty-three years. It was administered from Caesarea, Herod's new city on the coast, which being largely Gentile in population had none of the limiting traditions of Jerusalem. In Caesarea, and on his visits to Jerusalem, the governor lived in the palaces built by Herod. He could call upon the services of a small garrison of auxiliary troops, under the immediate command of a tribune, such as Claudius Lysias (Acts 21.31); many of these were probably recruited inside Judaea, at first from the army of Herod and Archelaus, but the great majority of them would have been Gentile, not Jew. In times of crisis requiring larger forces the governor would look for help to Syria, whose governor commanded four legions as well as some auxiliary units.

Although the province of Judaea was small –

only about the size of Wales – it was in a thoroughly unsettled condition. The Jews felt themselves to be a unique people, and, though the basis of this claim was religious, under conditions of unpopular foreign domination its manifestations were bound to be political. Each of the main religious sects thus had its own political 'line' – most obviously, the extreme nationalism of the Zealots. The governors of Judaea varied a good deal in type and origin – Pilate, for example, was probably by birth a provincial Italian, rather than a Roman, while Tiberius Alexander was a renegade Jew of the Dispersion – but one forms the impression that generally speaking they were men of insufficient calibre to cope successfully with the peculiar complexities of their office.

It is impossible to give a full narrative of the events occurring in each governor's term of office, but the disturbed situation of the province, with brigands – or nationalist insurgents – active in the countryside and frequent changes of high priest – now appointed by the Roman governor – increasing tension in Jerusalem, needs to be remembered as the background to the ministry of Jesus.

### 3. *Pilate, procurator of Judaea*

Pontius Pilate was the fifth governor of Judaea, in office from AD 27 to 36. His picture in the Gospels is well-known, but we also have information about him from two other sources, Josephus and the Jewish writer Philo of Alexandria, who was a contemporary of Pilate. It is Philo who relates Pilate's behaviour in the matter of the golden shields already mentioned; he describes him as 'naturally inflexible and stubbornly relentless' and accuses him of 'arrogance, repeated murders of innocent victims, and constant and most galling savagery'.

As Philo was arguing to prove a case, his evidence may be unreliable.

Neither is Josephus unbiased, for he was attempting to prove that the Jewish War of AD 66-73 was not started by irresponsible fanatics but by men who had already endured a succession of incompetent and cruel governors with the utmost patience and who only took to war reluctantly and as a last resort; it is thus in his interest, too, to blacken Pilate's character. He records three incidents in Pilate's governorship. The first was a tactless attempt to send troops into winter quarters in Jerusalem carrying standards bearing a representation of the emperor's head. The Jews protested; there must be no 'graven images' in the Holy City. Pilate attempted compromise unsuccessfully, and the matter was referred to Tiberius, who decided in favour of the Jews. The second incident underlines the extreme difficulty of Pilate's position. He used some of the temple money to improve the water supply to Jerusalem and to the temple itself. Although this use of the fund was specifically permitted by the Law, there was rioting in Jerusalem, which Pilate put down violently. Finally, Pilate massacred some Samaritans who were caught up in a messianic movement; a complaint to Vitellius, the governor of Syria, to whom Tiberius had entrusted a general oversight of eastern affairs, resulted in Pilate's removal from office and return in disgrace to Rome.

Apart from the Gospel descriptions of Pilate's part in the trial of Jesus, there is a reference to Pilate in Luke 13.1, 'Galileans, whose blood Pilate had mingled with their sacrifices'. It is just possible that this incident was the cause of the enmity referred to in Luke 23.12 between Pilate and Antipas, the tetrarch of Galilee.

### 4. *Pilate and the trial of Jesus*

The accounts of Jesus' trial before Pilate provide a good example of a Roman governor's judicial powers and of the way in which these would operate. It is one of the chief differences between Roman and modern English law that in the former very few crimes were clearly defined and provided with a set range of penalties and that even in these the procedures laid down applied only to Roman citizens. In all other matters brought before a magistrate (in this case, the governor) it was his first task to decide whether to listen to the accusers, for his power to dismiss a case was absolute. If he thought the matter deserved his attention, he would hear the trial and decide upon the sentence and penalty; from these, too, there was no appeal, though, before proceedings started, a Roman citizen could claim the right to be tried in Rome before the emperor.

Cases concerning Jews would not usually come before the governor at all, for it was Roman practice to allow well-established communities as large a measure of self-government as was consistent with good order, and the Sanhedrin thus retained wide judicial powers. It could not, however, inflict the death penalty – except in the quite exceptional cases of Gentiles trespassing in the temple – though it is sometimes argued that it could sentence a man to death and forward its decision to the governor for confirmation. This probably misstates the position. It is more likely that when the Sanhedrin felt the dealth penalty would be appropriate, it would institute proceedings before the governor; the Roman government was always particularly careful to retain life and death decisions in its own hands. At the same time, the prestige of the Sanhedrin must often

have made it successful in such actions, and it is easy to see how such a belief could have arisen.

All the Gospels make it clear that Jesus was first examined before the Sanhedrin and then taken to Pilate. The charge was one of sedition. It seems that Pilate would like to have dismissed the case, but, fearing to do so outright, availed himself of the fact that Jesus was a Galilean to send him to Antipas (Luke 23.7). As Antipas refused to deal with the case, he was sent back to Pilate. Pilate's reluctance to pronounce the death penalty remains clear, but, when he hesitated, the Sanhedrin played its trump card: 'If you let this man go, you are no friend to Caesar' (John 19.12). Pilate could not afford to provide grounds for an influential deputation to go from his province to Rome and accuse him before the emperor of unreliability. He submitted to this extra-legal pressure and gave orders for Jesus' crucifixion. Thus, though it is possible that the Gospel writers exaggerate Pilate's reluctance and Jewish guilt, the trial as recorded in the Gospels, with its curious laxity of procedure and combination of religious, political, and legal arguments, is exactly what one would expect in this situation.

Any final assessment of Pilate's character is made impossible by the scarcity of evidence, but it is perhaps worth mentioning that, in accordance with Tiberius' preference for long terms of office, Pilate was allowed to remain governor of Judaea for nearly ten years.

### *The later tetrarchs and governors*

Herod Agrippa I enjoyed the friendship of both Caligula and Claudius, the emperors who succeeded Tiberius. Caligula had made him king of the area which his uncle Philip had previously ruled as tetrarch and had then enlarged his kingdom by the addition of Antipas' tetrarchy. In AD 41 Agrippa had bravely used his friendship with Caligula to persuade him to countermand his orders for the erection of a large statue of himself in the temple. In the same year Caligula was assassinated, and Agrippa was largely instrumental in securing the succession of Claudius. He was handsomely rewarded. Claudius abolished the province of Judaea and added it to Agrippa's territory, thus reconstituting the kingdom of Herod the Great.

He reigned for only three years, but during that time he showed considerable ability. To demonstrate that Judaea was Jewish once more he made Jerusalem his official residence, and by remission of taxes and other conciliatory moves he became extremely popular with his subjects. His execution of James, the son of Zebedee, and arrest of Peter, two of the leaders of the growing Christian community (Acts 12.1–18), is hardly likely to have been widely unpopular. (Stephen, the first martyr, had been illegally executed by the Sanhedrin in AD 37 during the period immediately following Pilate's recall, in which Judaea had no governor.)

One of the main problems for the Jews of the Dispersion was the ill-feeling existing in many cities between the Greek majority and the Jewish community. Nowhere was this more true than in Alexandria. Matters came to a head once again in Claudius' reign, and rival deputations from the city appealed to the Emperor in Rome. Claudius' decree confirmed the traditional rights of the Jews and ordered the Greeks not to interfere with these; at the same time the Jews were not to try to increase their privileges and were not to seek converts.

On Agrippa's death, Claudius wished to appoint his son, Herod Agrippa II, to the throne of Judaea, but the boy was only seventeen, and Claudius was persuaded to make the area a province once more. (It now, of course, included the whole of Herod Agrippa's kingdom.) Four years later, Claudius made Herod Agrippa II king of Chalcis in the Lebanon.

The governors of the restored province seem to have continued the generally low standard set by their predecessors, although Josephus comments favourably on the first two, Cuspius Fadus and Tiberius Alexander, on the grounds that they 'left native customs alone and kept the nation at peace'. With the third, however, Cumanus, troubles began again, his governorship being marked 'by disturbances and further disasters to the Jews'. There was rioting at the Passover between the worshippers and the Roman garrison – which, if one may believe Josephus, led to the death of more than thirty thousand. There was trouble when Cumanus ordered his soldiers to sack some villages whose inhabitants he suspected of harbouring brigands, and there was a clash between Galileans and Samaritans, which ended in the now traditional way with each side sending a deputation to the emperor; the influence of Agrippa II with Claudius ensured a Jewish victory.

Of the next governor, Felix, the Roman historian Tacitus says that 'he indulged in every kind of barbarity and lust and exercised the power of a king in the spirit of a salve'. He was well connected at court – his brother was influential with Claudius and was said to be the lover of the Empress Agrippina, the mother of Nero – and clearly owed his position to this. Drusilla, described in Acts 24.24 as his wife, was the sister of Agrippa II and had been married to the king of Emesa, whom she had abandoned for Felix, although this was contrary to Jewish law. Among other injudicious acts, Felix procured assassins to murder the high priest Jonathan. In the atmosphere of terror that ensued many innocent men were killed. Others flocked to join various false prophets, of whom the most famous is the Egyptian, referred to in Acts 21.38, for whom Paul was mistaken; Felix crushed these with great severity. His high-handedness also shows in his dealings with Paul, whom he kept in custody for two years without bringing him to trial; Luke attributes this to his hope that Paul would offer him a bribe (Acts 24.26).

His successor, Porcius Festus, was more business-like, both in his dealings with Paul and in attempting to free the country of bandits. Unfortunately he died in office, and in the interval before a new governor could take office, the Sanhedrin once again took the law into its own hands and executed James, the brother of Jesus, who was the leader of the Christian community in Jerusalem.

Of the next governor, Albinus, Josephus says that he was 'guilty of every possible misdemeanour' – he mentions robbery, crippling taxation, and accepting bribes – and adds the significant detail that it was during his term of office that 'the revolutionary party in Jerusalem cast off all restraint'.

'Yet the endurance of the Jews lasted until Gessius Florus was governor.' So Tacitus; and Josephus comments that he made even Albinus seem an angel and claims that 'it was he (Florus) who compelled us to take up arms against the Romans, thinking that it was better to be destroyed at once than by degrees'. Florus took up office in AD 64, and the Jewish War – so named, typically, from the Roman angle – began in 66. What occasioned it?

### The Jewish war and the fall of Jerusalem

The first trouble was a clash in Caesarea between Jews and Greeks, in which Florus favoured the latter. Shortly afterwards, he provoked further antagonism in Jerusalem when he demanded a large sum of money from the temple treasury on the pretext that the emperor required it. Demonstrations followed, and, after failing to secure the arrest of those responsible, Florus allowed his troops to loot. Many innocent people were killed, including Jews who were Roman citizens. The Jews complained to Cestius Gallus, the governor of Syria, and he sent one of his officers to investigate the matter; no redress followed. At this stage Agrippa II, who happened to be in Jerusalem, and who realized that if war broke out his own position would be in danger, made a long speech to the inhabitants of the city urging submission. For a time it seemed as though he might be successful, but when he went further and advised them to obey Florus until a successor arrived, the people stoned him, and he returned to his own kingdom, clearly seeing that war was now inevitable.

The war began with seemingly unconnected acts of aggression against the Romans. Within a month the rebels had seized Jerusalem and the greater part of Judaea and had captured the fortress of Masada with its huge arsenal. The disturbances spread to the predominantly Greek cities of the Decapolis and the coast, and even to Alexandria; in all of them there was violent fighting between Greeks and Jews. Cestius Gallus was compelled to intervene and marched south with an army of thirty thousand men, but, despite early success, he failed to press home his advantage.

Nero realized the need for rapid action; the fighting must not be allowed to spread to the frontiers and endanger his recently won settlement with the Parthians. He appointed an experienced general, Vespasian, to the command of Judaea. In AD 67 Vespasian reconquered Galilee, where the young Josephus was in command, and the next year pressed on into Samaria and Transjordan. Meanwhile, in Jerusalem, factional struggles which amounted to civil war were rife and must seriously have weakened the capacity of the inhabitants to resist.

This was the situation in Jerusalem in AD 70 when Titus, the son of Vespasian, who had been left in command when his father returned to Rome to become emperor, came to attack the city. The story of the siege is graphically told by Josephus. The natural position of the city was immensely strong, and it was impressively fortified. Attack was only possible from the north or north-west, where the assailants would have to breach three walls in turn; even then, there remained the temple itself and the upper city, both of which could serve as well-defended inner citadels. The siege began in May. The Romans employed all their skill in siege warfare, building huge ramps and towers, attempting to mine the walls or battering them with huge boulders thrown from their artillery, and eventually constructing a wall of five miles in length running right round the city, but the defenders resisted heroically. Not until the end of September was the whole city in Roman hands. City and temple were razed to the ground. (Titus' achievement was recorded on a triumphal arch set up in the forum at Rome; its sculptures show the temple treasures, including the seven-branched candelabra, being carried in procession through the streets of Rome.)

Mopping-up operations continued for a further three years, culminating in the long siege and heroic defence of Masada, the great fortress which towers over the western shore of the Dead Sea. (The site has recently been excavated, and Josephus' account of the siege can now be compared with the findings of the archaeologists in Y. Yadin: *Masada*.) When further resistance proved impossible, the surviving defenders – to the number of nearly a thousand – set fire to the fortress and killed themselves; two women are supposed to have hidden in the underground water cisterns and thus to have furnished Josephus with details of the siege.

The result of the war was the end of a specifically Jewish state. The Sanhedrin and the high priesthood were abolished, and worship at the temple was forbidden.

Even so, for the Romans the Jewish problem continued, and two further revolts must be mentioned. In 115, while the emperor Trajan was campaigning against the Parthians, a rising started among the Jews of Cyrene and soon spread to those resident in Egypt, Cyprus, and Mesopotamia. In origin this seems to have been another in the long series of inter-racial and inter-cultural clashes between Jews and Greeks. In Cyprus, for example, the revolt was marked by hideous atrocities; a quarter of a million Gentiles are said to have perished, and the Greek city of Salamis was destroyed. Trajan, probably remembering the Jewish War of 66–73, obviously feared its effects on his eastern policy and crushed the rising with great severity. On this occasion Judaea itself remained at peace.

The last great rebellion of the Jews occurred in 132, in the reign of Trajan's successor,

Hadrian. When Hadrian visited Judaea in 130, he decided that it would be unwise to leave Jerusalem in its ruined state as a focus for Jewish nationalism and announced plans for its refoundation as a self-governing city with the name Aelia Capitolina (Hadrian's family name was Aelius); its inhabitants were to be Gentiles, and Jews were not to be permitted to enter it except on one day a year; moreover, on the site of the temple would be built a pagan temple dedicated to the worship of Jupiter and the emperor.

In 132, the Jews reacted to this insensitive decision by breaking out into revolt. They were led by Simon bar Kochba, whose recognition as Messiah by the Rabbis rallied support to him. At first the guerilla tactics of the Jews were successful, but the rebellion was finally crushed in AD 135, and Hadrian's new city was built.

### The Roman administrative system

The provincial system established by Augustus after the battle of Actium (31 BC) lasted without essential change throughout the period covered in this section. Under it, the provinces were divided into two groups. The older-established and more peaceful provinces were governed by proconsuls appointed by and responsible to the Senate. An example is Achaea, where Gallio was proconsul (Acts 18.12), but the most important of them were Africa (Libya and Tunisia) and Asia (the Aegean coast of Turkey). The remainder came under the direction of the emperor, who appointed their governors himself. They included most of the frontier provinces, and others where trouble might be expected and contained twenty-four of the twenty-five or so legions of the regular army. The most important of them in the eastern part of the empire was Syria.

An apparent exception to this division are the client kingdoms, of which Judaea under Herod the Great was the most important. Despite their title, these were not truly independent territories, for whatever internal autonomy they enjoyed might be withdrawn at any time by the emperor. However, the uniqueness of Judaea, a country with a well-established tradition of social organization quite different from that of the Greek cities in other parts of the East, made this the obvious solution in this case and the degress of freedom from ostensible Roman control must have been very considerable until the deposition of Archelaus.

The imperial provinces were themselves divided into two classes. The more important of them were governed by legates, men of considerable military and administrative experience. Their main functions were two – military and judicial. The legate of Syria, for example, commanded four legions and various auxiliary units. These guarded the frontier with Parthia, policed the mountains and cities of the province, and could be used to intervene in the client kingdoms or minor provinces surrounding Syria. We have already seen that the cities of the Empire often enjoyed wide judicial powers, and the governor's chief duty in this field was to serve as a court of appeal from the judgments of local magistrates. The governorship of Syria was regarded as the senior appointment in the imperial provinces and enjoyed enormous prestige throughout the East.

The smaller provinces of the second class, to which Judaea belonged, were governed by officials of less experience and standing. They are usually called procurators, the title used by the Roman historian Tacitus, but until the reign of Claudius their correct title was prefect, as an inscription found at Caesarea and dating from Pilate's governorship shows. Although they did not usually command legions and certainly enjoyed less prestige, their powers were basically the same as those of the legates.

So far, no mention has been made of the third main administrative field – the financial. To ensure control of the revenues of his provinces and to prevent corruption among their governors, Augustus separated this field from the military and judicial and created a new class of officials to deal with it, also called procurators. They were concerned with collection of the two regular taxes – the *tributum soli*, levied on land, and the *tributum capitis*, levied on other forms of property. To ensure that they were levied fairly, the holding of an accurate census was one of the first acts upon formation of a new province and was regularly repeated thereafter. There were also certain indirect taxes, including, for example, import/export dues of five per cent and taxes on the sale of slaves. These were not collected by the procurator's staff, but under contract by companies of financiers, who usually employed local assistants – the 'publicans' of the New Testament. All these taxes had, of course, to be paid in Roman currency, and the use of this – carrying as it did a representation of the emperor's head – inevitably caused unrest in Judaea.

### The Decapolis

The Decapolis was a league of cities created by Pompey in 62 BC, probably for mutual defence against the neighbouring Semitic tribes. The individual cities, however, were probably much older. The Roman writer Pliny (*Natural History* V, 74) gives a list of the members, but, as the membership fluctuated, they were not always ten in number. Together they formed a fairly continuous block of territory east of the Sea of Galilee and the Jordan.

Among the certain foundation members were Scythopolis (which Josephus describes as the greatest city of the Decapolis at the time of the Jewish War and which was the only one of the cities to be situated west of the Jordan), Pella, Gadara, Hippos, Dium, Canatha, Philadelphia (now Amman, capital of Jordan), and Gerasa (modern Jerash, the best preserved of the cities and containing many fine buildings dating from this period). Abila was probably a foundation member. By the second century AD Damascus was also a member and had become the metropolis (chief city) of the League.

Jesus crossed the Sea of Galilee and visited the Decapolis on several occasions (Matt.8.28; Mark 7.31). He would have found in them a very different atmosphere from that in Galilee itself, for their population and way of life were Graeco-Roman.

MARGARET J. THORPE

5 Accepted Ideas in First-century
Palestine

All Jews had in common the religious beliefs expressed in the Old Testament. This is the first and most obvious thing that can be said about their outlook on life. They were educated in the Scriptures in the synagogue schools, and what they learned there would be consolidated later by their attendance at worship on the sabbath and also by means of the great festivals of the Jewish year which celebrated the mighty acts of the God they believed in. But religious thinking had not come to an end when the last book in the Old Testament had been written. The Pharisees, the Zealots, and the Qumran sect were all influential, and all of them produced ideas which gradually became popular among ordinary Jews who were not specifically attached to any religious party. Many of these ideas are reflected in the New Testament. In the minds of ordinary people they would tend to intermingle and coalesce, so that the general climate of thought was characterized by a mixture of them all.

To have been born a Jew meant that a man inevitably lived his life within some kind of a religious framework. He might or might not profess a high degree of individual piety. As a Jew, however, he believed himself to belong to a nation which had been specially chosen by God as the instrument of his divine purpose, and which was therefore protected and favoured by him. He believed that God had rescued the Israelites from slavery in Egypt, and that, if they obeyed his commands, he would regard them as his 'peculiar treasure', his 'kingdom of priests', and his 'holy nation' (Ex.19.3–6). This

conviction was reinforced by the yearly celebration of the Passover, which commemorated the deliverance from Egypt. God was also naturally understood as demanding the exclusive loyalty of the whole nation. The worship of any other god was decisively to be condemned. In the past history of the Jews there had been occasions when they had indulged in heathen cults. But in the time of Jesus this was no longer true. Religious practice corresponded with official belief. Popular religion conformed to the words of the ancient prayer: 'Holy art thou, and thy Name is to be feared, and there is no God beside thee' (*The Eighteen Benedictions*). God was the Creator and Preserver of the world, and he was unique. Furthermore, the national way of life symbolized the conviction that God was to be obeyed as well as worshipped. The Jews believed that their function as a nation was to display the greatness of their God through their obedience to his law. In this way they distinguished themselves from other nations. They insisted on keeping the sabbath as a day of rest from work, and they insisted that certain foods, such as pork, were unclean and not to be eaten. By these and other means they symbolically demonstrated their belief in the uniqueness of their God, through their witness to the demands he made for their total devotion to his will. All this gave meaning and purpose to their national life. It was through them that God's plan for the whole world was to be carried out. They believed that the underlying purpose of world history was that the will of the God of Israel should be acknowledged and obeyed.

They showed the rest of the world what this meant, and by their own obedience to the law they assisted in the fulfilment of the divine plan for humanity.

## Evil and suffering

This brings us to another important aspect of Jewish thought during the first century. The actual state of affairs in the world appeared to disprove some of their religious beliefs. There was a great deal of evil, sin and suffering which was surely contrary to God's intention, and yet the world's sole purpose was to conform to the divine will. They themselves were oppressed beneath the tyranny of a heathen government, and yet God had specially chosen them to enjoy his favour and protection. So there was a conflict between belief and reality. The Jews had to ask themselves what explanation there was. And they naturally indulged in hopes of a better future for themselves and their nation.

Why, then, did the God of Israel allow the Romans to continue to occupy Palestine, the holy land of his chosen people? Some of the Pharisees provided an answer. The Jews were in servitude to the Gentiles because they had sinned. The Roman occupation was a sign of God's wrath. This state of affairs would continue until the Jews repented. A similar explanation was often given of individual suffering as well, for it was a common belief that illness was a punishment for sin. The idea is reflected in the question asked by the disciples of Jesus in the story of the man born blind: 'Rabbi, who sinned, this man or his parents, that he was born blind?' (John 9.2). If one asked the further question, why do men sin, the Pharisees would probably have replied that there is within

man an evil impulse, but that this can be held in check by keeping the law. Sin results from the failure to use the law as a remedy against the evil impulse.

Side by side with these explanations of sin and suffering, there is to be found a rather different way of looking at the situation. The present state of affairs is evil because the world and mankind are in the power of Satan, the prince of evil, and a host of lesser demons. The Qumran sect believed this. They regarded themselves as the children of light and the rest of mankind as the children of darkness. The children of darkness were under the dominion of the angel of darkness, who is also called Belial. All other evil powers were subordinate to this prince of evil. He was thought of as making war on the children of light and attempting to lead them astray. There are similar ideas in the New Testament. In the story of the temptation of Jesus (Luke 4.1–13), the devil is made to say that all the kingdoms of the world are in his power, and at the end of I John the writer says that the whole world lies under the sway of the evil one (I John 5.19). Jesus is accused of curing the demon-possessed by means of the diabolic power of the prince of the demons, and he asks in reply, How would it be possible for Satan to drive out Satan (Mark 3.22 f.)? In the background of this story there lies the idea of a kingdom of evil spirits ruled over by Satan. For Satan to assist in the exorcizing of demons would be for him to promote a state of civil war in his kingdom.

What was thought to be the function of the evil spirits? In the first place, they tempt men to evil conduct, such as idolatry, strife, and bloodshed, and set them against God. In the story we have already referred to (Luke 4.1–13), Satan is represented as trying to persuade Jesus to adopt courses of action which he knows to be contrary to God's will. Secondly, they do people physical and psychological harm. The idea that many illnesses were caused by demons was very common. The diseases themselves were spoken of as a 'spirit of leprosy', an 'asthma spirit', a 'spirit of heart disease', and the like. In the Gospels, the demon-possessed whom Jesus cures are variously afflicted. Some show symptoms of madness (Mark 5.1–20), some may be sufferers from epileptic fits (Mark 9.14–29), others may be dumb or blind (Matt.9.32–34; 12.22).

There were, therefore, two different ways of explaining the world's evil state. It could be regarded as the divine punishment for sin. Or it could be attributed to the activity of the demonic powers. Whichever way the Jews looked at it, the remedy, they believed, was ultimately in the hands of God. God alone would be able to bring about a radical alteration in the fortunes of their own nation and of the world at large. So they looked hopefully to the future.

### The presence of God

Before we discuss their future hopes, however, we must say something about their ideas of God's presence and God's activity in the interim period before the moment of his final intervention to put things to rights. Did they in fact believe that God was still present with his people and active to secure their welfare ? Or was he absent from the world he had created and from the nation he had chosen as his own ?

There is no single answer to this question, since there seem to have been varying ideas about the presence of God in the world – ideas which do not perhaps completely contradict each other, but which are difficult to combine in an entirely logical pattern.

In Pharisaic circles there was a strong conviction that God was present in the world everywhere in a quite direct way. No sin escaped his notice. Conversely, he cared personally for all his people, taking an interest in the ordinary joys and sorrows of everyday life. He was said to bless bridegrooms, to visit the sick, and to comfort mourners. He was believed to be present when men met to pray or to study the Law. He heard every prayer, however privately and quietly it might be uttered, as though he were taking part in a human conversation. Pious Jews addressed him in prayer as 'Our Father'. This shows that God was not thought to be wholly remote and unapproachable.

Nevertheless, there was a sense in which he was believed to be inactive, if not absent. In the past history of Israel, so the Scriptures related, God had bestowed his Spirit upon kings, warriors and prophets, and so had given them a dynamic divine energy and wisdom which was lacking in ordinary men. This gift of divine energy and insight now seemed to be no longer available. Of particular importance to the Jews of this period was the belief that the Spirit of God had inspired the prophets, and so had enabled them to understand and communicate their divine message. But by the time of Jesus prophecy had ceased. God no longer spoke by the Holy Spirit through the prophets.

Two qualifications are necessary at this point, however. God was believed sometimes still to speak to man directly, though not through the Holy Spirit. He spoke by means of a mysterious voice from heaven. We can see an example in Matt.3.17, where it is claimed that at the baptism of Jesus a voice from heaven declared him to be God's beloved son. Also, the members of the sect at Qumran believed that they were guided by a divine spirit which they spoke of as the spirit of truth.

Belief in angels was a more popular expression of the conviction that God was still present and active in the world. The angels are God's messengers, and members of his celestial court. They are spirits of fiery substance with the appearance of blazing light, but they appear to men in human form. Sometimes they appear in dreams (Matt.1.20), sometimes in visions experienced during the day (Acts 10.3). Gabriel is the angel who reveals God's plans to men – hence his appearance in the annunciation story (Luke 1.26–38). Michael is the champion of God's people against their enemies. In the Dead Sea scrolls he appears as the prince of light, or the angel of God's truth, and assists the children of light in their struggle against the prince of darkness. Often the individual was believed to have his own guardian angel, and, on a wider scale, different angels were regarded as responsible for the affairs of the different nations. The angels also administer the realm of nature. They regulate the movements of the stars, and control the sea, the rain and the thunder.

## Hopes for the future

So much for belief in God's activity in the present. What kind of future did the Jews hope for? And how did they expect that it would come about? Again, there are several different answers. Some thought of the better time to come, and of the means of its achievement, in ordinary, this-worldly terms, while others indulged in hopes of a more supernatural kind. Often the two ways of looking at the future merge and intermingle.

The Zealots cherished this-worldly hopes. They looked for a time when God alone would rule Israel, and this meant that his holy land must be taken out of the hands of the Romans. Nor were they the only people to hope for the end of Roman rule in Palestine. In one of the Psalms of Solomon (composed in Pharisaic circles after the first conquest of Jerusalem by the Romans in 63 BC), we find the following prayer for the expected messianic king:

> And gird him with strength, that he may shatter unrighteous rulers,
>
> And that he may purge Jerusalem from nations that trample her down to destruction (Ps.Sol.17.24).

The conquest of Israel's enemies is a necessary prelude to the betterment of her situation. And high hopes may be entertained of her future glory. In another first-century work, the *Assumption of Moses*, we have this description of Israel after the punishment of the Gentiles:

> And God will exalt thee
>
> And he will cause thee to approach to the heaven of the stars,
>
> In the place of their habitation.
>
> And thou shalt look from on high and shalt see they enemies in Gehenna (Ass. Moses 10.9 f.).

This means that Israel has reached 'the height of national, political and spiritual success alike'. In addition, it is expected that the Jews of the Dispersion – those living outside the borders of Israel – will return to Palestine, and that all God's people will be endowed with the gift of the Holy Spirit and purified from evil.

There are differing opinions about the fate of the rest of mankind. In many descriptions of the future the judgment and punishment of the wicked is a prominent feature, together with the judgment and vindication of the righteous.

The vindication of the righteous tends to be synonymous with the restored fortunes of Israel, which have just been described. The judgment and punishment of the wicked is often synonymous with the fate of the Gentiles and their rulers. But other hopes are expressed for the Gentiles as well. They are not necessarily all to be destroyed. They may remain in existence and acknoweldge the supremacy of the Jews. They may even be converted to genuine obedience to the God of Israel.

God's people are to be rescued from supernatural as well as from human enemies. The hope is expressed that the power of Satan will be destroyed:

> And then his kingdom shall appear throughout all his creation,
> And then Satan shall be no more (Ass. Moses 10.1).

In the Dead Sea scrolls, Satan is to be finally and decisively defeated at the end of the war between the children of light and the children of darkness.

### The glorious future

At this point we begin to approach the otherworldly type of hope for the future. The sect at Qumran believed that after the final battle the earth would be miraculously renewed, and that it would be restored to the state of perfection which it had possessed at its original creation. There would be a new temple in a new Jerusalem. God's people would inherit the glorious nature which had once belonged to Adam in the Garden of Eden, and they would enjoy the gift of eternal life. In other writings of the period similar ideas occur. In the book of Enoch, for example, eternal life is granted to the righteous. The distinction between heaven and earth will disappear, and the saints will dwell with the angels for ever.

The two forms of the future hope gradually came to be distinguished more clearly, and the one was thought of as the prelude to the other. First there was to be a better state of affairs in this world. The power of Rome would be vanquished by the messianic king sent by God, who would rule the whole earth, and there would be no more evil, pain, or sorrow. This period would be limited. It was a means of transition to the second, and final, state of existence. When it came to an end, the dead would be raised to life and the great world-judgment would take place. Then the righteous would be received by the angels, become like the stars, and dwell for ever in the heavens.

How did the Jews suppose that the better situation of the future would be brought about? As we have already said, they all took it for granted that fundamentally it would be God's doing. There were, however, different ideas of how he would choose to act.

The Zealots believed in initiating political and military action themselves. But they were also convinced that if they themselves took the first step in provoking a revolt against Rome, then God would fight with them and for them, and would win them a miraculous victory. Had they not believed this, they would never have taken up arms at all. A realistic appraisal of the military situation in purely human terms would make it obvious that a small subject nation, such as the Jews, could not possibly hope to stand out against the organized might of imperial Rome.

Other Jews believed that the initiative rested with God alone. Sometimes he would act without any human assistance at all. The *Assumption of Moses* shows us God and his angel acting to deliver Israel:

Then the hands of the angel shall be filled
who has been appointed chief,
and he shall forthwith avenge them of their
enemies.

. . . . . .

For the Most High will arise, the Eternal
God alone,
and he will appear to punish the Gentiles,
and he will destroy all their idols (Ass.
Moses 10.2,7).

Elsewhere, however, a human agent of the divine will enters the picture. He is to be a king chosen and endowed with authority by God, and a descendant of the royal house of David. He is often called the Messiah, i.e., the anointed one. (Anointing with oil symbolized the choice of a man for high office.) He will secure both the political and the spiritual welfare of the nation of Israel. There is an impressive description of such a Messiah in the Psalms of Solomon. As we have seen, he will drive the Gentiles from Jerusalem. He will set up a great kingdom which will be the centre of the whole world, and all the heathen peoples are to serve him. All this suggests military might, and yet it is clearly stated that he will not put his trust in weapons of war but in God. There is some suggestion that he asserts his supremacy by means of moral and spiritual force:

For he shall not put his trust in horse and
rider and bow,
Nor shall he multiply for himself gold and
silver for war.

. . . . . .

The Lord himself is his king, the hope of him
that is mighty through his hope in God.
All nations shall be in fear before him,
For he will smite the earth with the word of
his mouth for ever.

. . . . . .

He will rebuke rulers, and remove sinners by
the might of his word (Ps.Sol.17.37–39,41).
He himself is righteous and holy, and rules justly, caring for his people like a shepherd for his flock. But he does all this because God has endowed him with the power of his Spirit.

The Qumran sect also believed in a Davidic Messiah who would conquer the heathen. He is to be the military head of the community in the final war against their enemies. This war, however, has a twofold character. It is certainly a war against earthly foes, the heathen nations, and here the Messiah, also called the prince of the congregation, has his part to play. But at the same time it is a war on the supernatural plane, between the prince of light and the angel of darkness. It is the archangel Michael who fights against Belial on behalf of God's elect. 'This is the day appointed by him for the defeat and overthrow of the Prince of the kingdom of wickedness, and he will send eternal succour to the company of his redeemed by the might of the princely angel of the kingdom of Michael. . . He will raise up the kingdom of Michael in the midst of the gods, and the realm of Israel in the midst of all flesh.' It is just possible that the Messiah himself begins to take on a supernatural character, as he appears to be closely connected with the angelic hosts.

Whether or not this is so, there did exist in some Jewish circles the idea of a transcendent, supernatural being who would appear at the end and take part in the judgment, and with whom the blessed elect would dwell in the life of eternity. In the book of Enoch this being is called the Elect One and also the Son of man. He is a heavenly figure accompanying God himself:

And there I saw One who had a head of days,
and his head was white like wool,

And with him was another being whose
countenance had the appearance of a man,
And his face was full of graciousness, like one
of the holy angels (I Enoch 46.1).

He is to be enthroned in glory and he will judge
all the nations and their rulers. He will also
judge angels, likewise the evil spirits and their
chief Azazel. He will save the righteous, and
dwell in their midst forever. Because he is
himself close to God they also will enjoy the
divine presence:

And the Lord of Spirits will abide over them,
and with that Son of man shall they eat
And lie down and rise up for ever and ever
(I Enoch 62.14).

This sort of discussion of Jewish hopes
perhaps gives the impression that they were
chiefly concerned with their own national
misfortunes and chiefly preoccupied with
dreams of future bliss for themselves as God's
elect. It may be useful, in conclusion, to
emphasize once again that what the best
religious minds were concerned with was a
genuine theological problem: if God is Lord of
the whole world, why is the present state of
affairs so obviously contrary to his will ? And
the fundamental hope was that in the end he
would fully establish his authority and demonstrate his absolute sovereignty. This is what is
meant in the New Testament by the coming of
the Kingdom of God.

MARGARET THRALL

| **Matth 13** 18–23 | **Mark 4** 13–20 | **Luk 8** 11–15 |
|---|---|---|
| ¹⁸ Ὑμεῖς οὖν ἀκούσατε τὴν παραβολὴν τοῦ σπείραντος. | ¹³ Καὶ λέγει αὐτοῖς· οὐκ οἴδατε τὴν παραβολὴν ταύτην, καὶ πῶς πάσας τὰς παραβολὰς γνώσεσθε; ¹⁴ ὁ σπείρων τὸν λόγον σπείρει. | ¹¹ Ἔστιν δὲ αὕτη ἡ παραβολή. ὁ σπόρος ἐστὶν ὁ λόγος τοῦ θεοῦ. |
| ¹⁹ παντὸς ἀκούοντος τὸν λόγον τῆς βασιλείας καὶ μὴ συνιέντος, ἔρχεται ὁ πονηρὸς καὶ ἁρπάζει τὸ ἐσπαρμένον ἐν τῇ καρδίᾳ αὐτοῦ· οὗτός ἐστιν ὁ παρὰ τὴν ὁδὸν σπαρείς. ²⁰ ὁ δὲ ἐπὶ τὰ πετρώδη σπαρείς, οὗτός ἐστιν ὁ τὸν λόγον ἀκούων καὶ εὐθὺς μετὰ χαρᾶς λαμβάνων αὐτόν· ²¹ οὐκ ἔχει δὲ ῥίζαν ἐν ἑαυτῷ ἀλλὰ πρόσκαιρός ἐστιν, γενομένης δὲ θλίψεως ἢ διωγμοῦ διὰ τὸν λόγον εὐθὺς σκανδαλίζεται. ²² ὁ δὲ εἰς τὰς ἀκάνθας σπαρείς, οὗτός ἐστιν ὁ τὸν λόγον ἀκούων, καὶ ἡ μέριμνα τοῦ αἰῶνος καὶ ἡ ἀπάτη τοῦ πλ... | ¹⁵ οὗτοι δέ εἰσιν οἱ παρὰ τὴν ὁδὸν ὅπου σπείρεται ὁ λόγος, καὶ ὅταν ἀκούσωσιν, εὐθὺς ἔρχεται ὁ σατανᾶς καὶ αἴρει τὸν λόγον τὸν ἐσπαρμένον εἰς αὐτούς. ¹⁶ καὶ οὗτοί εἰσιν ὁμοίως οἱ ἐπὶ τὰ πετρώδη σπειρόμενοι, οἳ ὅταν ἀκούσωσιν τὸν λόγον εὐθὺς μετὰ χαρᾶς λαμβάνουσιν αὐτόν, ¹⁷ καὶ οὐκ ἔχουσιν ῥίζαν ἐν ἑαυτοῖς ἀλλὰ πρόσκαιροί εἰσιν, εἶτα γενομένης θλίψεως ἢ διωγμοῦ διὰ τὸν λόγον εὐθὺς σκανδαλίζονται. ¹⁸ καὶ ἄλλοι εἰσὶν οἱ εἰς τὰς ἀκάνθας σπειρόμενοι· οὗτοί εἰσιν οἱ τὸν λόγον ... καὶ αἱ μέριμναι τοῦ ... | ¹² οἱ δὲ παρὰ τὴν ὁδὸν εἰσιν οἱ ἀκούσαντες, εἶτα ἔρχεται ὁ διάβολος καὶ αἴρει τὸν λόγον ἀπὸ τῆς καρδίας αὐτῶν, ἵνα μὴ πιστεύσαντες σωθῶσιν. ¹³ οἱ δὲ ἐπὶ τῆς πέτρας οἳ ὅταν ἀκούσωσιν μετὰ χαρᾶς δέχονται τὸν λόγον, καὶ οὗτοι ῥίζαν οὐκ ἔχουσιν, οἳ πρὸς καιρὸν πιστεύουσιν καὶ ἐν καιρῷ πειρασμοῦ ἀφίστανται. ¹⁴ τὸ δὲ εἰς τὰς ἀκάνθας πεσόν, οὗτοί εἰσιν οἱ ἀκούσαντες, καὶ ὑπὸ μεριμνῶν καὶ ...θίου |

# 6 The Writing of the First Three Gospels

| | | |
|---|---|---|
| συμπ... λόγον, καὶ ἄκαρπος γίνετ... ²³ ὁ δὲ ἐπὶ τὴν καλὴν παρείς, οὗτός ἐστιν ὁ τὸν λόγον ἀκούων καὶ συνιείς, ὃς δὴ καρποφορεῖ καὶ ποιεῖ ὃ μὲν ἑκατόν, ὃ δὲ ἑξήκοντα, ὃ δὲ τριάκοντα. | ...καὶ αἱ μέριμναι τοῦ... τὸν λόγον καὶ παραδέχονται, καὶ καρποφοροῦσιν ἐν τριάκοντα καὶ ἐν ἑξήκοντα καὶ ἐν ἑκατόν. | ¹⁵ τὸ δὲ ἐν τῇ οὗτοί εἰσιν οἵτινες ἐν καρδίᾳ καλῇ καὶ ἀγαθῇ ἀκούσαντες τὸν λόγον κατέχουσιν καὶ καρποφοροῦσιν ἐν ὑπομονῇ. |

---

Mark 4, 19 ἡ ἀπάτη τοῦ πλούτου] αἱ (< D) ἀπάται τοῦ κόσμου D Θ it
Luk 10, 24 καὶ βασιλεῖς > D it

# (a) What Kind of a Book is a Gospel ?

Literary criticism of any book rests on the belief that to know what a book is good for and what may be expected from it depends to some extent on knowing what sort of a book it is, and how it has come to be the kind of book it is. The same holds good for the Gospels. What kind of a finished article is each of the Gospels ? In what category do they belong ?

Supposing someone living towards the end of the second century AD had made a present of the four books we call Gospels to the famous library at Alexandria, which was the most scholarly place in the world at that time, what would the librarian have thought of these books, and how would he have set about cataloguing them ? He might have considered putting them under the section headed *Bioi* or 'Lives'. These tended to be rather discursive accounts of philosophers, literary men or statesmen – the most famous to come down to us are Plutarch's *Lives* of famous Greek and Roman statesmen, which he arranged in pairs to illustrate some moral virtue. But the librarian might have been puzzled by the fact that two of these books, Mark's and John's, gave no account of the birth of Jesus, but started as it were in mid-stream. So he might have considered putting them under the section headed *Praxeis* or 'Acts'. These were narratives of the heroic deeds of notable people – for example, the Acts of Alexander the Great – and the title was eventually adopted rightly or wrongly for one of the books of the New Testament, the Acts of the Apostles. But the librarian might have thought that Jesus was not a sufficiently well-known public figure to have Acts – he is, after all, represented in these books as being put to death by the government – and that there was too much teaching in them, and too much about God, to go under the title of Acts. So he might have thought of putting them under a category called *Apomnemoneumata* or 'Memoirs'. These were collections of individual anecdotes about, or sayings of, a famous figure, generally supposed to come from someone who knew him well, as, for example, the famous *Memoirs of Socrates*, written by the Greek historian Xenophon. There was in fact one early Christian writer who did speak of these Gospels in these terms. He was a man called Justin, a Christian teacher living in Rome about the middle of the second century, who in his Apology, or Defence of Christianity, addressed not to his fellow-Christians but to the general public, refers to what he calls 'The Memoirs of the Apostles'. Judging from what he quotes from these memoirs it looks as if he is referring to something like some of our Gospels. A sentence from his description of Christian worship, which is actually the earliest we possess, goes as follows: 'And on the day called Sunday there is a meeting in one place of those who live in cities or the country, and the memoirs of the apostles or the writings of the prophets are read as long as time permits.' In another place he writes of the 'memoirs of the apostles which are called Gospels . . .'. This shows that Justin, in using the word memoirs, was doing his best to give his non-Christian audience some idea of what the Gospels were like in terms with which they were familiar; *but*, he also indicates that the word for them among Christians was not memoirs, and indeed this title for them does not appear again in any Christian writing after Justin. What they were called among the Christians themselves was 'Gospels'.

This fact is remarkable in two respects. In the first place, it shows that the Christians had an instinctive feeling that these books did not fit into any of the current categories of literature. They were not *Bioi*, lives; they were not *Praxeis*, deeds; they were not even *Apomnemoneumata*, memoirs. A new genre of literature had been born, which required a new name. In the second place, the name is a very odd one and without parallel. The word 'gospel' was not often used in the plural anyhow, and it had never before been a name for a book. Of course the word 'gospel' in the singular was very common in the church – it is particularly common in Paul's letters – and it was not unknown outside the church. Its basic meaning was 'good news', especially the good news of salvation or deliverance from some threat of catastrophe. There is, for example, an inscription from Asia Minor dated 9 BC, which speaks of the birth of Augustus, who brought peace to the Roman Empire after its long and catastrophic civil war, as 'good tidings for the world'. But the word is much more frequent in the New Testament, where it has a precise meaning, and it is always used there in the singular; for the Christians it was axiomatic that there was, and could only be, one gospel. It was almost a synonym for what we would call Christianity. It is God's gospel, that is, it belongs to the God of the Old Testament, and it is the message of his final deliverance of his people from what threatened them, and it is in fulfilment of his promises in the Old Testament. But in the New Testament 'gospel' is never a book. It is always a spoken message and what that message says. The verbs used with it are never verbs like 'write' or 'read', but always verbs like 'announce', 'proclaim', 'speak' or 'receive', 'hear', 'obey'. When, therefore, it became a title describing a certain kind of book, the word was being put to a new use. This means that the first Christian readers had an instinctive feeling that these books were something which did not fit into any of the known type of literature. It also means that they had a feeling that what made these books new was their close relation with the original spoken gospel or message, which was also something new in the world. So the word was transferred from one to the other, and took on a new meaning as the title of a book.

### External evidence

What is the explanation of this development, and how did these books come to be what they are, and what are they good for ? The quickest short cut to an answer would be, of course, if we had enough reliable information from the horse's mouth about who wrote the Gospels, and when and how and why they were written, and in what relationship the writers stood to the events that they were talking about. Suppose, for example, that the gospel writers had talked about themselves and their work in their own books, or others who lived near enough to the time of the writing of the Gospels to have had reliable information written about them, and their works had come down to us. This is what would be called external evidence about a book. But this short cut is denied to us, because very little indeed of this kind has been handed down to us, and what little has come down appears to be not very reliable – some would say it is largely guess-work and worthless. As to the Gospels themselves, Matthew and Mark are completely anonymous; the writer nowhere speaks of himself or his work. So is John, though at the end someone else, writing in the plural, says that the Gospel was written by the beloved disciple – but we do not know who he is; and when this note was added, and how reliable it is, we do not know. Luke does say something in the dedicatory preface he has attached to his two-volume work – the Gospel and Acts; he says that many had written before him, that their work had been based on traditions coming from eye-witnesses of the events and preachers, and that he himself had followed all things accurately. Unfortunately this tells us much less than we might at first sight imagine, because this preface is written in the somewhat stilted and conventional phraseology in which such prefaces were usually couched. It was the custom to refer to one's predecessors, and to say that one's information came from reliable sources and so on, and since the language is conventional we cannot press it too hard – for example, when he says that 'many' had written before him, we cannot take this as reliable information that there were already a considerable number of Gospels in existence.

As to the information coming from outside the Gospels themselves, it really reduces itself to little more than two quotations from a certain Papias, who was a bishop in Asia Minor round about AD 130 (his exact date is not known). These quotations have come down to us because they are preserved by Eusebius, the first church historian, writing at the beginning of the fourth century. Papias lived at a time when, in his own words, he still preferred oral tradition about the Christian message to books. Nevertheless the written Gospels of Matthew and Mark were already in existence and in use, and he made statements about them. About Matthew he said: 'Matthew drew up a compilation of the Lord's utterances in the Hebrew language (meaning either Hebrew or Aramaic), and everyone translated (or interpreted) them as he was able.' About the Gospel of Mark he made a longer statement, which he said he had got from a certain 'elder'. This was to the effect that Mark's Gospel was not written in an orderly fashion (he may mean it was not like Matthew's), and that the reason for this was that Mark was Peter's disciple and interpeter, and Peter did not preach in an orderly manner, but as the occasion demanded; thus Mark's lack of order is due to his exactly reproducing Peter's preaching. What is this information worth ? That is a much disputed question. So far as his statement about Matthew is concerned it would seem to be worthless, since if Papias is talking about the Gospel of Matthew we know – and there is no good evidence that he is not – then it is quite clear that our Matthew is not a translation from anything, but his own book written in Greek from the start. Is Papias' statement about Mark's Gospel also worthless ? Some would be inclined to say no, and that there may be some connection between Mark's Gospel and Peter, though perhaps not as precise as Papias makes out. Others would be inclined to say yes, and that Papias, or his informant, is making a guess to account for what he regards as the lack of smooth orderly writing in a book which had already become an accepted book in the church. Subsequent Christian writers who say anything on this matter do not add to our information. They would seem to be repeating what Papias said and embroidering it.

## Internal evidence

This point had to be discussed in some detail because it is precisely the dearth of reliable external evidence about the authorship and origins of the Gospels which compels us to embark on the long, delicate and difficult process of analysing the Gospels themselves. People do sometimes think of the gospel critic as a kind of wanton wrecker who pulls a Gospel to bits just for the fun of the thing. But this is not the case. His method of internal analysis is forced on him by the lack of reliable external evidence. To give another example, we have no precise information about the date at which each Gospel was written. We are not, of course, entirely in the dark. It is probable that the earliest was written somewhere about AD 65 – that is, later than Paul's letters, though not necessarily later than the other letters in the New Testament. We have seen that Papias, writing about 130, or earlier, refers to Matthew and Mark as established and accepted books in the church, and a piece of papyrus has been recently discovered containing a fragment of the Gospel of John, which the experts date with some confidence early in the second century. This shows that the Gospel of John was already current by that time. So we would not go far wrong if we put the date of the writing of all the Gospels somewhere between AD 65 and AD 100. But we have no more precise information than that, and therefore the critic is compelled to examine the Gospels themselves by any means to hand to see whether they can yield up their secrets about themselves, just as a literary critic does with a play of Shakespeare, or a historian with an ancient document, or even a scientist when he frames his hypothesis and constructs his experiments to test it.

How does the critic set about his work ? First, there is a preliminary job to be done which can only be mentioned briefly. It is a well-known fact that when we copy anything of any length we make mistakes – we leave out words, we misspell, we make alterations and so on. This has happened down the centuries in the copying of the Gospels. As a result the text of the Gospels varies from manuscript to manuscript, varies very often in small ways, varies occasionally in bigger ways. It is the job of the textual critic to decide which are the most reliable manuscripts, and to judge in each case between two different versions of a word or sentence which it was that the evangelist actually wrote. Did Matthew write the Lord's Prayer with the doxology, as some manuscripts have it, or without it as others ? In this way the textual critic attempts to get back to a purer form of the text, free from error – if we compare the Revised Version or the New English Bible with the Authorized Version we can see that they are translations of a Greek text which in many places is different from the Greek text behind the Authorized Version, and a purer one. The work is delicate and technical, but that is partly because there are so many manuscripts available for the New Testament, far more than for any other ancient text whatever. It is unlikely that we cannot restore what the evangelists actually wrote except in comparatively few cases of any importance.

## The Synoptic problem

Taking this for granted, how does the critic go about his work ? It really begins from the point when a certain German scholar named Gries-bach in 1776 printed the Gospels of Matthew, Mark, and Luke in columns alongside one another in such a way that the passages which were similar in all three stood opposite one another. This procedure was revolutionary. Already early in the second century we have evidence from Christian writers that the exist-ence of four Gospels and not one single authoritative account was felt to be a problem, and the problem was all the more acute in that the four accounts were often different from one another. One way of getting over this problem was to try to turn them into a single account by fitting them together, perhaps by taking John's as the framework, because he appears to have a ministry lasting three years, and then placing the material from all four to form as near as possible a single continuous story. It cannot really be done; it is like trying to make a jigsaw out of several different jigsaws. But this is how the Gospels were studied for centuries, and so it was impossible to look at each one critically on its own, and to ask questions about their origins and their relations to one another. But when Griesbach printed the Gospels in this way – incidentally he called his work a synopsis, and that is why the first three Gospels are called Synoptic Gospels – certain things came out into the light. The first was how different the Gospel of John was from the other three. This was shown by the fact that it was impossible to make a fourth column alongside the other three. There was hardly anything to go in it; only very occasionally does the Gospel of John overlap with the other three, so that it stands on its own, and has to be studied in a different way. The second was that the three Synoptic Gospels had a remarkable character. Although they differed from one

another considerably, so that there was often material in one column which had nothing corresponding to it in the other two columns, it was also the case that again and again the material in all three columns was not only similar but almost identical in wording. There is an example opposite.

The phenomena here pose a scientific problem. It arises because, as is well known, there are any number of ways of telling the same story, and no two people will use identical sentences and words. If a teacher found two essays with this amount of agreement, he would assume that one pupil had been cribbing from another.

What is the explanation of these phen-omena ? Is it sufficient to say – and this was the first solution to be offered – that the individual gospel stories had been so often repeated that in the telling they had become stereotyped in form and wording, so that when Matthew, Mark and Luke, whoever they were, acting independently, at different dates, in different parts of the church, came to put down their traditions, their Gospels agreed at these points because the form and wording had become fixed ? There is an important point to note here. The early church was a teaching body rather than a writing body, and the eastern memory is much more retentive than ours. Nevertheless, as a solution this would not do, and for two reasons. First, the agreement in wording was so close, at times extending to even the most minute Greek words, that it was straining the evidence to say that wherever these stories were told in the church, perhaps over a period of forty years, they were always told with exactly this wording. And secondly, the stories which were so similar in wording were also told in the same order. This would not be surprising if the stories in the Gospels

| Mark 2.3–12 | Matthew 9.2–8 | Luke 5.18–26 |
|---|---|---|

3 And they came, bringing to him a paralytic carried by four men.

4 And when they could not get near him **because of the crowd**, they removed the roof above him; and when they had made an opening, they let down the pallet on which the paralytic lay.

5 And when Jesus saw their faith, he said *to the paralytic*, 'My son, your sins are forgiven.'
6 Now *some of the scribes* were sitting there, questioning in their hearts, 7 'Why does this man speak thus ? It is blasphemy ! **Who can forgive sins but God** alone ?'
8 And immediately Jesus, perceiving in his spirit that they thus questioned within themselves, said to them, '**Why do you thus question** in your hearts ? 9 Which is easier, to say to the paralytic, "Your sins are forgiven," or to say, "Rise, take up your pallet and walk" ?'
10 But that you may know that the Son of man has authority on earth to forgive sins' – *he said to the paralytic* – 11 'I say to you, rise, take up your pallet and go home.'
12 *And he rose*, and immediately took up the pallet and went out before them all; so that they were all amazed and glorified God, saying, 'We never saw anything like this !'

2 And behold they brought to him a paralytic, lying on his bed;

and when Jesus saw their faith he said *to the paralytic*. 'Take heart, my son; your sins are forgiven.'
3 And behold, *some of the scribes* said to themselves, 'This man is blaspheming.'

4 But Jesus knowing their thoughts, said, 'Why do you think evil in your hearts ? 5 For which is easier, to say, "Your sins are forgiven," or to say, "Rise and walk" ?'

6 But that you may know that the Son of man has authority on earth to forgive sins' – *he* then *said to the paralytic* – 'Rise, take up your bed and go home.'

7 *And he rose* and went home.
8 When the crowds saw it, they were afraid, and they glorified God, who had given such authority to men.

18 And behold, men were bringing on a bed a man who was paralysed, and they sought to bring him in and lay him before Jesus;
19 but finding no way to bring him in, **because of the crowd**, they went up on the roof and let him down with his bed through the tiles into the midst before Jesus.
20 And when he saw their faith he said, 'Man, your sins are forgiven you.'
21 And the scribes and the Pharisees began to question, saying, 'Who is this that speaks blasphemies ? **Who can forgive sins but God** only ?'
22 When Jesus perceived their questionings, he answered them, '**Why do you question** in your hearts ? 23 Which is easier, to say, "Yours sins are forgiven you," or to say, "Rise and walk" ?

24 But that you may know that the Son of man has authority on earth to forgive sins' – he said to the man who was paralysed – 'I say to you, rise, take up your bed, and go home.'
25 And immediately he rose before them, and took up that on which he lay, and went home, glorifying God. 26 And amazement seized them all, and they glorified God and were filled with awe, saying, 'We have seen strange things today.'

*Words underlined are identical in all three Gospels; words in italics are common in Mark and Matthew; words in bold print are common in Mark and Luke; a broken line indicates close similarity.*

had a necessary order about them, and if they were closely connected with each other by a careful date, or by precise information as to where and when each incident took place. But this is not the case. Some of them are simply connected with phrases like 'and then . . .'. Again it would be straining the evidence to say that wherever these stories were told in the forty years they were always told in the order – A B C D E. If this solution had to be excluded, there was only one possibility left; someone must be copying somebody else. (In the ancient world it was not considered reprehensible for one man to use another man's work without acknowledgment. It was only the invention of printing which made it so, as then a man's writing became his possession, and had to be protected by copyright.) The question now was: which evangelist was borrowing from which ?

After many years of trial and error, stretching over the best part of a century, in which one hypothesis after another was tried and rejected, the solution which has come to be almost universally accepted as best satisfying the evidence is that the first of the three Gospels to be written was Mark's, and that Matthew and Luke, independently of each other, used Mark's Gospel as the framework of their own Gospels. The grounds for this conclusion are basically three. First, while almost all the material in Mark, in column one in the synopsis, has an equivalent in column two or column three, the reverse is not the case. There is a great deal in Matthew's column and in Luke's which is not in Mark's. This, of course, is not conclusive in itself, but it points in a certain direction. Secondly, some of the words and phrases common to all three look like phrases characteristic of Mark's style, and where Matthew and Luke differ it looks as if they are

altering and improving what is in Mark. And thirdly, the stories they have in common are either in the same order in all three, or when they are not it is either Matthew and Mark who agree together in having the same order and Luke not, or it is Mark and Luke who agree together and Matthew not. It is not the case that Matthew and Luke agree against Mark in the matter of order. The conclusion then is that Mark's Gospel is the common denominator of the other two, and the reason for the agreement in wording is the use made of Mark by Matthew and Luke.

This solution has immediate consequences. In the first place, it focuses attention on the Gospel of Mark for the first time in Christian history. Early Christian writers very seldom quote from Mark. It looks as if it was comparatively neglected in the church. Nobody wrote a commentary on it until the sixth century. It is almost a miracle that it has survived. But now it appears in a quite different light. We can see that Mark was the first to put the material together in this way, that he was probably the inventor of this new genre of literature which required a new name to describe it. In the second place we can see that Matthew's was not the first Gospel, and that it cannot have been written by an apostle, for his Gospel now appears to be a fresh edition of Mark's with additions, and it is incredible that an apostle, who was an eye-witness of the events, should have used another book as the basis of his own. This discovery overturns a tradition of the church, which dates from soon after the appearance of the Gospel of Matthew, that it was the first to be written and came straight from the pen of an apostle. Then, thirdly, it is now possible to examine those passages where all agree, and to observe carefully the changes which Matthew and Luke make in Mark – how they improve his style, how they shorten him, correct what they think are his mistakes, how they tone down what they find offensive. For example, in the passage about Jesus blessing the children who were brought to him (Mark 10.13–16 = Matt.19.13–15 = Luke 18.15–17) the accounts are almost word for word the same, except that in Mark Jesus is angry when the disciples rebuke those who brought the children. In Matthew and Luke Jesus' anger is omitted. It is characteristic of Mark that he does not mind presenting Jesus as angry, and that he does not spare the disciples, while it is also characteristic of Matthew and Luke, from their later point of view, that they do not like referring to violent feeling on the part of Jesus and that they have a more reverential attitude towards the disciples. So we can now begin to get behind Matthew's and Luke's Gospels as finished articles, to peer in, as it were, through the window of the workshop where they are being made, and to see them in the making, and

to get some idea of what went on in the minds of the editors, Matthew and Luke, as they reacted to Mark. The Gospels cease to be static, and we see them in the process of growth.

But the Synoptic problem is not finished with here; there is still something to be explained. If we take out of Matthew and Luke all they got from Mark, there are still some two hundred verses in which they agree with each other in wording, sometimes very closely. An example is the preaching of John the Baptist (see below).

The agreement is obviously very close indeed, but Matthew and Luke cannot have got this from Mark because Mark has nothing like it. What is the explanation ? Here the answer is not so certain and not so widely accepted. We could say one of three things. Either Matthew, as well as having Mark in front of him, also had Luke, and got these verses from Luke; or Luke, as well as having Mark in front of him, also had Matthew, and took these verses from him. But the difficulty about either of these explanations is that Matthew and Luke use this common

| Matthew 3.7–10 | Luke 3.7–9 |
|---|---|
| **7** But when he saw many of the Pharisees and Sadducees coming for baptism, he said to them, 'You brood of vipers! Who warned you to flee from the wrath to come? **8** Bear fruit that befits repentance, **9** and do not presume to say to yourselves, "We have Abraham for our father"; for I tell you, God is able from these stones to raise up children to Abraham. **10** Even now the axe is laid to the root of the trees; every tree therefore that does not bear good fruit is cut down and thrown into the fire.' | **7** He said therefore to the multitudes that came out to be baptized by him, 'You brood of vipers! Who warned you to flee from the wrath to come? **8** Bear fruits that befit repentance, and do not begin to say to yourselves, "We have Abraham for our father"; for I tell you, God is able from these stones to raise up children to Abraham. **9** Even now the axe is laid to the root of the trees; every tree therefore that does not bear good fruit is cut down and thrown into the fire.' |

*Words underlined are identical in the original; a broken line indicates close similarity.*

77

material in such different ways and put it in such different contexts in their Gospels. So the solution which is most widely accepted is that they were using a common source, largely made up of the sayings of Jesus, and that each used it in his own way as he fitted it into the framework supplied to him by Mark. Scholars denote this source by the symbol 'Q'. There are, however, considerable difficulties when it comes to reconstructing 'Q' out of Matthew and Luke, and in such a way that it carries conviction. Do we follow Luke's version when it differs from Matthew's ? Do we follow Luke's order rather than Matthew's ? So there are some scholars who still prefer to say that Luke used Matthew as well as Mark.

If now we take out of Matthew and Luke not only all they owe to Mark but also what they have in common which is not in Mark, then we are left with what Matthew alone has and what Luke alone has. For these two lots of material the symbols used are 'M' and 'L'. But it is very doubtful whether these two symbols should be used to denote single written documents. It is not at all clear, for example, that Luke got his stories of the birth of Jesus which he alone has from the same place as he got the parables of the Good Samaritan and the Prodigal Son, which he alone has. It is probable that at this point we get back to oral traditions which the evangelist was the first to put into writing when he included them in the pattern of his book. So we could represent the Gospel of Matthew by a kind of algebraical formula: the Gospel of Matthew = Matthew, the editor (Mark + 'Q' + 'M'), and the Gospel of Luke = Luke, the editor (Mark + 'Q' + 'L').

By such methods as these, which are called out by the nature of the evidence which demands to be explained, the critic is led on from one point to another and to test one hypothesis after another. He is able to make the Gospels begin to talk and to tell us something about themselves, and about how they came into being within the life of the church to express the gospel message which the church was preaching and living by. At this point the further question opens up, can we go any further back and get nearer to the point where the material which composes the Gospels and the spoken message of the gospel are closely related to each other ? Can we, for example, get behind the Gospel of Mark as a finished product and break it down into component parts ? If so, will these component parts show us anything of their relation to the single gospel ? Can we do the same with 'Q', and with 'M' and with 'L' ? If we are to be able to do this we cannot go any further along the lines of literary analysis I have been describing because there are no more agreements in wording in the Gospels to be explained. We shall have to come at the material by some different method.

C. F. Evans

# (b) What Actually Happened?

Matthew and Luke were like most other historical writers, at any rate to this extent, that they used written sources. Indeed they seem to have drawn on previous writers for a very large part of what they had to say.

There is nothing particularly surprising about that, but it does tell us something important about them; namely that they had not themselves taken part in the events they describe. For a person who is talking about something that he has actually seen, though he may borrow a phrase, or even an occasional paragraph, from a previous account, will want to tell his story in his own words and not copy slavishly the words of others.

Once it was recognized that Matthew and Luke were, in this sense, secondary authorities, attention naturally switched to the sources on which they relied. What were the character, age, and origins of these sources? Were they, too, secondary or were they the work of eye-witnesses?

All except one of them seem to have disappeared, but luckily the one that has survived is the most extensive and important – the Gospel according to Mark, and as a result Mark's Gospel has been minutely studied in the past century. No one who is not a specialist in these matters can easily imagine the amount of attention scholars have lavished on the sixteen short chapters of the Gospel of Mark in the endeavour to find out how it came into existence and what sort of reliance can justifiably be placed upon it.

## The shape of Mark's Gospel

There is very little external evidence to help in answering these questions and what there is gives rise to some suspicion, so scholars have rightly felt that in the first instance, at any rate, they must rely on the internal evidence of the Gospel itself. What does that evidence tell us?

The first thing that was noticed, when the Gospel was studied from this point of view, was that it divided fairly sharply into a number of short paragraphs. There is nothing remarkable about that; but when these paragraphs were studied individually a fact of considerable importance emerged. Each one is a self-contained unit which tells of some one deed or saying of Jesus and can perfectly well be understood in isolation from its context. The point may be illustrated from a short section of Mark's Gospel, especially if attention is concentrated on the first and last parts of the paragraphs in question.

He went out again beside the sea; and all the crowd gathered about him and he taught them. And as he passed on, he saw Levi the son of Alphaeus sitting at the tax office, and he said to him, 'Follow me.' And he rose and followed him.

And as he sat at table in his house, many tax collectors and sinners were sitting with Jesus and his disciples; for there were many who followed him. And the scribes of the Pharisees, when they saw that he was eating with sinners and tax collectors, said to his disciples, 'Why does he eat with tax collectors and sinners ?' And when Jesus heard it, he said to them, 'Those who are well have no need of a physician, but those who are sick; I came not to call the righteous, but sinners.'

Now John's disciples and the Pharisees were fasting; and people came and said to him, 'Why do John's disciples and the disciples of the Pharisees fast, but your disciples do not fast ?' and Jesus said to them, 'Can the wedding guests fast while the bridegroom is with them ? As long as they have the bridegroom with them, they cannot fast. The days will come, when the bridegroom is taken away from them, and then they will fast in that day.

No one sews a piece of unshrunk cloth on an old garment; if he does, the patch tears away from it, the new from the old, and a worse tear is made. And no one puts new wine into old wine-skins; if he does, the wine will burst the skins, and the wine is lost and so are the skins; but new wine is for fresh skins.'

One sabbath he was going through the grainfields; and as they made their way his disciples began to pluck ears of grain. And the Pharisees said to him, 'Look, why are they doing what is not lawful on the sabbath ?' And he said to them, 'Have you never read what David did, when he was in need and was hungry, he and those who were with him: how he entered the house of God, when Abiathar was high priest, and ate the bread of the Presence, which it is not lawful for any but the priests to eat, and also gave it to those who were with him ?' And he said to them, 'The sabbath was made for man, not man for the sabbath; so the Son of man is Lord of the sabbath.'

Again he entered the synagogue, and a man was there who had a withered hand. And they watched him, to see whether he would heal him on the sabbath, so that they might accuse him. And he said to the man who had the withered hand, 'Come here'. And he said to them, 'Is it lawful on the sabbath to do good or to do harm, to save life or to kill ?' But they were silent (Mark 2.13–3.4).

Each of the sections is a self-contained unit, which can be understood without any reference to what comes before or after.

Now contrast with that an ordinary piece of biographical writing, for example, this page from Lord Eustace Percy's *Life of John Knox* (p.208):

That, however, was not his destiny. He had hardly installed himself and opened his books when he received a letter from Mrs Bowes. Sir Robert, presumably the chief obstacle to Marjorie's marriage, had died in late February or early March. Sir Richard, no longer captain of Norham, had (we must suppose) withdrawn his opposition. Let Knox therefore return. They could meet at Berwick; and, if England could not offer a home to Marjorie and him, perhaps Scotland would.

The venture did not at all appeal to Knox. It was *most contrarious to his own judgment.* Nevertheless he set out. If he had received any communications from Scotland itself suggesting his return, they did not weigh much with him. Mrs Bowes alone, he said, had *drawn* him *from the den of* his *own ease.*

His reluctance was natural. He had had few influential friends in Scotland. His connections there had been only with the Lothian lairds and with the company of St Andrews. To the lairds he was known as little more than an upper servant; but among the company of St Andrews he had enjoyed a rather surprising prestige.

Here it will be noticed that each paragraph only makes sense in the light of what comes before; for example, one paragraph begins 'The venture did not at all appeal to Knox'. What venture ? You only know if you have read the paragraph before. The thing holds together, and that is what you would expect, for a writer normally constructs each paragraph as he goes along and specially designs it to lead on from what he has said before to what he plans to say next. Why should this not apply to Mark ? The obvious explanation would seem to be that Mark's paragraphs were not specially constructed for their present position in the Gospel; indeed that they were not constructed by Mark at all, but simply taken over ready-made. They each had a life of their own before ever Mark put pen to paper. Each one existed as a separate story, intended to be understood on its own, without reference to the others. What Mark in fact did was not to write a book *de novo* but to string together a series of already existing, originally self-contained paragraphs. Scholars have a special name to distinguish paragraphs of this kind – they call them *pericopes* (which is simply the Greek word for 'paragraphs' or 'sections').

## The purpose of Mark's Gospel

But now some obvious questions arise. How came Mark to write in this extraordinary way and how did the *pericopes* he incorporated come into existence ? If we take a closer look at these *pericopes*, two further facts appear. First, every *pericope* is designed to make some religious point or to convey some religious impression. You never feel that any of these *pericopes* is meant simply to satisfy your curiosity or add to your stock of historical knowledge for its own sake. Some of them give us sayings about religious and moral topics, sayings which demonstrate Jesus' perfect widsom, for example, the *pericope* about the basis of Jesus' authority (Mark 11.27b–33) or that about the rights and wrongs of paying taxes to the Romans in Mark 12.13–17 (cf. also Mark 10.17–22 and 12.28–34). Others describe deeds of Jesus, but they are always deeds which impress us with his perfect moral goodness or his supernatural power; examples of this type of story are Jesus' blessing of the children (Mark 10.13–16) or his healing of a deaf-mute (Mark 7.32–37, cf. also Mark 1.23–27 and 4.35–41). When we have read one of these stories we are left feeling as people often felt in the stories themselves, 'Surely anyone who could do things like that must have stood in some very special relationship with God.' So in Mark we read: 'And they were filled with awe, and said to one another, "Who then is this, that even wind and sea obey him ?"' In fact these stories all have a religious slant; they are all angled in such a way as to emphasize some aspect of Jesus' *religious* significance.

And that brings us to the second characteristic of these stories; every fact or detail, however interesting it might be, which does not contribute towards the religious theme of the story is omitted. An example will make that clear.

Another time he entered a synagogue, and a man was there with a withered hand. And they watched to see if he would heal him on the sabbath, hoping to find a charge to bring against him. Then he said to the man with the lame hand, 'Stand forth.' And he asked them, 'Should one do good on the Sabbath, or evil ? Save life, or kill ?' But they answered nothing. Then he looked at them with anger, grieved at their hardness of heart. And he said to the man, 'Stretch out your hand.' He held it out and it was restored (Mark 3.1–5).

You notice we are not told the day or time or the place. We are not told the crippled man's name, or age, or occupation. We are not told who the people were who tried to entrap Jesus, and at the end we learn nothing about their subsequent history or that of the man who had been healed. We are told only what is necessary to convince us that Jesus was totally in the right as against his opponents and that he was possessed of a power so remarkable that, at any rate in first-century eyes, it was nothing short of supernatural.

If we study Mark's Gospel carefully we find that this story is typical of practically all the others, and so the question we have to ask is: In what circumstances are stories with these particular characteristics likely to have arisen? Is not the most likely answer: In church? When a preacher tells a story about Jesus, is not this exactly the sort of way he does it? When he is expounding a saying of Jesus he does not mind whether it was spoken at ten in the morning or six in the evening, at Capernaum or at Bethsaida, to a man called Benjamin or a man called Eleazar. What concerns him is simply the meaning of the saying and its relevance to his hearers; and he only deals with the historical background so far as it is important in making that meaning clear.

It is to this sort of context that New Testament scholars point us for an explanation of Mark's *pericopes*. No doubt in the years immediately after Jesus' lifetime, when his original friends and disciples spoke about him, their narratives came tumbling out with all the wealth of detail that filled their memories. But as the years went by and the stories were repeated in public contexts, in church sermons and catechism classes, and in Christian missionary work, often by people who had never seen Jesus themselves, all purely picturesque detail will have fallen away and the stories will have become progressively streamlined into a concise, severely practical form. And naturally, once a story had attained the form best adapted for such practical religious uses, it will have tended to become more or less stereotyped in that form, especially as the oriental memory, in those days before the wide dissemination of books, was very tenacious and accurate. In fact the form in which these stories were told was so largely governed by the purposes for which they were told, that we can still very often tell from the form in which a story has come down to us what particular impression the early preachers or teachers intended it to make, and for that reason the branch of New Testament study which deals with these *pericopes* has come to be known as *form-history* or *form-criticism*.

It is demonstrated by form-critical study, for example, that if the point to be brought out in connection with some incident was the comment the Lord made upon it, then, in the telling of the story, the comment itself would be reported in full and given prominence, while the rest of the incident would be related as briefly as possible, just the minimum being retained that was necessary to provide the Lord's words with an intelligible setting. A story of this kind about Jesus is usually referred to in English as a 'pronouncement-story'. The point will be clearly understood if Mark 2.18–20 (? and vv. 21 f.), for example, or 2.23–27 is contrasted with Mark 5.25–34. If, on the other hand, the aim was to stress the remarkable nature of some *action* of Jesus, as evidence of his supernatural power, then any words that might have been spoken in connection with it would be briefly reported and little emphasized, and the emphasis would be concentrated entirely on those features of the incident which underlined its supernatural character – for example, in the case of a healing, the chronic and deep-seated nature of the illness, the ease with which Jesus cured it, the impression of amazement made on the bystanders and the completeness of the cure as evidenced by the healed man's ability to run or shout or carry his own bed (see, e.g., Mark 5.25 f.; 9.20–22; 2.12). Such stories are usually referred to in England as 'miracle stories', although the actions they describe are not always miracles in the strict sense.

This suggestion about the origin of Mark's *pericopes* has a further fact to recommend it: it provides an explanation of the independent, self-contained character of the stories. For the natural thing would be for the preacher or teacher to repeat one such story at each service or instruction class, and not to confuse his hearers by adding other stories with a different moral or lesson. And so the tradition about Jesus would naturally tend to circulate in the form of a large number of short, separate, self-contained stories, each one relating a single incident and doing it in such a way as to make as clear as possible its religious bearing. At the earliest stage the stories circulated mainly by word of mouth. Probably by the time Mark came to write, a certain number had already been collected and committed to writing. For example, in the opinion of many scholars, the six stories in Mark 2.1–3.6 had already been collected and written down before Mark incorporated them in his Gospel.

For the most part, however, Mark probably knew the stories only in oral form, and what he did in effect was to collect and write down some of the stories about Jesus with which he had become familiar through hearing them repeated in his own and neighbouring churches.

## The stories in Matthew and Luke

If now we look at those sections of Matthew and Luke which they derived from sources other than Mark, we discover that they too are made up almost entirely of similar *pericopes*, presumably for similar reasons. This applies both to the material which Matthew and Luke appear to have derived from a common source, or sources, e.g., Matt.8.5–13 (cf. Luke 7.1–10); Matt.11.7–11 (cf. Luke 7.24–28); Matt.12.43–45 (cf. Luke 11.24–26) and to the material which is peculiar to each evangelist, e.g., Matt.2.1–12; Luke 2.41–50; 10.17–20. In reading these and the other *pericopes* referred to in this article it is important to remember that in the text as we have it the evangelist has sometimes added phrases at the beginning and end to link them with what precedes and what follows.

So we seem justified in formulating the conclusion that virtually all the material in our first three Gospels reached the writers or their sources in the form of the sort of short, separate, self-contained stories we have been describing. If the question is raised why Mark was no longer content to leave the stories in their oral form but committed some of them to writing; and why Matthew and Luke followed his lead, the answer must be that the evidence does not allow us to say with any certainty. The suggestion is sometimes made that it was because eye-witnesses were dying off and hopes for a speedy end of the world were dying out, but at any rate in the case of Mark and

Matthew, that explanation will hardly bear investigation. More probably, Mark's church commissioned a written version of certain of the well-known stories to meet some specific liturgical or catechetical need no longer known to us, and then the resultant book of stories proved so valuable that other churches followed suit, though their needs, being somewhat different, gave rise to rather different Gospels. Indeed on one view Matthew's Gospel is essentially a new and expanded edition of Mark's.

Whatever the evangelist's motives, if we try to imagine him starting to work on the basis of a tradition of this kind, we are bound to ask: 'On what basis did he select the particular *pericopes* to be included and on what principles did he arrange them?' As far as arrangement goes, the answer that springs to mind immediately is that he arranged the stories in the order in which they occurred. But would he in fact know in what order they occurred? In view of what we have seen about the circumstances in which the individual stories were preserved, it does not seem very likely. New Testament scholars are not as yet entirely at one on this matter, but it is pretty generally agreed that to a considerable extent, at any rate, when it came to the arrangement of their *pericopes* the evangelists had to use their own judgment. In some cases the answer was obvious enough – for example, the birth narratives had to come at the beginning and the trial and crucifixion stories somewhere near the end; but for the most part, we have to reckon with the possibility that the arrangement of the material was the work of the individual evangelist, and what is more that it was largely governed by the same sort of practical considerations that had led to the preservation of the stories in the first place.

One such practical consideration would be convenience of reference; this seems to have been what was in Matthew's mind, for example, when he collected the teaching of Jesus on the basis of subject matter and arranged it in five large blocks each dealing with a single general topic (5–7; 9.3–11.1; 13.1–53; 18–19; 24–25. Professor G. Bornkamm denies that this five-fold arrangement is conscious or significant, but he is almost alone in that view). Matthew may also have been influenced by his belief that Jesus was a second Moses and a desire to show that the new law he brought was given in five blocks, corresponding to the five books of the Old Testament law.

Another consideration governing the evangelists' arrangement of their material will have been the light that one story can throw on another, if the two are placed side by side, just as a poem may gain new meaning if it is read alongside another poem in an anthology. For example, in Mark 8 the story of how the disciples gradually recognized the truth about Jesus comes immediately after the story of Jesus gradually restoring sight to a blind man. Probably what Mark had in mind was not that the one incident occurred immediately after the other as a matter of historical fact, but that if we read the two stories side by side, we may be brought to see that when people recognize the truth about Jesus they are not making a discovery by the exercise of their own unaided wits, but are having their eyes opened by God, just as the blind man had his physical eyes opened in the story.

## Interpreting the Gospels

If all this is true about the origins of the Gospels, two conclusions follow – one positive, the other negative. The first is that in reading the Gospels we must always be on the lookout for the practical aims which controlled the writer's choice and arrangement of his material. We must always be asking: What truth did he mean to bring out by selecting this particular story and including it in this particular context in his Gospel? We must regard him in fact as an evangelist, a preacher, who sought to bring out certain vital religious truths about Jesus by the way he selected, formulated, and arranged his *pericopes*.

Negatively, all this means that we can draw only very limited historical conclusions from the order of events in the Gospels. We cannot really reconstruct from it the course of Jesus' life. And to that is added a further consideration: we saw that those responsible for preserving the *pericopes* in the early church were not interested in purely picturesque and personal detail. It is not only that they say nothing about Jesus' appearance or health or how he dressed or how long his ministry lasted: they were not interested in his *inner* development either. What concerned them was what Jesus' deeds and sayings meant to them and their contemporaries, not what they had meant to Jesus himself; and so they told nothing about how or why Jesus came to act or speak as he did, or how his thought and outlook developed. Obviously, what is absent from the *pericopes* must be absent from the finished Gospels, and that means that the Gospels afford no basis for a Life of Jesus in the sense of an accurate account of the outward course of events and a tracing of the inner spiritual pilgrimage which accompanied and controlled those events.

Before we pass finally to consider the significance of that, let us go back behind the finished Gospels and take another brief look at the individual *pericopes*. How far do these narratives correspond to incidents which actually occurred? Clearly it is very difficult to generalize, and competent scholars are considerably divided on this issue. Some insist on the retentiveness of the oriental memory and point out that the early Christians believed their very salvation to depend on these historical events, so they would have had every ground for complete accuracy with regard to them. Accordingly, their accounts of Jesus can be regarded as generally trustworthy, unless in a particular case we have special indications to the contrary.

Other scholars are not so sure. They argue that stories handed on by word of mouth always get modified in the process and that that is especially likely to have happened in this case, where the tradition was handled by comparatively poorly educated folk, who were not accustomed to scholarly standards of accuracy, and in any case lived before the rise of modern scientific historical study.

In trying to decide on this issue, it is extremely important to preserve a sense of proportion. No one is accusing the early Christians of any dishonesty or intent to deceive. What the second group of scholars is suggesting is that any new insight about Jesus which came to the early Christians in the period after the resurrection was almost bound to be reflected, often quite unconsciously, in the way they narrated his earthly life. For example, if the early church became convinced that the Lord was (in their sense of the term) the Son of God, it was natural that some of the *pericopes* should come to be told in a way that implied as much, even if they had not done so in their earlier form (e.g., contrast Matt.14.33 with the earlier form in Mark 6.51; or Matt.16.16 with

Mark 8.29 and Luke 9.20). And that may also be the reason why some *pericopes* suggest that Jesus claimed to be Son of man, while others suggest that he did not (on the one side, cf., e.g., Mark 2.10; Luke 7.34; 9.58; 22.48 and Matt.16.13 – even though the AV reading is the wrong one; on the other side cf. Mark 8.38; Luke 9.26; 12.8 f.; Matt.19.28, where 'Son of man' seems to refer to someone other than Jesus himself. In fact what the *pericopes* give us is not *directly* the life of Jesus but what the early Christians believed the life of Jesus to have been like. And in that connection we have to remember that their interpretation of a whole lot of things differed from ours. If, for instance, they heard of Jesus having cured a case of what we should call epilepsy, they unhesitatingly interpreted it (as no doubt Jesus did himself) as the casting out of a demon.

So there is no escaping the fact that these stories present us with an inextricable combination of history and interpretation. But that is not for a moment to say that they are pure fiction or that the interpretation they contain is worthless. In the first place, the interpretation is not the work of any eccentric individual or minority group. The first three evangelists drew their material from many sources and many parts of the church, yet the overall picture in all this material is remarkably consistent. And even if we date the Gospels later than many scholars would, the material was only circulating in oral form for fifty years or so, which is hardly long enough for even an oral narrative to get completely out of hand. When Mark's Gospel was written, there must still have been plenty of people alive who had known Jesus, though it is difficult to be sure that they had any *direct* influence on its composition. What is more, the picture of Jesus that the

Gospels give is remarkably true to the conditions in Palestine in Jesus' time – and we now know quite a lot about Palestine at that time. The people, the institutions, the questions in the gospel stories, for the most part fit remarkably well with what we know – which is quite an impressive fact when we remember that many of those who passed on the tradition were living a good deal later and a long way from Palestine. We may feel sure that if they had simply been inventing, their inventions would have reflected much more closely the circumstances of their own times and places, in the same sort of way that mediaeval painters portray the Madonna in mediaeval clothes.

Still, the fact remains that what these stories, and the Gospels based on them, present to us is an inextricable interweaving of history and interpretation. About that two things may be said. The first is that it is not a matter simply for regret. If we are Christians and believe that the New Testament writers were in some sense inspired, we shall want to take their interpretation of Christ's life very seriously. We shall believe that their interpretation of him in the first century is meant to help us to interpret him in the twentieth century. Indeed some modern theologians have taken this line of thought a very long way. They argue that from the religious point of view the Christ of the early church's preaching, the *interpreted* Christ, is all that matters. According to them, God's way of saving us is to confront us, through the church, with this Christ of faith and to challenge us to accept and follow him. On such a view the question how far there was a historical figure corresponding to this Christ of faith is a comparatively unimportant one, but this is a position which seems to many people impossibly paradoxical, and in recent years a group of scholars in Germany have been examining this whole question in a quite novel way. These scholars fully accept the sort of account of the Gospels I have been giving and they agree that a Life of Jesus in the modern sense is impossible. But then, they say, a life in that sense is not what we want. We do not need for religious purposes to be able to trace Jesus' inner psychological development; what we are concerned about is Jesus' claims about himself and his will for us. What relationship did he claim to have with God, and what relationship did he desire that we should have with him? And this is precisely the sort of information the Gospel *pericopes* were intended to give.

But do they give it correctly? To put it simply, the way to find out is this. Take the interpreted picture of Jesus presented in the Gospels and look for any passages which do not square with it – which have slipped through the interpretative net, so to speak. For example, according to the interpretation of the church, Jesus claimed to be Son of man, and yet we come across a passage like this: 'For whoever is ashamed of me and of my words in this adulterous and sinful generation, of him will the Son of man also be ashamed, when he comes in the glory of his Father with the holy angels' (Mark 8.38); at any rate, on the most obvious interpretation, Jesus here seems to *distinguish* himself from the Son of man. The early church will hardly have invented such passages, for they seem to contradict its general picture of Jesus, so they are presumably original and provide a starting-point for a historical reconstruction. Clearly there is no room for dogmatism here, but this is the *sort* of line along which a good deal of recent scholarship has been working; and the upshot so far appears to be something like this. Although the historical Jesus probably differed in certain quite important respects from the picture conveyed by the finished Gospels, he was in fact such that the gospel picture can justly be described as 'fair comment' – legitimate deduction from the genuine historical facts.

In order to fill that out, notice first the 'authority' or 'directness' of Jesus. In his teaching and activity he was not dependent on any support from outside himself. For example, he did not say, as the Rabbis tended to say, 'Things are thus and so because that is what the Old Testament means if properly interpreted.' Nor did he say, 'So and so is going to happen because if you add up the numbers in Daniel or Jeremiah that is how it works out'. He just boldly claimed, 'I tell you . . .'

And what did he tell them? That God's kingdom was coming and they would soon be finding themselves face to face with God — inescapably involved in dealing with God, in a situation in which his will prevailed completely, and everything had been brought into conformity with it. Jesus probably envisaged this in terms of the end of the world and God's appearing, with clouds descending and trumpets blowing, very much along the lines of contemporary thought; and he may have expected it very soon. But that, it is argued, is not really vital, because it was not the whole, or even the centre of Jesus' concern. He was not just concerned to point men to something God would do in the future – he believed God was *already* doing something in and through him. When he was able to cast out demons, for example, he interpreted that as God's power at work in him, starting the final overthrow of the forces of evil. And even more important, he believed that in his dealings with other human beings God was also at work. Jesus had certain attitudes and standards; he demanded honour, goodness, consecration, unselfishness, and love – what he called 'perfection' – from everyone, and he would settle for nothing less; he would not abate his demands by so much as a jot or tittle. But yet he welcomed people into his company and full friendship without their having come anywhere near meeting his demands. He freely gave his friendship to extortioners and prostitutes and all sorts of people who came nowhere near having attained the perfection he demanded. He called people to come and stand beside him, to adopt his relationship and attitude to others. They were to come without any pretence of having attained perfection; and yet without any fear of being rejected by Jesus. His principle seems to have been that his free acceptance of those who came into contact with him and the influence of his love on them would lead them to contrast their previous attitudes with his, and would create his attitude in them.

And all this he did *in God's name*. His attitude, he said, is God's attitude and if men have accepted his call and entered into relationship with him, then they are in that same relationship with God. Jesus' unconditional promise of love and acceptance was in fact God's promise made through him, so that in all he said and did he claimed to be confronting men directly and immediately with God. That was the meaning of his 'authority' and 'directness'. As one of the German scholars put it, 'His attitude is not that of a prophet or a sage; it is that of a man who dares to act in God's place.'

This means that as he saw it, people's relationship with God was essentially bound up with their relationship to him. To 'follow' Jesus, to accept his call and forgiving friendship *is* to partake in God's kingdom, to be in the true relationship to God. Therefore Jesus believed that with his appearance the time of salvation had arrived; the time, that is, when people can enter into a decisive relationship with God. Jesus' aim was not so much to introduce a new concept of God as to open for men a new relationship with God, a relationship which means the certainty of being accepted, and so freedom from anxiety; and thus sonship, liberty, simplicity, love.

And all this Jesus offered without being other than a man among men. The choice he offered was what is sometimes called an 'existential' choice. There was no 'proof' – no outward 'reason' on which people could base their acceptance of his claim or promise; they had to take it or reject it according as their own deepest being responded. 'What think you . . .', he said, and again, 'Blessed are they who are not offended – i.e. put off, moved to objection – by me.'

If there is any truth in all this – and it is of course still very much *subjudice* – it is obviously important. When New Testament writers spoke of Jesus as a supernatural figure who had come down from heaven to live on earth, they were only drawing out, in the ways of speaking natural to them, the basic truth which Jesus himself had affirmed in his own way. That is to say, while Jesus, so far as we can now reconstruct him, was not by any means identical with the figure portrayed in the finished Gospels, or in St Paul's epistles or in the creeds of the church, he was such – and his words and actions were such – that these later descriptions were legitimate ways, for their own respective periods, of saying about him what he would have wanted said in those periods. Which still, of course, leaves open the question: 'What would he want said today ?'

D. E. NINEHAM

# (c) The Gospel Makers and their Message

What was it that the writers of the Synoptic Gospels wanted to convey to their respective readers by the way they arranged and edited the materials they had to hand? This is a question which has to be kept in mind all the time a Gospel is being studied. A full answer would involve a detailed examination of all parts of a Gospel and of those parts in relation to the whole. What is set out below can only be in the form of brief guidelines.

## The Gospel according to Mark

The Gospel according to Mark is the one of which it is the most difficult to trace the pattern, and many different views are held about it. It has a kind of prologue (1.1–15) which gives some clue to the whole. It begins very abruptly, not with the birth of Jesus but with John the Baptist's preaching as the fulfilment of Old Testament prophecy and his promise of the mightier one who would baptize with Holy Spirit. This is Jesus, who is baptized by John, receives the Holy Spirit and is acknowledged by God as his Son and Servant. Jesus is tempted in the desert, but no details are given. A summary of his message, God's gospel, is given as 'the appointed time has come, the rule of God has drawn near' (1.15). From 1.15 to 10.31, Mark places nearly all the material in Galilee, perhaps because this is for him the chosen place of God's revelation where Jesus' ministry is received by crowds. The build-up of this ministry by Mark is through a succession of paragraphs, for the most part of two kinds: (a) stories of Jesus' work

of power; (b) teaching through controversy with his opponents.

### 1. The acts of power

In one story after another (sometimes with little connection between them) Jesus is shown to be victorious over various kinds of physical and mental disorder – over demoniacs by exorcism, over fever, paralysis, haemorrhage, death, deafness, blindness. He is even in control of disorder in nature, and can multiply food. Occasionally a meaning is suggested, as when the healing of the paralytic is evidence of the forgiveness of sins, or exorcism a sign of the defeat of the rival kingdom of Satan. But for the most part these acts are unexplained, and sometimes, when Jesus demands silence and secrecy, a mystery is suggested about them.

### 2. Controversy

Interspersed with the works of power are controversial dialogues in which Jesus is the victor in debate with opponents (often Pharisees) in bringing to light God's will in relation to various aspects of life and religion – sinners and the righteous, fasting, the sabbath, what is clean and unclean, marriage and divorce, children, wealth. The effect of all this is to present a figure of tremendous and mysterious power and authority: in two places (2.10,28) he is referred to as 'the Son of man'. This power and authority is also shown in Jesus' capacity to draw huge crowds and to detach men from their occupations to become his personal followers. He teaches these disciples, despite their inability to understand, and they share his power.

### 3. *Death and resurrection*

In ch. 8 the disciples, in contrast with others, confess Jesus to be the Christ, but are told to be silent, and from this point the mysterious and unexplained title 'the Son of man' reappears. Now the Son of man must undergo a divinely ordained suffering and rejection and death at the hands of the authorities. This death will be followed by resurrection and glory. The disciples, three of whom see a glimpse of Jesus in his future glory at the transfiguration, must also expect suffering. From 10.32 ff. the story moves to Jerusalem, the scene of this rejection. Again, there is power and authority – in the entry into Jerusalem, the cleansing of the temple, the cursing of the fig tree; in controversies over taxes, resurrection, the commandments, the messiahship and in the words which will 'never pass away' in which Jesus instructs his disciples in advance of the trials that lie ahead and of the ultimate consummation of all things by God through the Son of man. But now this is a prelude to the condemnation of Jesus by the authorities for his acknowledgment of himself as the Christ and the coming Son of man, and his crucifixion by the agency of the Romans. The scene is one of total desertion by men and apparently by God, until a centurion confesses that Jesus was 'a son of God'. The Gospel ends as abruptly as it began with a visit by women to the tomb and their encounter with an angel there who gives them a message for the disciples that the risen Jesus is to go before them into Galilee.

> . . . and they went out and fled from the tomb; for trembling and astonishment had come upon them; and they said nothing to anyone, for they were afraid (16.8).

### 4. *Authorship*

According to tradition, some of it going back to the second century AD, the author of this Gospel was a certain Mark, who was a companion of Peter, from whose preaching he derived his materials, and he wrote in Rome. (New Testament references to a Mark are Acts 12.12; 12.25; 15.37–39; II Tim.4.11; I Peter 5.13.) The tradition could be correct, at least in part, but it throws no light on the Gospel itself, unless it is that the stress in this Gospel on the suffering of the Son of man and his disciples is due to the situation of Christians at Rome under their persecution by Nero in AD 64. Mark's paragraphs do not read like first-hand transcripts from an apostle who was an eyewitness. The author could have written to stir up his church to a renewed mission to the Gentile world through the message of the powerful and authoritative Christ who broke with Judaism.

## The Gospel according to Matthew

The Gospel according to Matthew is easier to analyse, as in general it has a clearer structure. It is like Mark, and has been called 'a fresh edition of Mark', but it is also very unlike Mark.

It is like Mark because there is little in Mark's Gospel which has not been taken over into Matthew. Thus the story from the entry into Jerusalem to the empty tomb (Matt.20.17–28.7) is a writing out of Mark's story with the addition of a few incidents and of much parable material. In the Galilean ministry (3.1–20.16) the narrative framework as well as some of the material is from Mark.

It is unlike Mark because Mark's narrative,

with some slight alterations in order, is used as a framework for collections of largely non-Marcan material in the form of discourses on a theme. The result is that compared with Mark it lacks vigorous movement, and the story often stands still – e.g., in 8.1–9.34 most of the miracles are gathered together and are strung one after another, and so are the parables in 13.1–52. What stands out and gives this Gospel its special character is the five collections of teaching, each rounded off with the formula 'It came to pass when Jesus had finished . . .' (7.28; 11.1; 13.53; 19.1; 26.1).

### 1. *Shape and contents*

The pattern of the Gospel appears to be somewhat as follows:

(a) It begins (chs. 1–2) not abruptly but with a theological genealogy, tracing the descent of Jesus from the father of the Jewish race, Abraham, in three periods of fourteen generations (perhaps the equivalent of six sevens, leading to Jesus at the beginning of the seventh seven, a perfect number), and with the birth of Jesus, five episodes each built round the fulfilment of an Old Testament text.

(b) The Marcan beginning of the Galilean ministry is expanded and leads to the first of the discourses in which Jesus is the giver of the new Law on a mountain (chs. 3–7).

(c) The Marcan miracles, with expansions, and his call of the twelve leads to a missionary charge to them (8.1–10.42).

(d) Marcan and non-Marcan material leads to an expansion of the Marcan section of parables by additional parables on the nature of the kingdom of heaven (11.2–13.52).

(e) Marcan incidents, including the confession of Peter (here the rock of the church), the transfiguration and a dispute by disciples over greatness, lead to instruction of the disciples on behaviour in and the discipline of the church (13.54–18.35).

(f) Matthew's re-telling of Mark's account of the entry into and the ministry in Jerusalem leads to an expansion of Mark's eschatological discourse (Mark 13) and to parables of judgment (19.1–25.46).

(g) The narrative of the passion and resurrection, ending not abruptly but with the command of the exalted Lord to go to the whole world and the promise of his permanent presence.

These collections of teaching are carefully constructed, especially the first, the Sermon on the Mount. Eight beatitudes express the grace of the gospel, leading to two addresses to disciples as salt and light, five illustrations of the statement 'I came not to destroy but to fulfil', each introduced by 'It was said . . . but I say', the three religious duties of almsgiving, prayer and fasting, etc. Behind these constructions may lie what the Jews called 'Targum'. This began as translation of the Old Testament out of Hebrew when people no longer understood that language, but it also came to include interpretation and application of the text, sometimes by the use of similar passages from elsewhere in the Old Testament. It may be that Matthew is a kind of 'Targum' of Mark, and that this kind of activity had been going on in Matthew's church before he began to write.

The result is that this Gospel assembles sayings on a particular subject and their application, and reads more like a manual of instruction for Christians on the Gospel and its demands, on the nature of the Christian life in the church, and the severe judgment upon belief without practice. It has been suggested that this Gospel was written for reading in church. For these reasons it certainly became from the first the most popular Gospel. But there is a further element. The fact that so much of Matthew's special material is Jewish in tone and is concerned with Jewish matters, and that the author appeals so much to the Old Testament to prove a point, may indicate that his church had lived close to Jewish communities. It may be that this teaching had been hammered out in the face of Jewish opponents who denied the Christian claims about Jesus, and in order to show that Jesus was the Jewish Messiah, his disciples the true Israel or people of God, and the Old Testament and the Law, when interpreted by Christ, belonged to the Christians.

### 2. *Authorship*

The author is unknown. His dependence on Mark makes it unlikely that he was an apostle, and it remains a mystery how the name 'Matthew' became attached to this Gospel. It was probably written after the fall of Jerusalem (AD 70: Matt.22.7 seems to refer to this). There is evidence that it was known to Ignatius, the bishop of Antioch in the early years of the second century, which may indicate that it was written somewhere in Syria.

## *The Gospel according to Luke*

The Gospel according to Luke is constructed to a considerable extent from the same or the same kind of material as Mark and Matthew, but the result is different from either. This is partly because, unlike them, it is not a complete work in itself, but the first volume of a two-volume work, Luke-Acts, which has been separated from its sequel in order to be brought into the Gospel section of the New Testament.

Luke was the only one of the evangelists to think and plan in this way, or to speak about the origin and purpose of his work, as he does when he addresses Theophilus in a preface (1.1–4). The writing there is in the conventional literary language of prefaces, and for that reason cannot be pressed too hard. Thus in view of Luke's dependence on Mark, 'Q' and other material ('L'), made up of independent stories, it can hardly be the case that there were 'many' Gospels in existence when he wrote or that he had been in personal touch with events 'from the beginning'.

As generally translated, 1.4 gives the impression that Luke is writing to give Theophilus further instruction in his Christian faith. However, the NEB translation 'so as to give you authentic knowledge about the matters of which you have been informed' could mean that Theophilus was not a Christian, and that the whole two-volume work was being written to give an account of the origins of Christianity so as to commend it to the outside world, and to defend it against the charge of being treasonable to the state (this theme appears in Luke's account of the Passion, and is dominant in the second part of Acts). In any case, the style of the preface shows that Luke thought of himself as a literary person writing to some extent like a Greek historian.

### 1. *The pattern of the Gospel*

Luke is dependent upon Mark, but in a different way from Matthew. He places what he takes from Mark in blocks alternately with his non-Marcan material and does not mix them together, and in the non-Marcan material what he gets from 'Q' and what he gets from 'L' are not much mixed together. Scholars are divided over what this implies. Some hold that if all that he derives from Mark is taken out of Luke's Gospel, what is left still makes a continuous narrative from John the Baptist to the resurrection, and they conclude that this was Luke's first version (Proto-Luke = 'Q' plus 'L'), which Luke later filled out with blocks inserted from Mark, who was thus not a primary but a secondary source for him. Others hold that this is not so, and that Mark supplies the basic framework in the Galilean ministry and the passion narrative, but that Luke has used it and edited it more freely, and for his own purposes has chosen a non-Marcan in preference to a Marcan story (e.g., the call of Peter [5.1–9]; the visit to Nazareth [4.16–30]; the anointing by a woman [7.36–50]).

There is no clearly pronounced pattern as in Matthew, but the narrative is more flowing than in Mark. Luke intended to write 'in an orderly manner' (1.3), and by this he seems to mean the treatment of one subject at a time (e.g., all the material gathered in 3.1–20 makes up a little account of the career of John the Baptist), with smoother transitions from one section to another so that the whole is more intelligible. He can write vividly in more than one style, including that of the Greek Old Testament. This versatility, and the fact that some of his special material – parables of the Good Samaritan, Prodigal Son, Dives and Lazarus, and episodes such as the Call of Peter, the Visit to Nazareth and the Anointing, the Walk to Emmaus, etc. have a highly graphic character, gives his Gospel a special appeal.

The birth stories are quite different from Matthew's. They trace parallel births of John and Jesus; they are not written around Old Testament texts as fulfilment of past prophecy, but in Old Testament style and as occasions of the revival of prophecy itself (the Canticles:

1.14–17, 32–34, 46–55, 68–79; 2.29–35). The Galilean ministry is largely Marcan, but Jesus is depicted more than in Mark as one who is on a journey (4.14 f., 16, 31, 44; 5.12; 7.1, 11; 8.1 f.). The journey from Galilee to Jerusalem, only briefly referred to by Mark and Matthew, becomes for Luke a framework for the whole middle section of his Gospel (9.51–19.28; cf. 10.38; 13.22; 17.11; 18.31), which as far as 18.14 is made up entirely of non-Marcan material. This concept of the journeying healer and preacher occurs again in Acts in relation to Philip, Peter and Paul, and is a common feature of Hellenistic literature. Luke's passion narrative has additional material and, like the rest of his Gospel, many human touches. It is rounded off by resurrection stories concerned not with Galilee but with Jerusalem, which also provide a bridge to the second volume, the Acts of the Apostles.

There are some threads which run through the two volumes and therefore affect the choice of material for the first volume and the way in which it is presented. One is the theme of the Spirit, through whose agency Jesus is conceived, which he receives at his baptism and which controls him in his temptations. By its power he heals and teaches (4.16 ff.). The same Spirit is his gift from the Father to the disciples (24.49; Acts 1.8) and directs the church throughout Acts. Also Luke is the only evangelist to say that Jesus named the twelve 'apostles' (6.13), and these are the chief recipients of his teaching and the nucleus of the church in Acts. Luke's version of this teaching is more immediately directed towards the moral guidance of men.

### 2. *Authorship*

According to tradition, Luke was Paul's

travelling companion. This may be correct, but it may have been arrived at by deduction that among the 'we' mentioned in Acts was Luke the physician, referred to in Col.4.14; Philemon 23 f.; II Tim.4.9–12. Even if it is correct, it throws no light on the Gospel, as this is derived from Mark and other such sources, but not from Paul. The Gospel was written after AD 70 (the fall of Jerusalem is reflected in 21.20), but it is not known where.

C. F. EVANS

7 The Miracles

## The nature of miracle

What is a miracle? Philosophers and theologians have argued long over the question and have produced some complex and sophisticated definitions. When it comes to ordinary discussions, however, the starting-point is clear enough. A miracle is usually taken to be an action or event which apparently violates the accepted order of nature. The sea is suddenly turned back, the sun stands still, water is changed into wine, a small quantity of bread feeds a vast crowd, the sick are suddenly healed and the dead are revived.

Miracles like this are still discussed because they are to be found in the Bible; not only on its fringe, but at crucial points in the story which Old and New Testaments tell. Of course, they are not confined to the Bible. Miracle stories are also common in the ancient Near East outside the Old Testament and in the first-century Mediterranean world outside the New Testament. They appear in Buddhism, Hinduism and Islam, and in later Christian tradition, right down to the present day. But only the biblical miracles are generally thought to be a problem worth devoting attention to.

These biblical miracle stories belong to a pre-scientific outlook, and are part of a completely different approach to the world from the one to which we have become acclimatized. This approach may best be called 'mythical', provided that the term is understood correctly. 'Myth' is a way of looking at the world which presents what we would be more likely to call dimensions of personality, of experience (including what man believes to be experience of the divine), in an objective, tangible, pictorial form. In a three-decker universe, with heaven above and the underworld below, with divine and demonic forces at work, the story, the description, the picture takes the place of abstract analysis or philosophical and psychological argument. This is the setting where miracle belongs.

Miracle and myth are by no means identical. What we would call miracle is often absent from a 'mythical' view of the world. But in such a view, where there is nothing like modern science to draw a line with a reasonable claim to authority between what is theoretically possible and what is theoretically impossible, the distinction between a factually correct historical account and a religiously significant symbol inevitably becomes blurred. Just how blurred this line could be is not easy to establish. How literally, say, the first-century world understood the language oyth and accounts of miracle is a puzzling question. Attitudes probably varied widely, just as do miracle stories themselves.

Even in a mythical setting, miracles appear in some places and not in others. They cluster round the exodus from Egypt, the lives of Elijah and Elisha, the ministry of Jesus and the work of the apostles as told, e.g., in Acts. On the other hand they are almost completely absent from the primary traditions of the great prophets, the wisdom literature, the apocryphal I Maccabees (but compare II Maccabees) and the letters of Paul and his successors. Outside the Bible, from the time of the early church, one might compare the more or less rational approach of Plutarch and Josephus and the scepticism of Lucian of Samosata with the excessive credulity of Philostratus, author of a life of the wonder-worker Apollonius of Tyana, and Antonius Diogenes, whose *Incredible Things beyond Thule* which included a trip to the moon was accepted even by quite respectable philosophers. Perhaps the most interesting example of different attitudes to miracle comes from the eleventh century. The historian R. W. Southern, writing about Anselm and his biographers, notes how the famous Archbishop of Canterbury was at one time accompanied on his travels by two companions; of these, one regularly saw miracles, while the other did not!

This differentiation in the appearance of miracle also extends to the kind of miracle stories that are told. Not all of them have the same profundity. On the one hand, there are the miraculous legends or semi-edifying tales which great figures or events seemed to attract almost automatically. Many of these stories are popular in character; they are often unedifying and superficial, and reduce miracles almost to the level of the conjuring trick. Examples of this type are the elaborations of the plagues of Egypt, most of the Elisha stories, the incident of the coin in the fish's mouth (Matt.17.24–27), some of the miracles attached to Peter and Paul in Acts (5.12–16; 9.32–41; 19.11 f.; 20.7–12), and above all the stories of the boy Jesus in the apocryphal gospels. In the Infancy Gospel of Thomas, for example, Jesus becomes a little menace, cursing those who annoy him so that they die (and then reviving them). The apocryphal Acts of the Apostles take the biblical Acts even further, with talking animals, obedient bed-bugs and swimming kippers. By this stage

miracle has virtually become popular entertainment.

On the other hand, miracle can be an attempt at representing the profound and the mysterious character of people or events through which a new dimension seems to be present, exhausting ordinary language and ideas. Something of this very different atmosphere can be seen in, say, the story of the burning bush at the call of Moses, in the central event of the exodus from Egypt which kindled the faith of a nation, and above all in the work of Jesus, at the centre of the New Testament.

Those who told miracle stories thus saw miracles as the working of supernatural power in the world. This power was not necessarily good; miracles could be worked by the devil as well as by God. For example, in the story of the Egyptian plagues (Ex.7–11) there is virtually a competition between Moses and Aaron and the Egyptian magicians; Jesus himself is accused of casting out demons by demonic power (Matt.12.24; for an amusing sideline on the whole question see Acts 19.13 ff.). So in the early days, the problem for Christians was not so much in establishing that miracles had happened as in demonstrating what they meant.

## Miracles and science

As we have seen, even against a mythical background, miracles were 'miraculous'. The first century AD was probably one of the most credulous periods of history, but even then the restoration to life of a corpse was not an everyday occurrence. On the other hand, when so many marvellous stories were going the rounds, such a happening would have been that much easier to credit. The problem of miracle really became serious when the growth of science provided rational explanations for hitherto unexplained happenings, reducing phenomena which might be attributed to divine intervention and establishing consistent 'laws of nature'. Once this scientific approach had been established, miracle tended to be detached from its context in myth and examined in physical terms.

How was a miracle possible? That was the key question, but alongside was another, equally important. Was the old view that what could not be explained in natural terms had to be supernatural still valid? Suppose a 'miracle' occurred; did it necessarily point to divine action? It might be a fraud or a misunderstanding. It might be explicable in other terms if all the facts were available. It might be explicable in the future, with an increase in scientific knowledge. It might be an oddity, a freak. In short, not only did the possibility of miracle seem more remote; because the whole world view of which miracles had been a part gave way to a new approach, miracles were no longer accepted as the kind of pointers which they once seemed to be.

This new situation led to three different approaches to miracle:

1. *Science and belief in miracle conflict: belief in miracle is to be retained.* In a famous book on miracles, C. S. Lewis defended the old, supernatural view of miracle against all objections. For him, Christianity itself was based on the Great Miracle, that God had become man; given this, was it not fitting that other remarkable happenings should follow? A 'naturalistic' approach was not enough; Christianity demanded a supernaturalist view of the world. In its time, this attitude was very popular; it does, however, leave the Christian fighting rather a lone battle as the man who can believe 'eight impossible things before breakfast', and with more recent developments in theology as a whole is increasingly difficult to sustain. (Bruce Marshall's book, *Father Malachy's Miracle*, is a vivid fictional account of a similar point of view.)

2. *Science and belief in miracle conflict: miracles are to be rejected.* It is regularly argued that scientists have discovered enough to establish a system of natural laws which rule out the possibility of miracle. There is some truth in this argument. We do not see miracles happening, and our day-to-day life and our reconstruction of the past are based on the presupposition that nature is regular. On the other hand, with science has also come the insight that our knowledge is based on observation and experience and can never be absolute. So while scientists and historians may be very sceptical indeed, strictly speaking they can never rule out completely the possibility of miracle.

3. *Science and belief in miracle can be reconciled.* The discovery of quantum physics and the principle of indeterminacy appeared to some people to make science far more open-textured. The impossibility of predicting the behaviour of nuclear particles led to revised statements like, 'Scientifically speaking, a miracle is a highly improbable, statistically rare, but not impossible event.' Such a view builds heavily on the objections to the second view mentioned above, supported by the feeling that the categories of science cannot by themselves explain every dimension of human life. But this is an irrational combination of thoughts and is certainly a misinterpretation of recent scientific developments. While it is true that twentieth-century science is very different from that of the nineteenth century, responsible scientists

(including many Christians) seem agreed that the new developments do not in themselves alter the problems of the relationship between miracle and science.

## *Do miracles happen ?*

Is it, then, possible to come to any provisional conclusions about miracle ? One of C. S. Lewis' important points was that the ideas with which a person approaches a miracle story will determine what he makes of it: 'Those who assume that miracles cannot happen are merely wasting their time by looking into the texts; we know in advance what results they will find, for they have begun by begging the question.'

It is difficult to seem not to beg the question, for a straight answer to the question 'Do miracles happen ?' is not easy. As we have seen, the historian can reconstruct the past only on the assumption that the world is regular and constant, i.e., that miracles do not happen. He naturally fears that excessive credulity will corrupt his judgment as a historian. On the other hand, he has to accept that his method, by its very nature, could not accept a miracle even on the strongest testimony. That is its limitation.

Perhaps the most satisfactory reply, in the circumstances, is to stress the need to look at particular miracles against their proper background and thought-world. Sometimes close examination of a miracle will show it to be of a kind that can reasonably be dismissed or explained in another way; sometimes the dimension of mystery will simply have to be acknowledged and it will have to be recognized that something really beyond our understanding may have taken place.

The more general issues are certainly rele-vant, but without detailed application they will only remain abstractions. This will become clear if we look more closely at the miracles in the Gospels; the principles applied here can be extended to the treatment of miracles else-where in the Bible.

## *Miracles in the Gospels*

As we have seen, miracles were attributed to Jesus by later writers as they were to other famous men. Sometimes this wholesale attribu-tion of miracles hinders our understanding rather than helping it. The Jesus who conjures a coin out of the mouth of a fish to pay his tax, who makes sparrows out of clay or stretches with his bare hands a piece of wood which is too short for Joseph's purpose is more grotesque than anything else. Nor are we really enlight-ened by the elaborations to Matthew's passion narrative, stories of saints appearing out of their graves and of angelic guardians at the tomb. We can see why these stories were told, but they seem artificial; even the incident in Luke's Gospel, where Jesus heals the ear of the man wounded by Peter at the time of his arrest, strikes us as being little more than an embell-ishment.

On the other hand, there are other stories told about Jesus which seem to have much deeper roots. There are the miracle stories themselves (e.g., the stilling of the storm [Mark 4.35–41], the healing of the Gerasene demoniac [Mark 5.1–20], the healing of Jairus' daughter [Mark 5.21–43], the feeding of the multitudes [Mark 6.30–44; 8.1–10], the walking on the water [Mark 6.45–51]) which occur in the earliest tradition and focus interest in various ways on the power of Jesus and the impression he made. There are also incidental references to miracles in contexts where the miracle itself is of subsidiary interest. Thus in Mark 3.1–5, the healing of the man with a withered hand on the sabbath is secondary to the main controversy, what is permissible on the sabbath. Similarly, among the sayings of Jesus, the famous remark, 'If I by the finger of God cast out devils then is the kingdom of God come upon you' (Luke 11.20; cf. Matt.12.28), takes the miracles as its basic premiss; the dispute is over what the miracles mean (see above).

One of the firm facts in the tradition about Jesus therefore seems to be that he performed miracles. Is it then possible to go further and to say more closely what these miracles were ?

Two categories are usually distinguished: the healing miracles and the 'nature' miracles. The first group includes exorcisms and the cure of the crippled, blind, deaf, dumb (and even the raising of the dead); the second comprises, e.g., the stilling of the storm, the walking on the water, the feeding of the five (four) thousand. The distinction is a useful one, not because the first group is less problematical for our modern views than the second (i.e., there might well be a psychological explanation for the cures), but because with the nature miracles the relationship between the story as we have it and an event behind it seems that much more complex.

With their overtones of Old Testament (and other ?) imagery, the nature miracles in fact come quite close to stories like those of the temptation and the transfiguration, where the basic event (if there was a single event at all) lies buried under a very considerable amount of interpretation. Given this position, rather than trying to penetrate the interpretation, it is better to look for the meaning it is intended to convey.

It is, then, perhaps justifiable to see the healings and exorcisms as most characteristic of Jesus' own work, and the other miracles as above all ways of understanding him. But this is not, of course, a distinction which would have occurred to the evangelists themselves.

The evangelists have an important part in the miracle stories. They have selected these stories, arranged them and even retold them to fit their own wider purposes. This means that the same story may have a different emphasis from Gospel to Gospel.

Miracles have the most positive role in the *Gospel of Mark*. Almost one third of Mark consists of miracle stories, immensely varied both in form and subject-matter. Some have a biblical flavour, but many are closer to the atmosphere of the first-century world. Mark uses these miracle stories to highlight Jesus as above all the destroyer of unclean spirits and the forces of chaos by his greater power of the spirit; Jesus is the victor who emerges triumphant from his contest with the demons – it is a case of the Holy Spirit (1.8) overcoming the 'unclean spirits'.

This dynamic use of the miracle tradition is absent from the other two Synoptic Gospels. *Matthew* takes over the Marcan miracles and adds some of his own. But by keeping them all together in a group and thus in essentials confining them to one part of his Gospel (8.1–10.42), he reduces their prominence so that the figure of Jesus is no longer predominantly that of a doer of mighty work, but that of a teacher. Where Matthew himself introduces miracles outside this section (e.g. 17.24–27; 27.52 f.; 28.2–4), they tend to be much more legendary in character.

In *Luke*, the opening scene of Jesus' ministry (4.18 f.) links the miracles directly with the Holy Spirit, which is such a prominent concern of

Luke's throughout the Gospel and Acts. A summary of the ministry of Jesus in Acts 10.38 mentions 'how God anointed Jesus of Nazareth with the Holy Spirit and with power and how he went about doing good and healing all that were oppressed by the devil, for God was with him'. To a degree this resembles Mark, but there is a real difference: the element of mystery and awe which is so characteristic of Mark almost completely disappears; Luke's Jesus is a much more human figure, and comes much closer to the type of the first-century travelling wonder-worker.

The *Gospel of John* differs greatly from the Synoptic Gospels in its treatment of miracle, as in so much else. It only has a few miracles, which are called 'signs', a word which 'indicates that John has made a selection of those actions which for him were most significant because in their outward and physical circumstances they served as the clearest pointers to what in Christian experience believers had come to see Jesus to be and his gifts to be'. Signs by themselves are not enough. They need to be interpreted and understood properly. And in the end they can be dispensed with.

The different approaches of the Gospels to miracle indicates the kind of questions which should be asked of the stories they contain. Seen as part of a portrait of Jesus, what do the miracles convey ? Are they cheap and superficial marvels, with a superficial view of God ? Or are they part of a mythical approach in which writers are struggling to convey and interpret the mystery of an overwhelming experience which sometimes takes the form of miracle because it refers to something beyond common words and experiences ?

## The Resurrection

It is sometimes said that the resurrection is 'the greatest miracle of all'. This may, however, be a misleading way of putting it. For the resurrection of Jesus comes close to those stories, mentioned above, where interpretation and original occurrence are so intertwined that it is very difficult indeed to see what actually happened.

The customary ways of approaching the resurrection closely resemble the alternative approaches to miracle mentioned earlier.

1. *The traditional faith of the church in the physical resurrection of Jesus' body is straightforward, and to be accepted.* The tomb was empty; Jesus appeared to his disciples and later ascended to heaven. The New Testament says so. Why complicate things further ? Of course, there are discrepancies (both between individual Gospels and between the Gospels and I Cor. 15.1–8), but these are only to be expected when the same event is told by several different people.

2. *The bones of Jesus lie buried somewhere in Palestine.* Bodies, once dead, cannot be revived. There can be no exceptions to the scientific law that all men must die. Furthermore, to insist on the physical resurrection of Jesus is to introduce at the wrong point a stumbling-block in the way of belief. What matters is not so much whether or not one has the capacity to believe in a physical resurrection of Jesus, but rather commitment to the way of Jesus, to the new life which is made possible in the fellowship of his church, where his spirit lives on.

3. *Both the preceding views are too simple.* For others, it is impossible to prove the question either way in definite terms. So the resurrection might be presented as John Hick presents it:

We shall never know whether the resurrection of Jesus was a bodily event; or consisted instead in visions of Jesus; or in an intense sense of his unseen personal presence. But we do know the effects of the event and we know that whatever happened was such as to produce these effects. The main result was the transformation of a forlorn handful of former followers of an executed and discredited prophet into a coherent and dynamic fellowship with a faith which determined its life and enabled it to convince, to grow, to survive persecution and become the dominant religion of the Roman Empire.

This view takes from the first approach the conviction that *something* happened, and from the second the conviction that human reaction to Jesus was a constituent part of the event; but it is unwilling to go as far as either to their respective extremes.

A view of this kind would certainly seem to fit the evidence best. The resurrection is a complex event. New Testament writers talk about it in different ways and differ in more than detail. But they agree in including in this 'event' the consequences of the death of Jesus, up to and including the conviction of the church that Jesus, who had died, was the Risen Lord. What is to be singled out from all this complex as the essence of the resurrection is less easy to say. Paul, for example, shows no knowledge of the empty tomb, and his use of the phrase 'he appeared' (I Cor.15.5) allows of no conclusions as to the nature of the Risen Lord. An examination of the Gospel accounts of the resurrection will show a wide divergence; the contributions of the evangelists themselves seem to be considerable. Compare, for example, Matthew, Luke and John, the three Gospels with resurrection appearances; is it not significant that the Christ who appears is in Matthew a Matthaean Christ, in Luke a Lucan Christ and in John a Johannine Christ? The more deeply we penetrate the more mysterious it becomes.

There are indeed questions here. Nevertheless, the main fact, that those who doubted were transformed into a dynamic new movement, would still seem to be best explained by a recognition that this change had been produced by something which had happened, and which they knew to have happened, to Jesus of Nazareth.

JOHN BOWDEN

# 8 The Ministry of Jesus

The most striking thing about Jesus is his immense influence over the heart and imagination of ordinary men and women. He has shown a persistent and enduring power of haunting – to put it no higher – the minds of all sorts and conditions of men, contradicting the prescriptions of friends and surviving the criticisms of enemies. He has been profoundly involved in the rise and fall of civilizations. He has had more to do with the rise and attitudes of the modern world – its scientific inquiry and its secular convictions – than most of us are aware of. He has made himself at home in races other than his own. Whatever the problems – and they are not a few – with which the earliest records of his story present us, we must remind ourselves, as we set out to tell his story, that we are not dealing merely with a misty figure half-seen in debatable documents, but with a man whose three brief public years have left an indelible mark on all men's life and thought, and whose character and ministry and remembered words have an incredible power of awakening the imagination and opening the minds of men twenty centuries after his death, one Friday afternoon, somewhere about the year AD 29.

Writing about Jesus can so often get lost in the bogs of the important but limited discussion of documents and of the uncertain events of the rise and spread of the Christian community in the first decades after his death, that we must remind ourselves of what we are now attempting. We are scrutinizing the earliest records to find a clue to the widespread and profound personal influence of Jesus. Who *is* he who can speak to us through the etchings of a Rembrandt or the sculpture of an Epstein, the paintings of a Spencer or a Rouault, the poetry of an Eliot or Auden, the work of a Gandhi or a Dr Luther King; and who, beyond this, can be the inspiration and guide of steel-workers, shop-keepers, farmers, housewives today ? Though, before we have finished, we may have other things to say about him, we must begin with an awareness of the public facts of his influence in the world. This is the man on whose story we are now embarking.

Those who have tried to write his story have often been charged with painting it in their own likeness. There is truth in this charge (it is true of all biographies); but we cannot escape this dilemma. We must be bold. We must not be frightened of asking our own questions and being ourselves in his presence. We must listen to historian and biblical scholar and take a proper note of what they have to say; but we must not be intimidated by them. We must constantly remember who it is whose story we are telling.

### The evidence for the story

The evidence on which any account of Jesus must be founded has already been discussed in some detail. It is necessary, however, to make some comments about it here; we must keep in mind what kind of evidence it is.

Three things only need be said:

1. The indisputable fact with which we begin

is the existence, in the later decades of the first century, of small Christian communities scattered throughout the Mediterranean world. Their records – Gospels, letters, the remarkable Fourth Gospel, The Revelation – have been subjected to the most intense scrutiny that has ever been given to any ancient documents. It is clear that they are religious documents – church books – 'reflecting in manifold ways,' as one writer has said, 'the experiences and reflections of the churches in the final decades of the first century and adapted to meeting the felt needs of these primitive communities'. What we find, then, in the letters as well as in the more apparently 'historical' Gospels, is *the memories of his friends*, set down in the way they needed them and as they understood them.

2. These are, therefore, not 'historical documents' in our twentieth-century meaning of the words. Historical investigation as we understand it is a recent discipline. But *this does not mean that their authors were indifferent to authentic information about Jesus*. Their conviction that in him 'God acted' required of them that, as far as they could, they should make sure that what they said had happened had really happened. They must get right 'the plain story of what had happened in the ministry of Jesus'. If they knew they were freely inventing a story, the very ground of their convictions would have been cut from beneath them. We have much sorting out to do and we must be careful how we use their evidence, but their reports are honest reports, not deliberate fiction.

3. What we have, therefore, before us in the letters and the Gospels are *portraits* of Jesus. There has been much discussion about what knowledge Paul had of Jesus, but no one can read through Paul's letters without being aware of the portrait of Jesus which illuminated his

mind – a portrait painted from knowledge, as his 'thumb-nail sketch' of Jesus in I Cor.13.5–7 seems to imply. We meet different portraits of Jesus in the first three Gospels, and another bolder portrait in the Fourth Gospel. We are free to examine these portraits, question details and comment on their broad strokes. But, finally, we must stand back from the portraits; when we do so, we become aware, as we note their different colours and pattern, of a recognizable figure, of a real person, at once strange and familiar, at once confirming and challenging our impressions and assumptions. Above and beyond the questions and hesitations which arise as we read, the total impression which these portraits make upon us is of a real story in a real world: that face was once seen, that voice was once heard.

## The presuppositions of the story

But before we begin to sketch that story out, there are two other important questions to take note of – questions which perhaps more than others make this story seem to many people remote and unreal.

1. The reports about the events with which we are concerned belong to the pre-scientific world. Men's assumptions about the world they lived in and the way they thought and talked about it were very different from our assumptions and the way we think and talk about it. This is no insuperable obstacle to our understanding of them. Their different assumptions and idioms no more inhibit dialogue with them than a similar situation inhibits dialogue with present-day pre-scientific people, if we take the trouble to learn something of their language, idiom and approach. But it does mean that we must take trouble; we must not read the

accounts in the Gospels as though they had been written in our own century by people who think about the world as we do. We have to ask about their reports – 'Why did they put it like this?' 'What happened to make them talk like this?' 'How would we put it today?' Anybody who has lived among civilized but pre-scientific people knows how inescapable these questions are. We have to ask them of the events before us.

2. But more important is another question. We have noted that the records in which the story of Jesus is found are religious records. Their writers were concerned with getting clear the meaning of their new religious experience which was rooted in events that had happened a few decades before in Palestine. They wanted to know what actually happened; but they described the events that happened – and only so much of them as mattered to them, for they were not attempting a full historical account – in religious language. These events had evoked for those who were first involved in them a new awareness of God, and they used language which brought this character of the events out. For example, such a word is 'miracle', a word which has been in recent centuries a storm-centre of debate. It does not, as has been said, necessarily mean something which breaks 'the regularities and consistences of nature and history', as by many people then and now it has been assumed to mean. The characteristic word for 'miracle' in the New Testament is not 'wonder', but one of two other words – 'power' and 'sign'. Hence it may best be defined as 'an event which through its unusual character attracts our attention, but also awakens or deepens our awareness of, our faith in, and our assurance of, the love of God'. The question of what actually happened in what the New Testament writers describe as 'a power' or 'a sign' is open to inquiry, and we may have to admit that for many such occasions we have to say 'We do not know'; but what we cannot do is to dismiss it as if that was the end of the matter. This event awakened the sense of God's presence – made God real – for them. We must ask why. We must remember, then, what our authors are doing and what kind of language they are using.

## The background of the story

We come now to the story of Jesus itself. It is a story we shall never begin to understand unless we place it firmly against the background of his day – a country occupied by Roman troops whose presence provoked not only a general feeling of resentment and frustration but also the bitter activities of a Resistance Movement, the Zealots. Jesus was no rootless individual. He grew up in Galilee where the Resistance Movement was very much alive; Nazareth was about two miles from Jaffa, 'the oldest and most important settlement in this part of the hill country . . . and a rallying point for the armed opposition to the invading Roman Army' in AD 66. Its bitter resistance must have had a long history behind it; and it is likely that Jesus grew up in a strong resistance atmosphere.

We have learned much in our own day about resistance movements – how they dominate and determine the mind and mood of a people under the apparent calm of ordinary life, and how their very secrecy gives them an indisputable authority over the activities of ordinary citizens. Their clandestine character offers room for a wide variety of opinions among ordinary people which only become acute when full-scale fighting breaks out. It is against such a background that the ministry of Jesus must be seen; his sayings and actions take on new meaning against it; the brevity of his ministry and his political murder outside Jerusalem become intelligible. For the fact is that he came to his convictions the hard way – he was not day-dreaming about some ideal world, but making a costly and dangerous attempt to ask real questions about a real world. His criticism of the common assumptions of his day, arising as they did from his own profound experience of God's presence and a life-time's meditation on the history of his people, made him, when his attitude became recognizably clear, suspect with Resistance Movement, people and government alike, and disowned by many of his friends (John 6.66).

Jesus' ministry falls midway in the story of the three hundred years' Jewish war for religious and political freedom. The war began with the Maccabaean rebellion of 168 BC and ended with Bar Kochba's revolt in AD 132. Its story is the theme of Josephus' *The Jewish War*, a book to be used, indeed, with caution, but where we may find 'set down both clearly and accurately the main course of events . . . the long-drawn agony of the war (AD 66-70) and the happenings which preceded it, with such a wealth of detail that his work is a major contribution to the history of a crtical century'. The reading of this book is a prerequisite for the proper reading of the Gospels.

The Gospels, as we have said, are church books, written for the guidance of the early Christian communities and concerned with their religious life. These communities, after AD 70, were predominantly non-Jewish in their membership; for many Christians then the incidents in Palestine from AD 29 to 70 were mere episodes in a far-off province on the eastern edge of the Roman Empire, as interesting to them as a colonial war in Africa probably was to an ordinary British citizen in the late century. But the brutal and violent story of what had happened pushes through even these religious records. It is the critical context against which the very meaningfulness of Jesus' 'Good News' is to be grasped – even his phrase 'The kingdom of God' may have been the watchword of the Zealots. What he did and said was meant for men and women there and then; only because this was so, could it also have a meaning for all mankind.

A story which Josephus tells about Pilate is a fitting quotation to give us the feeling of what it was like to live in Palestine in Jesus' day.

As procurator of Judaea Tiberius sent Pilate, who during the night secretly and under cover, conveyed to Jerusalem the images of Caesar known as *signa*. When day dawned this caused great excitement among the Jews; for those who were near were amazed at the sight, which meant that their laws had been trampled on – they do not permit any graven images to be set up in the City – and the angry city mob were joined by a huge influx of people from the country. They rushed off to Pilate in Caesarea, and begged him to remove the *signa* from Jerusalem and to respect their ancient customs. When Pilate refused, they fell prone all round his house and remained motionless for five days and nights.

The next day, Pilate took his seat on the tribunal in the Great Stadium, and summoned the mob on the pretext that he was ready to give them an answer. Instead he gave a pre-arranged signal to the soldiers to surround the Jews in full armour, and the troops formed a ring three deep. The Jews were dumbfounded at the unexpected sight, but Pilate, declaring that he would cut them to pieces unless they accepted the images of Caesar, nodded to the soldiers to bare their swords. At this the Jews as though by agreement fell to the ground in a body and bent their necks, shouting that they were ready to be killed rather than transgress the Law. Amazed at the intensity of their religious fervour, Pilate ordered the *signa* to be removed from Jerusalem forthwith.

We can imagine the talk and comment in the streets of Jaffa and Nazareth. Among such people Jesus had to think his own way to the truth about God and man; such were the people he attempted to persuade when he made his public appeal after the arrest of John the Hermit; and from such people came his first friends. He was living in a real world and dealing with real situations.

The Resistance Movement was not a bid for mere political freedom. Politics and religion were, for Jews, two sides of one coin. Hence among the people of the country, many different religious movements made a bid for their allegiance – Pharisees who were popular with the common people, groups such as we meet in the monastery of Qumran in the Jordan valley, Sadducees (wealthy priestly families) in Jerusalem, and followers of John the Hermit. The common people, as at all times, had their own varying ambiguous attitudes. But it was the political situation which gave all these movements their focus; it is not an accident that Jesus was its victim.

## The outline of the story

No biography of Jesus can be written; what we find in the Gospels, as we have said, are portraits of Jesus, painted some years later in a very different situation by people with deeply religious convictions. When we look at them we are looking at their portraits of their Master and Lord.

It has been widely held that, because this is so, we can know nothing of the actual story of Jesus and that it is impossible to separate the religious story from the originating incident which lies behind it. What is more, it is said, all we have are isolated stories strung together on a framework which is the creation of the evangelists themselves. There is no questioning that the theological convictions of the writers – and of the communities they speak for – are deeply impressed on the stories they have given us. But is this all that can be said ?

We have already emphasized that among the convictions of the early friends of Jesus was the conviction that the story which lay at the heart of all they most deeply believed was an authentic story – it had really happened. There is much evidence that they cared enough about the authenticity of their fundamental story to put down their memories of what Jesus actually did and said even when they themselves were puzzled about them and perhaps did not really understand why on these occasions he should have done and said what they reported. Is it likely that they did not remember also something of the broad outline of the course of his ministry ?

Dr C. H. Dodd once wrote a famous article in the *Expository Times*, which is worth considering, though it has been questioned by some scholars. He looked at the editorial notes with which Mark linked his various stories about Jesus together ('generalizing summaries' which other more radical scholars admitted as such) and noted that, if we put them together, the striking thing 'is the way in which the summaries fall naturally into something like a continuous narrative'. Here they are:

After John's arrest Jesus came into Galilee proclaiming the Kingdom of God in the words, 'The time is fulfilled, and the Kingdom of God has drawn near: repent and believe in the Gospel.' He entered Capernaum; and on Sabbath days he would go to the synagogue and teach. All were in a state of astonishment at this teaching; for he used to teach them as one with authority, and not like the scribes. He went proclaiming in the synagogues throughout Galilee, and casting out demons. He went out to the seaside, and the whole crowd would come to him, and he would teach them. From Judaea and Jerusalem, from Idumaea and Peraea, and from the districts of Tyre and Sidon, a great throng, hearing what he was doing, came to him. He told his disciples to have a boat waiting for him because of the crowds, so that they should not throng him; for he healed many, so that all who had plagues kept pressing upon him to touch him. The foul fiends, whenever they saw him, would fall before him, and cry out, 'Thou art the Son of God.' He would enjoin them not to make him known. He went up into the hill-country, and summoned those whom he himself wanted, and they came to him. He appointed the Twelve that they might be with him and that he might send them out to preach and to have authority to expel demons. So he appointed the Twelve (and here follows their names). He summoned the Twelve and began to send them out two by two; he used to give them authority over foul fiends; and they went out and preached repentance. They kept expelling demons and anointing many sick folk with oil and healing them. The apostles gathered to Jesus and reported to him all that they had done and said.

So, if this argument is accepted, behind the individual stories (which came to Mark without any indications of time and place), behind the larger groups of material (genuinely continuous narratives, stories strung upon an itinerary, and stories connected by unity of theme), we can discern 'an outline of the whole ministry, designed, perhaps, as an introduction of the passion story, but serving also as a background of reference for the separate stories'.

What, then, is this broad 'outline' of the story of Jesus ? We can mark these decisive moments:

His Call (the Baptism and Temptations)

The Proclamation of the 'Good News' ('Gospel') in Galilee

The Desert Meal ('The Feeding of the Five Thousand')

A Period of Retirement

The Incident near Caesarea Philippi and the Mountain Climb ('The Transfiguration')

The Journey to the South

The Last Days

Most of the older attempts to write 'the story of Jesus' took the whole structure of the gospel narratives as their pattern, beginning with the birth stories and proceeding to the stories of his death and resurrection. This procedure suits well if what we are concerned about is a meditation on the whole ministry of Jesus. But it gets the real story out of focus and blurs the edges of the dramatic and urgent quality of what seems actually to have happened. Let us approach the story in another way, and paint our own portrait of him, as far as the evidence permits.

## The climax of his death

A cursory reading of the gospel material reveals the startling way in which the passion narrative – the story of the last few days – dominates the whole record. It was that death in the afternoon which not only haunted the imagination of his first friends but was for them the clue to the whole story.

The passion narrative (Mark 14 f.; Matt.26 f.; Luke 22 f.; John 18 f.) was probably the first account to be given permanent oral – and, later, written – form. From the earliest days, when his friends met to 'break bread' together and remember what happened on the night before he died, this story had been told as part of their meeting. Three different versions seem to have survived, those in Mark, in Luke (where it is now interwoven with Mark's account) and in John (where, if Dr Dodd is right, we find the third account). Some scholars, however, would explain the differences between the passion narratives as due simply to the extra-material the evangelists used and to their special theological views. This story of the passion dominates the whole account of the ministry of Jesus, occupying a predominant place in the telling.

Let us summarize it in its Roman version as we find it in Mark.

It begins a few days before the Passover feast with Jesus' sudden return, incognito, to the capital city. He had already apparently made arrangements for the hiring of a house. He sent two carefully chosen friends to a pre-arranged rendezvous, to be guided by a man 'carrying a water-jar' to an unknown house. Here they prepared a meal; here, after dark, came Jesus and his other friends.

The meal does not seem to have been a Passover meal, though this has been its association in Christian practice from earliest times. The evening meal had taken a prominent place in the common life which Jesus and his friends lived together; this was the last of such evening meals. Jesus gives it a unique meaning – giving himself, in the giving of the bread and the wine, to and for his friends, and through them, to all mankind. The earliest record we have of what happened is found in one of Paul's letters:

The Lord Jesus, on the night of his arrest, took bread and, after giving thanks to God, broke it and said: 'This is my body, which is for you; do this as a memorial of me.' In the same way, he took the cup after supper, and said: 'This cup is the new covenant sealed by my blood. Whenever you drink it, do this as a memorial of me' (I Cor.11.23–25 NEB).

Whatever the debates in Christian circles about the precise meaning of his words, their overwhelming significance is plain. His death was to make utterly clear all that he had lived for, and be the means by which his Father would 'reconcile the world to himself', at once the reality and hope of all humanity.

Meanwhile, Judas had left the company – a strange, enigmatic figure whose motives and intention have troubled the Christian conscience ever since. Whether it was his rigid loyalty to Jesus ('I know what he ought to do and I will force him to be himself'), his passionate belief that Jesus was the Messiah (but the Messiah of the Resistance Movement), his isolation from the others (he seems to have been the only southerner among them) can only be a matter of conjecture. Something like this, however, may be the explanation of his sudden suicide when all his dreams crashed about him and he realized the enormity of what he had done.

The others walk through the dark streets and

out to the Olive Orchard, Gethsemane, perhaps on their way to Bethany where they may have been staying. Here they stayed, and here Jesus felt the crisis he was facing suddenly overwhelming him – 'horror and dismay came over him'. 'My heart is ready to break with grief,' he said. He felt, apparently, some contradiction between his own judgment and what he knew, deep in his heart, was his Father's will: 'Not what I will, but what thou wilt', he prayed.

Suddenly a posse of armed men break into the orchard. They seem to have thought that in the darkness they might arrest the wrong man; Judas makes identification unmistakable by kissing him.

The meeting of the Jewish Council and the trial before Pilate follow, with Peter's cowardly disavowal and the soldiers' horse-play, and by nine o'clock in the morning, he was crucified outside the city. The agony dragged on into the afternoon.

Then Jesus gave a loud cry and died. When the centurion who was standing opposite him saw how he died, he said, 'Truly this man was a son of God.'

It was a dramatic ending.

Whatever stories precede this plain and moving account of the death of Jesus are an exploration of how and why it ever happened. For his friends, it was not just a brutal political murder – its political background counted least in their minds. It was its theological significance that mattered, and raised for them the whole character and work of God for all humanity. The reasons for their belief are found in their own accounts – in their selection of story and saying and their references to the Old Testament – and in other New Testament documents like the letter of Paul and that Fourth Gospel. But neither was it a mere political event for

Jesus. It had long been clear to him that there was no escaping a brutal death (they are common in occupied countries); during the last months he had spoken of it to his friends to their consternation and bewilderment. It was bound up for him with what he believed was the whole work God was doing in and through him – the climax of human history.

That Jesus thought all this through in the light of the actual situation among his own people, their hopes and fears, their wild dreams and military preparations – asking himself how ordinary men and women can be persuaded to see what God is really like and what he actually is doing, criticizing their own assumptions and breaking the entail of their own history – is clear from the way in which the Desert Meal (Mark 6.30–44) was for him the great critical moment between his baptism and his death (see below, p. 115).

Such is the story which dominates the records. What brought him there ?

### His call

The beginning of the story is the incident by River Jordan (Mark 1.9–11; Luke 3.21 f.; Matt.3.13–17).

The story of what happened by the river – and in the wilderness above it – must go back to Jesus himself. It is the story of his call – the first great crisis he had to face. It was a profound personal experience, not a public event as later it seems to have been thought (Matt.3.14; Luke 3.22). No man talks easily of his profoundest experiences, and then only to his closest friends when some crisis demands it of him. The incident at Caesarea Philippi (Mark 8.27–30) was such a crisis for Jesus. His language and theme change after this – about God as 'Abba'

('Father'), about the kingdom of God and about his death. It is not improbable that his friends knew nothing about his experience at River Jordan and in the wilderness until Jesus, knowing they were completely misconceiving the work God had given him to do, for the first time told three of his closest friends on the Mountain Climb what had happened and what it meant to him in the light of the history of his people.

Jesus must have long pondered God's work among his own people and in the life of mankind during the years in Nazareth. His own deepening experience of God's presence, his prolonged study of the Scriptures, his participation in village debates led him to make up his mind about the nature of that work. News of the preaching of John the Hermit in the Jordan valley reached Nazareth. It was the moment when he must act. He went down to take his part in this moment of prophetic revival – and found himself face to face with his unique destiny.

Luke tells us that Jesus was praying after his baptism when he suddenly became aware of this unique destiny. In words reminiscent of a royal Psalm (Ps. 2) and one of the Servant Songs (Isa.42.1), he heard God calling him to his unique relationship with him and to the unique work he had to do. Whatever he may have thought before of his place in the renewal of God's real work to which John called men back, he knew now that into his hands was given its leadership. The words 'Son', 'the Beloved' (meaning 'Messiah' but not using the word), and 'Servant' were typical of his own thought and approach, revealing his intimate sense of God's presence ('Father') and his relationship to his fellow-men. They were to recur again and again, and they colour parable and poem.

He now knew his destiny, but he had again to think through what his destiny involved. This is the theme of the days he now spent in the loneliness of the wilderness of Judaea. The character of God's work among men was to be the principal point of disagreement between himself and his own countrymen, and he summarized his thinking in this critical period in parabolic form – a form in which his mind was most at home – for his friends. His work was to be concerned neither with the dream of some early paradise ('bread alone') nor with political power ('all the kingdoms of the world') nor with browbeating the minds of men with winders ('the pinnacle of the temple'). Persons can only be treated as persons ('You must love God with all you are, and your neighbour as yourself'); the intimate reality of God's love can only be made known in personal friendship. He chose to be a teacher and to wander through the villages – meeting people, talking to them, offering them his friendship, being their servant, proclaiming the Good News of the kingdom of God. There was no other way if God whom, in the depth of his being, he knew as 'Father', was to be made plain to ordinary men and women – to men even of the Resistance Movement – not as an abstract truth but as a living experience changing their lives and refashioning the world they lived in. He was no dreamer. He knew well the complexity of human nature and the titanic task to which he was committed. He had his feet planted firmly on the ground. The range and depth of his thinking in the wilderness are distilled in the bold words in which Mark summarizes the theme of his Galilean campaign:

The time has come;
The kingdom of God is upon you;

Repent;
Trust in the Good News.

## In Galilee

'After John had been arrested, Jesus came into Galilee proclaiming the Gospel of God' – so Mark (1.14 NEB); 'armed with the power of the Spirit' – so Luke (4.14 NEB).

Why Galilee ? At first sight, this strikes us as a most unexpected decision for anyone who claimed to stand in the prophetic tradition. We can understand the fascination of the Jordan valley and the desert beyond (John's choice) with its symbolic harking-back to the desert traditions of the Jewish people and the story of their founder Moses. To Jesus, with his forward-looking mind, Jerusalem, the heart of the nation, would surely seem to be the one place where the 'Good News of God' should be proclaimed. We know how deeply the old city touched his imagination:

O Jerusalem, Jerusalem, the city that murders the prophets and stones the messengers sent to her!
How often have I longed to gather your children as a hen gathers her brood under her wings! (Luke 13.34 NEB)

It was to the capital city he came to make his last and final proclamation to his people.

Why Galilee, then ? It was the 'foreign province', suspect in the eyes of the more orthodox south, only recently – a hundred or so years before – reoccupied by a Jewish population. 'Are you a Galilean, too ?' the Jewish authorities once rebuked Nicodemus. 'Study the scriptures and you will find that prophets do not come from Galilee' (John 7.52 NEB).

The answer may lie in the freshness, original-ity and imagination with which Jesus had thought out the strategy of his work. Galilee was, of course, his home territory, a countryside and people he knew and understood and loved – his precise observations of them gave him the imagery of parable and poem. But it was perhaps the independence and liveliness of its people, their unorthodoxy, that made him feel that here was the opportunity – which the rigid society of the south forbade – of his really being listened to. He was a northerner, and the north, which comes out so badly in the great southern histories of the Old Testament, had stubbornly held that there, rather than in the compromising south, the real religious traditions of the covenant had been maintained. Here, too, were large populations of foreigners – Greek cities, foreign landowners; such a mixed population was a more congenial centre for that public criticism of popular assumptions which he knew was to be part of what he had to say. All this is conjecture; we do not know. But we should note the boldness and originality of his decision.

Nazareth was no possible northern centre: 'A prophet will always be held in honour except in his own home town, and among his kinsmen and family.' The story of his visit there (Mark 6.1–6) is one of sullen resentment: 'What surprised him was that the people of his own village didn't trust him.' There is a story, too, of his mother's and brother's bewildered concern and his refusal to go outside to meet them. Looking round at those who were sitting in the circle about him he said 'Here are my mother and my brothers. Whoever does the will of God is my brother, my sister, my mother' (Mark 3.35 NEB).

Capernaum, the busy fishing-town on the north-west shore of the Sea of Galilee, became his centre. It was a customs station and an out-post of the Roman army, and close by passed the great road from Egypt to Damascus. Here he lived – he seems to have owned his own house – and from here he climbed the hills to the many villages and small towns.

Nobody remembered the details of these exciting months. Mark begins by giving us what we might call 'A Day in the Life of Jesus' (1.21–38), where the sort of man he was, his informal way of dealing with people, his concern with human need are clearly painted. It ends with a story that highlights the dilemma that constantly faced Jesus.

Very early next morning he got up and went out. He went away to a lonely spot and remained there in prayer. But Simon and his companions searched him out, found him, and said, 'They are all looking for you.' He answered, 'Let us move on to the country towns in the neighbourhood; I have to proclaim my message there also; that is what I came out to do' (Mark 1.35–38 NEB).

We must come back to this dilemma; let us now look at the other memories of his friends.

The stories in Mark bring out vividly the character of Jesus' whole approach to his work – his profound concern with people, with 'all sorts and conditions of men'. No prejudices proscribed his meeting them; no taboos held him back. He would touch a leper in healing him (1.41) in spite of the irrational fears that popularly surrounded this skin disease. A madman, a little girl, an unknown woman in the crowd, a blind man stand witness to the quiet generosity of his spirit – a feature of his character that common people and artists and poets down the centuries have seized on as the most striking thing about him. The emphasis of these stories is not on their remarkable charac-

ter (this they assume but do not enlarge upon) but on their power and concern through which the reality of God's presence made itself known. 'Power' and 'concern' are linked inseparably together and lie at the heart of his impact upon ordinary men and women. No better commentary on these stories can be found than what may be Paul's thumb-nail sketch of Jesus' character in his letter to the Corinthian church (I Cor.13.4–7): 'He was never in a hurry and always kindness itself. He never envied anybody at all, never boasted about himself. He was never snobbish or rude or selfish. He didn't keep on talking about the wrong things other people do; remembering the good things was happiness enough. He was tough – he could face anything. And he never lost his trust in God, or in men and women. He never lost hope and he never gave in.'

Luke, who sets all these stories on a larger canvas, touches something of their deeper quality – the compassion of Jesus which crosses all the barriers which we so often, in a false self-defence, erect between one group and another, one person and another. His stories about Jesus and the Roman officer (7.1–10) and the woman 'who was living an immoral life in the town' (7.36–50) foreshadow that great concern for people of every race which dominates his Gospel. Here, in Jesus himself, we see the roots of that universality and catholicity which alone can match God's love.

Such overriding of the accepted religious taboos of orthodox society could only bring him into debate and conflict with the authorities. This is a developing theme of Mark's account. Here was a fundamental disagreement about the whole nature of real religion, and here is the explanation why, in the long run, Jesus' bitterest enemies were the good synagogue people. It is brought boldly out in the story of Jesus' evening meals in Capernaum. It makes utterly clear the divergence of concern:

When Jesus was at table in his house, many bad characters – tax-gatherers and others – were seated with him and his disciples; for there were many who followed him. Some doctors of the law who were Pharisees noticed him eating in this bad company, and said to his disciples, 'He eats with tax-gatherers and sinners !' Jesus overheard and said to them, 'It is not the healthy that need a doctor, but the sick' (Mark 2.15–17 NEB).

There follow the stories about fasting and the disciples' plucking ears of corn as they walked through the cornfields. That Mark was clearly aware of the significance of these incidents is shown by the sayings of Jesus he associates with the stories: 'Fresh skins for new wine !' and 'The sabbath was made for the sake of man, not man for the sabbath' – which put their finger on the revolutionary nature of the whole ministry of Jesus. He adds at the end of this group of stories the words: 'The Pharisees . . . began plotting against him with the partisans of Herod to see how they could make away with him' (Mark 3.6 NEB). No wonder; what his friends seem to have been unaware of was increasingly clear to the authorities.

But it was not only the religious authorities who came into conflict with him; Galilee was one of the strongholds of the Resistance Movement, and at last the issues between them and Jesus had to be brought into the open. The whole Galilean campaign is brought to an abrupt end at the Desert Meal (Mark 6.30–44). This provoked the great crisis in the ministry of Jesus. After this, he never went back to Galilee again – except once when he passed through it incognito (Mark 9.30 f.). Before that last

journey south, there intervenes a period of retirement where the whole struggle in the wilderness of Judaea is re-enacted, and Jesus seems to have been compelled to rethink through the principles and purposes of all that he was doing.

We are told that the incident of the Desert Meal happened almost by accident.

Jesus and his friends had set off in a boat to find a spot away from the crowds where they could find some rest from the incessant demands of the people. They were recognized in the boat and the crowds hurried along the coast. Jesus summed up the situation and put the boat into shore. The crowd was an organized crowd – five thousand men. Though this story had, by the time Mark was written, been the subject of much Christian meditation and preaching (in which its religious meaning had been predominant), it had not altogether lost touch with the original occasion. The grass was 'green' (it was spring) and at the common meal they sat down in military companies ('fifties' and 'hundreds'). The Fourth Gospel suggests that it was an informal meeting of members of the Resistance Movement. ('They meant to come and seize him to proclaim him king' – 6.15).

We are not concerned at the moment with all the details of this story, but with its main intention. Jesus recognized what was happening – 'His heart went out to them, because they were like sheep without a shepherd.' The words have Old Testament echoes. They echo the story of the prophet Micaiah and King Ahab where Micaiah describes a vision he had seen: 'I saw all Israel scattered upon the mountains, as sheep that have no shepherd; and the Lord said, "These have no master; let each return to his home in peace" ' (I Kings 22.17). Here the words 'sheep without a shepherd' mean a 'nation without a government, an army without a commander, a leaderless mob, a danger to themselves and to everybody else'. So the five thousand men in front of him seem to Jesus.

He now shows his superb ability to handle men. They shared a common meal together and the talk went on into the afternoon. Then he got the men to disperse without any outbreak of violence. 'After taking leave of them, he went up the hillside to pray.'

The aftermath was, at first glance, disastrous. 'From that time on,' says the Fourth Gospel, 'many of his disciples withdrew and no longer went about with him' (6.66 NEB). From now on Jesus is a lonely figure. Only a handful of his friends remained loyal; some months later, in Jerusalem, even they abandoned him. He died alone.

Such an event had to happen some time. Jesus had to make publicly clear that he could have no part in the Resistance Movement, that its ideals and his had no meeting place, that he was looking beyond the understandable political parochialism of his people to the wider world of God's whole work in the world of men.

Nothing is clearer from these stories than that Jesus had to come to his fundamental convictions and to hold them the hard way – as all of us have to win and hold our convictions. There is no royal road to certainty in these matters. The Desert Meal led inevitably to his obscure exile in the north, in alien territory across the borders of his homeland.

### In retirement

Jesus was not exempted from those inner struggles of the spirit which, in times of deep personal crisis, all men have to face. We cannot, with the evidence available to us – the memories of his friends – say very much about what he himself went through. But that he knew this darkness of the soul, the story of his wrestling in the wilderness of Judaea and the agony of Gethsemane are evidence enough. The silence that now shrouds his story needs some explanation. His friends knew little of what happened – what he did and where he went. They tell us a story of his meeting with a foreign woman when he wanted to remain unrecognized (Mark 7.24–30). Then silence until they meet him again near Caesarea Philippi and three of them climb a mountain with him (Mark 8.27–9.13). What we notice about these last two stories is their echoes of the baptism and the temptations, evidence of what he had been struggling to get clear in his retirement in the northern hills.

With these stories in mind, remembering the crisis of the Desert Meal, we catch a glimpse of the inner debate which must have occupied him in those lonely days.

The Galilean campaign has apparently ended in disaster – his friends still uncomprehending, the religious authorities suspicious, the Resistance Movement hostile. This wide rejection made him re-examine his methods. Was the way he had followed in Galilee the way in which the work God had given him to do ought to be done ? He had approached men as men; he had given himself to individual people; his only weapons – persuasion and the integrity of his own vision. Was this the only way – or was there some other ? Can the care and love of his Father be brought home to anybody by any other way than by loving them, and in his love of them trying to help them to see that this alone was the reality through which human life can have the depth and richness and joy which is our native heritage ? We put this in our own language; but this is the fundamental human issue that not only Jesus but all who are concerned with the remaking of human history have to face. He had settled it at the beginning in the Judaean wilderness; he now reaffirmed it in the northern highlands. There is no other way.

He takes up his work again, and meets his friends near Caesarea Philippi.

### Near Caesarea Philippi

Now there is a new note, as we have already hinted, in what he has to say. The way of love is the way of suffering. The shadow of his own inescapable death falls across his path.

The incident at Caesarea Philippi is crucial: On the way he asked his disciples, 'Who do men say I am ?' They answered, 'Some say John the Baptist, others Elijah, others one of the prophets.' 'And you,' he asked, 'who do you say I am ?' Peter replied. 'You are the Messiah.' Then he gave them strict orders not to tell anyone about him; and he began to teach them that the Son of man had to undergo great sufferings, and to be rejected by the elders, chief priests and doctors of the law; to be put to death, and to rise again three days afterwards. He spoke about it plainly. At this Peter took him by the arm and began to rebuke him. But Jesus turned round, and, looking at his disciples, rebuked Peter. 'Away with you, Satan', he said: 'you think as men think, not as God thinks' (Mark 8.27–33 NEB).

It was a great thing for Peter to say – when the desertion of Jesus by friend and foe alike was staring them in the face. But his words show that he still had little inkling of the radical newness of Jesus' own vision, a fact which

Matthew's expanded account misses (Matt.16.3–23). His loyalty to Jesus was unshaken; his understanding of Jesus had yet to begin. We can see in this conversation Jesus' own suspicion of conventional language – he did not like the word 'Messiah'. But it was something other that was now dominating his mind – the cost of love, and his whole-hearted acceptance of what he knew this involved for him. Words alone were no longer enough to shake men out of their conventional obsessions and open their minds to the only truth that mattered. He must face love's ultimate demand.

A week later, he took three of his close friends and climbed with them upward to the snowline of Mt Hermon. That they shared with Jesus some exalted spiritual experience – such an experience as he had had alone by River Jordan – is clear. He took them into his confidence and opened his heart to them. It was perhaps on this climb, as we have suggested, that they heard for the first time what had happened by River Jordan. Moses and Elijah were the theme of his conversation – Moses the founder of the people and Elijah the representative of the prophets, the whole history of God's dealing with humanity and his place in that great, strange work.

Mark's account is this:

Six days later Jesus took Peter, James and John with him and led them up a high mountain where they were alone, and in their presence he was transfigured; his clothes became dazzling white, with a whiteness no bleacher on earth could equal. They saw Elijah appear, and Moses with him, and there they were, conversing with Jesus. Then Peter spoke: 'Rabbi,' he said, 'how good it is that we are here! Shall we make three shelters, one for you, one for Moses and one for Elijah?' (For he did not know what to say; they were so terrified). Then a cloud appeared, casting its shadow over them, and out of the cloud came a voice: 'This is my Son, my Beloved; listen to him.' And now suddenly, when they looked round, there was nobody to be seen but Jesus alone with themselves.

On their way down the mountain, he enjoined them not to tell anyone what they had seen until the Son of man had risen from the dead. They seized upon those words, and discussed among themselves what this 'rising from the dead' could mean (Mark 9.2–10 NEB).

There was nothing more to do now, except to take up his work again in the only way he knew it could be done; but this time, not in Galilee but in the south. He passed through Galilee incognito.

### In the south

The journey south and Jesus' movements until the last week in Jerusalem are shrouded in obscurity. Dr T. W. Manson has called our attention to the importance of the brief sentence in which Mark summarizes it:

On leaving those parts [in the north] he came into the regions of Judaea and Transjordan; and when a crowd gathered round him once again, he followed his usual practice and taught them (10.1 NEB).

Judaea and Transjordan, the countryside east of the river, are now the area of his southern campaign, and the quoted words seem to imply a wider ministry than the account that follows seems to allow for.

Did he move south in the late spring, passing down the east side of the river, and come to

Jerusalem at the beginning of that last week? Such is the impression that the records give us; but we must remember that the account as we now have it had been used in the worship of the church where all the events of the Passion were celebrated together. Perhaps the journey took longer, and perhaps Jesus spent a much longer time east of the river (so Mark's brief words quoted above would seem to suggest) than a mere journey south would permit.

Dr Manson has suggested that Jesus came to Jerusalem in October when he entered the city on a donkey, dealt with the shopkeepers in the foreigners' court of the temple, and was engaged in open debate with the religious authorities. It was then that the authorities 'began to look for a way to arrest him, for they saw that the parable [of the Vineyard Tenants] was aimed at them; but they were afraid of popular feeling, so they left him alone and went away' (Mark 12.1–12).

Jesus had made up his mind to make his final appeal to his people when they gathered for the feast of Passover in the next spring. He did not intend to have his hand forced. So he spent the winter outside the jurisdiction of the Jerusalem authorities in Transjordan, and returned to the city a few days before he was arrested. It has always seemed that the elaborate preparations that were made to secure his secret arrest away from popular interference, to suborn one of his friends and to come to some agreement about all this with Pilate, would take far more time than a few days. If the course of events was as Dr Manson has suggested, there would be time enough.

The two incidents which need comment – whether they happened in the last week or whether the winter separated them from the supper in the upper room and his arrest – are

Jesus' entry into the city and his action in the foreigners' court of the temple (Mark 11.1–10; 15–19). They are both, along with his giving of the bread and wine in the upper room, 'acted parables', a form of proclamation which can be noticed in the stories of the prophets, especially Isaiah, Hosea and Jeremiah (cf. Isa.8.1–4; Hos.1.2–9; Jer.18.1–12).

The entry into the city made clear his whole approach to God's work. He had made secret preparations for it – arranging for the hire of a donkey with a farmer in a village near the city, as he made secret arrangements for the hire of the house. He rode in to claim his right as God's Chosen Leader. Did he remember those days a thousand years before when his ancestor David, after the southern rebellion, rode back on a warhorse, to reclaim the city along the same road (II Sam.19.15–20.2) ? He was no such leader. The words of Zechariah's poem were probably in his mind:

Lo, your King comes to you;
    triumphant and victorious is he,
    humble and riding on an ass,
    on a colt the foal of an ass (Zech.9.9).

All he had done and said in the preceding ministry was symbolized in this act. It must have been intended for his friends, as was the symbolism of the supper. If it happened in the October, he joined the pilgrims coming into the city for the feast of Tabernacles and used the occasion for his own purposes. Had it been a public claim to messiahship, it is strange that the authorities, looking round for evidence to incriminate Jesus, did not seize upon this occasion as the kind of evidence they were looking for. But the significance of the 'acted parable' is quite clear.

Jesus' 'Cleansing of the Temple' was the second acted parable, and was a public one. It is important to notice that the market was held in the foreigners' court. Jesus' action, taking the people by surprise, was a declaration of the universality of the Good News – 'My house shall be called a house of prayer for all nations,' he quoted, and added 'but you have made it a robbers' cave.' He was later asked by the authorities what right he had to act like this. It was on this occasion he told the story of Vineyard Tenants (Mark 12.1–9), whose unmistakable point precipitated the Jewish government's decision to get rid of him.

It was now clear that the Jewish leaders were going to stand no more nonsense. When Jesus returned in the spring, their plans were laid. They caught him at night in an orchard; his execution was now only a matter of time.

## The strategy of Jesus

We have sketched, in bold strokes, the course of the three brief years of Jesus' ministry as suggested by the 'framework' that lies behind the gospel material; the political and religious situation he had to deal with explains the brevity of that ministry and illuminates its pattern.

But one decisive aspect of his work – his strategy – must now be dealt with, an aspect which needs a broader background to bring its importance out into the open.

Jesus was a realist. God's work was, for him, not some ideal pattern forcibly super-imposed on the intractable material of human history; it was the inner pattern of history itself. God was 'Creator' as well as 'Father'; he was not, as it were, caught out by the recalcitrance of men and women. All history is the theatre of the drama of his love – he 'makes the sun rise on good and bad alike, and sends the rain on the honest and dishonest' (Matt.5.45). It is this conviction of Jesus which is brought out in the developing argument of the Fourth Gospel and is summarized in the words 'My Father has never yet ceased his work, and I am working too' (John 5.17 NEB).

How was God working out his purposes in the history of humanity ? Jesus had the Scriptures of his people as his guide. He had meditated deeply on them and he quotes them with an originality and insight which surprises us with its freshness still. The theme of the Old Testament – its 'salvation-history' – is that God does not dragoon men, but wins them through his 'steadfast love', speaking to the world through 'his people'. This is the insight of Moses; it is embodied in the idea of the covenant. But who are his people ? Moses welded the scattered tribes into a people, linked by their loyalty to Yahweh. The tribal confederacy was to be 'the people of God'. This proved politically unstable. David took the idea further by developing the tribal confederacy into a nation. Is then the 'nation' the instrument of God's active love in human history ? The deviating story of the southern and northern kingdoms raised serious doubts. The theme of the prophetic debate was the frustrating inadequacy of the political unit, the nation, as a vehicle of God's love, and the proposal of a more informal group (the 'remnant' of Isaiah's phrase) whose fellowship should be founded simply on loyalty to God who would be the leader of nation and world alike. The disaster of the exile and the rebirth of the city, the Maccabaean rebellion and the political and religious situation as he found it in his own day, were the background of Jesus' own thinking – a background exemplified in the ambiguity of the Pharisees and the anger of the Zealots.

Jesus went back to the heart of the Old Testament, the witness of the prophets, especially the books of Isaiah and Jeremiah – books some of whose profoundest words were in his mind at his baptism and at supper on the night before he died.

His reading of the Old Testament led him to the conviction that no *political* entity can be the effective vehicle of God's love, only a genuinely religious society the loyalties of whose members were to God alone, freely transcending and gathering up in themselves all the other loyalties of kin, race, nation, class. If his work was to go on, it would be through such a group or society. Hence his calling of disciples 'to be with him', with the 'twelve' as their centre. The very number 'twelve' recalls the tribal confederacy – they were to be the nucleus of God's 'people', to be in the wider life of mankind like 'salt' and 'leaven' and 'light', and to live, as he himself lived, as the 'servants' of their fellow-men. Through their life among their fellows, God's love, the fundamental fact of human history – the source of its reality and the principle of its existence – would be proclaimed and acknowledged. God's love would establish itself as the joyfully accepted way of life, not automatically or by threat, but through the gladly accepted sufferings of those who humbly received God's love themselves and, in its strength, lived for others, sharing their common life and being involved in their common destiny.

Two words bring out what Jesus intended their function in society to be. They were his 'apprentices' ('disciples') and they were to be 'mixers' ('apostles' – 'sent out'). They were to set the pace:

Don't judge and you won't be judged,
   don't condemn and you won't be condemned;

forgive and you will be forgiven;
give and you will be given;
  good measure,
  pressed down,
  shaken together,
  running over,
  will be poured into your lap.
The measure you give
will be the measure you get (see Luke 6.37 f.).

We can see something of Jesus' working-out of these convictions even in the fragmentary accounts of the men he chose as his closest friends – 'the twelve' – and particularly in the man he marked out as their leader – Simon 'the Rock' ('Peter') as he nicknamed him. The four surviving lists of the twelve (Mark 3.16–19a; Matt.10.2–4 – a second edition of Mark's list; Luke's two lists, Luke 6.14–16 and Acts 1.13 [the eleven]; there are further traditions about three of them – Andrew, Philip and Thomas – in John) are perplexingly different from one another and show that, by the time Mark was written, the twelve were 'traditional figures of the past'. Of eight of them we know little or nothing. Four of them come to life in the memories of Jesus' friends: the two brothers, James and John, whom he nicknamed 'The Thunderers'; Judas Iscariot, 'the man from Kerioth' (a town either south of Hebron or in old Moabite country); and especially Peter, of whom many stories are told both in the Gospels and in Acts.

We note that they were all laymen – a fact which, in the light of the subsequent history of the Christian community, is surely significant. Four of them we know were fishermen, one a customs-officer. The presence among them of a member of the Resistance Movement – Simon the Zealot – and the lone figure of Judas Iscariot show the risks Jesus was willing, like all true teachers, to take. All ventures in genuine fellowship involve immense risks – anything can happen in the close companionship of men of independent minds (which Jesus encouraged) and of different backgrounds and assumptions. This, too, in the light of Christian history, is startlingly significant.

But it is Peter of Bethsaida (John 1.44) whose rough but loyal heart speaks for the common man in whom Jesus, under God, put his trust for the future of humanity. In the stories told of him he is painted 'warts and all': his impulsiveness and dogged loyalty; his courage – and the breaking of his courage; his qualities as a 'Beloved Captain' – and his lack of imaginative insight (Gal.2.11–14); his slowness to understand (Mark 8.27–33) – and his fearless quickness to act when the truth came home to him (Acts 10.1–11.18); and his manly love of his Master which held him to the end (John 21.15–19). In Peter we meet the kind of 'apprentice' Jesus wanted, and in Jesus' handling of him we see his greatness as a teacher. Into such hands as Peter's he was ready to commit the whole destiny of his work.

As Jesus realized the realities of the human situation in which he found himself – the rigid and conventional and unimaginative habits of organized religion, the passions and blindness of existing political societies – he set himself to the work of calling into existence the nucleus of a new community (but a community which had its roots in the past history of his people): the community of his 'friends' (cf. John 15.15) whose principle of existence is their humble acceptance, centred in their loyalty to himself, of God's 'amazing love' as the source and principle of their own life, and through whom the whole world might become his Father's family. We touch here Jesus' profoundest political and social insight; and we note that its ground and justification are to be found in his religious insight: God as 'Abba' ('Father').

## The man behind the story

When we stand back and look at the story of Jesus as a whole, as we see it shining through the 'portraits' his friends painted, he stands before us in unambiguous clarity. Nobody can be in doubt about what sort of man he was, though we can confuse ourselves with a too particular concern with the debatable details.

What strikes us most forcibly about him is his sanity and his maturity. As we watch him through these brief years moving towards his tragic destiny – his execution outside his capital city – he stands out among his fellows as the *real man*. His sense of God's presence ('Abba !'), his life lived for his fellow men, his steady and penetrating vision make us aware that we are meeting for the first time a man who was 'true man', showing us the fullness and richness and joy of being really alive. We watch him dealing with men and women – and children; we say 'This is how we ought to live among our fellows'. We watch him dealing with the evil that shatters our common life and makes us act as caricatures of men; we say 'This is the sort of person we ought to be'. We watch him assailed and hurt by the brutal realities of his immediate society – 'man's inhumanity to man' – and marvel at his freedom from its corrupting obsessions; we say 'We ought to be free like that.'

We note other aspects of his life which reveal his insights and 'soaring mind'. He chose to be a *teacher*. He is the only great religious leader who seems to have asked himself questions like these: 'How do ordinary people learn ?' 'How

do they become aware of God's presence and their own destiny ?' and 'How can they be helped to make sense of their confusing experiences ?'. He is 'the greatest teacher of the western world'; his ways of dealing with ordinary people as a teacher have come to their own only in the context of our modern debate about education. His parabolic method – his approach to the minds of ordinary men and women – is not an imitation of old illustrative methods found in past teachers, but a new venture in opening men's minds and encouraging them to think for themselves and be critical of their prejudices, challenging their conventions and provoking them to ask questions.

When we come to look more closely at his reported sayings, we become aware that he brought to his whole presentation of his convictions a great poetic imagination – he was a *poet*, holding his own with Dante and Shakespeare. His simplicity is deceptive. He created a body of sayings which have caught the imagination of the world and provided the greatest minds with an enduring stimulus. 'He is the greatest artist of us all', said van Gogh. It is not an accident that the profoundest commentary of his life and words is to be found, not in the works of theologians and scholars, but in the works of artists and in the lives of countless ordinary men and women. His parables and poems have a profound imaginative unity.

We may pause, for a moment, to consider one implication of the fact that Jesus was, in the technical sense, a poet. We know nothing – except the story Luke tells (2.41–52) – about Jesus' boyhood. But if he was a poet, and if his parables and poems are not just teaching devices but the way in which he habitually thought and in which he himself came to his insights, then the imagery of parable and poem take on a new meaning. We know, from the continuing debate about the nature of poetry initiated by Wordsworth and Coleridge, how deeply the experience of a poet's boyhood moulds his later poetry. The imagery of Jesus' parables have every mark of being largely what he remembered from boyhood, used, remade, then formed into vehicles of his profoundest insights – the raw material of his mature vision. They are a surer guide to what boyhood meant to him than much of the guesswork in which we indulge.

But more than this, he was a *leader of men*. Members of the Resistance Movement wanted to 'make him king' – that needs some explanation. The story of Peter walking with him through the darkened streets after that final supper speaks for countless others.

Jesus said, 'You will all fall from your faith; for it stands written: "I will strike the shepherd down and the sheep will be scattered." Nevertheless, after I am raised again, I will go on before you into Galilee.' Peter answered, 'Everyone else may fall away, but I will not.' Jesus said, 'I tell you this: today, this very night, before the cock crows twice, you yourself will disown me three times.' But he insisted and repeated: 'Even if I must die with you, I will never disown you' (Mark 14.27–31 NEB).

Jesus had an extraordinary power of holding men. He was honest and direct and could be witheringly frank. He never played for popularity; his honesty cost him temporary rejection by many of his early friends. But immediately after his death five hundred of them (I Cor. 15.6) gathered together; and from that moment the circle of followers spread over the known world. There is no magic about this (though many other things must be said about it); he knew how to speak to men and how to lead them.

There is something else to be said. His hold over men was more than 'leadership'. There was a strangeness about him that puzzled and held men – especially those who came to know him intimately. His 'mighty works' were not just the sort of things Pharisees and others could do (cf. Luke 11.19). 'If it is by the finger of God that I drive out the devils, then be sure the kingdom of God has already come upon you.' These 'mighty works' were moments when, for those who could recognize it, the reality of God was brought home to them. There are other moments recorded when the 'strangeness' of Jesus scared his friends. 'They were on the road, going up to Jerusalem, Jesus leading the way; and the disciples were filled with awe; while those who followed behind were afraid' (Mark 10.32 NEB).

Here we perceive that aspect of Jesus' total 'witness' which, vaguely apprehended in his life-time, was seen and recognized by his friends after his resurrection with unmistakable clarity. He was not only leader; he was *Lord*. There was a strange authority about him which they found both disconcerting and arresting. He not only spoke with authority and not as the scribes (Mark 1.22); there was an authority about his whole life – an authority which still speaks through his life and words, and overrides the stumbling attempts of his friends to describe or explain it. This is the essential Jesus. In the light of later Christian experience, this is the central thing about him.

### The heart of the story

If any brief words could put what is the heart of the Christian faith, they might be these words:

'God is love . . . We love because he loved us first' (I John 4.8,19). Love – agape, to give the New Testament word – is the clue to our human story, because it is its originating fact and its enduring principle. The world is God's world; he is Lord of history; and he is love. Our awareness of this is supremely the work of Jesus; 'he made God real'. This is the heart of his story. For his story is the story of love in action. This is what it means to 'be human' – genuinely human: 'Jesus lived love; God is love and has made men for love'.

Love is not the weak and sentimental thing that we often make it. It is robust, venturesome, utterly open to the varied complexity of human relationships. It is tough, as Paul said – 'there is nothing that love cannot face' (I Cor.13.7). Jesus made this plain (cf. John 1.18).

The crowds of Galilee and Jerusalem pass through the stories which Jesus' friends told about him: farmers, fishermen, tax-collectors, housewives, children, religious leaders in village and city; members of the Resistance Movement and Roman soldiers; governor and high priest. Jesus meets them with openness and friendship; he is frank and critical and speaks in plain language; but behind agreement or disagreement, approval or reproof, stands his profound concern for people as people. He could mark insight and commend it – whether he met it in a doctor of the law or in a Roman officer.

His parables – and there are about sixty of them, whole or in fragment – are crowded with people. What marks them (if we could cease treating them as mere pious moral homilies) is the breadth of their sympathy (a rascal of a manager was the 'hero' of one of his stories) and their profound insight into human nature. Here are real people, and the situations in which we meet them are real situations. These stories are explorations of the meaning of love as the working principle of human action. Jesus expected ordinary men and women to see the point he was making – this was the only way in which human situations could be dealt with – and he put it so that hard-headed people could see what he was driving at and be in no doubt. He was revealing the way in which things actually work, situations actually develop, human meeting can be really human meeting. His charge against the people of his time was that they were like 'children sitting in the market-place and shouting to one another' (Luke 7.32) – they were not grown-up. Love is really grown-up; it is the way of maturity.

But most of all we see what love means when we come to the story of his death. It was his concern for men and women that brought him to that lonely hill – and his refusal to let any other way have any part of his decisions. It was precipitated by the treachery of one of his closest friends, but he stood his ground. The cross, for Christian and non-Christian alike, is the symbol and reality of the supremacy and triumph of love.

So the heart of the story (this should guide us to the way we should deal with it in our teaching) is the exploration of love; its character, its manner, its ability to deal with an unpredictable world, its maturity and its cost, its source in God's love of us. 'We must pass through many hardships,' as Paul is reported to have once said – what mother or father or friend, what person who has ever loved, does not know that ? There is no 'short cut' to dealing with human relationships; all our failures and disasters come from trying to take one. When we do so, we find ourselves driven to treat persons as less than persons – numbers, units, individuals. But we are persons; love is the only way persons can live as persons together.

This is the heart of the story of Jesus.

This is the point John is making when, at the very beginning of the Book of the Passion (John 13.1–9), the great conclusion of his dramatic presentation of the ministry of Jesus, he puts this story as the supremely characteristic story about Jesus:

The Great Feast of the Jewish people was near. Jesus was having supper with his friends.

He got up from the table and took off his long robe. He picked up a towel and tied it round him like a belt. He poured water into a basin, and began to wash his friends' feet.

When he had washed their feet, he picked up his long robe, put it on and sat down again at table.

'I have shown you what you must do,' he said. 'You must do what I have just done for you. Believe me –

A slave is not greater than his master,
a messenger than the man who sent him.

I hope you understand all this. You will be happy men if you live as I have shown you.'

### Not the end but the beginning

The death of Jesus, we now know, was not the end but the beginning. Indeed, the stories we have been examining are no cool historical accounts – they are all written in the light of the amazing new experiences which followed his death. It is this that gives them their peculiar elusiveness: they are about events that really happened, but events that had an original strangeness – a strangeness that could not be expunged from any record

of them if they were to be honestly reported; and more, events that were the prelude to the new shared experience which was at once an awareness of God's love 'shed abroad in their hearts' and an inescapable sense of the continuing presence of the risen Lord. Paul's words give this experience its classic expression: 'The life I now live is not my life, but the life which Christ lives in me; and my present bodily life is lived by faith in the Son of God, who loved me and sacrificed himself for me' (Gal.2.20 NEB).

Let us consider the reports of the decisive experiences which brought into being the Christian community and revolutionized for his friends the way they remembered his ministry and death and made them describe the story not as though it was just something that had happened in the past but had an enduring contemporary quality for all who accepted Jesus as Lord. There would have been no such community without them; only, possibly, a dwindling Jewish sect, one among many, to be scattered and destroyed by the war of AD 66-70.

The earliest account we have is found in one of Paul's letters written in Ephesus somewhere about AD 56 – nearly thirty years after the death of Jesus. But it probably goes back to within a few years of his death, Paul's words suggest, to his own baptismal initiation in Damascus City, about AD 36, some seven years after Jesus died.

I handed on to you the facts which had been imparted to me: that Christ died for our sins, in accordance with the scriptures; that he was buried; that he was raised to life on the third day, according to the scriptures; and that he appeared to Cephas, and afterwards to the Twelve. Then he appeared to over five hundred of our brothers at once, most of whom are still alive, though some have died. Then he appeared to James, and afterwards to all the apostles.

In the end he appeared even to me; though this birth of mine was monstrous, for I have persecuted the church of God and am therefore inferior to all other apostles – indeed not fit to be called an apostle. However by God's grace I am what I am (I Cor. 15.3–10 NEB).

We note the brevity and reticence of the report: 'he appeared' – a word which can describe visible sight or spiritual experience. Of the reality of what happened there was no doubt – the new life of his first friends was rooted in it; but to give an intelligible and coherent account of it was another matter. Paul's long discussion of the questions it raises that follows the account we have quoted, and the later records in the Gospels, are their attempt to do so.

The very divergences in the gospel reports bespeak their honesty – they give the stories that were current in the great centres of the Christian community and they do not try to make them fit. The ending to Mark is now lost; the present ending (16.8–20) is a much later addition, one among several added endings. The appearances they list are these: Matthew – to the women, to the eleven in Galilee; Luke – to two disciples (not of the 'twelve') on the road to Emmaus, to the eleven in the upper room; John – to Mary of Magdala, to the ten in the upper room, to the eleven a week later, again gathered there, to seven on the beach of the Sea of Galilee; the added ending to Mark – to Mary of Magdala, to two 'as they were talking on their way into the country', to the eleven 'at table' (this reads like a summary made from the earlier accounts). Paul's list is different still: to Cephas, to the twelve, to 'five hundred of our brothers at once', to James (Jesus' brother), to 'all the apostles', then 'to me'.

All the reports, except Paul's, agree that the tomb was empty (Paul did not mention the tomb). This was no proof of Jesus' resurrection – it was susceptible of several explanations, and it created its own problems – but it was a fact and they all report it. The account in the Fourth Gospel is supposed by some scholars to be a criticism of too naïve an understanding of what happened; at any rate, it calls attention, as Luke does, to another fact – Peter and the 'other disciple' were not deeply impressed by the discovery: 'As yet they did not know the scripture, that he must rise from the dead. Then [they] went back to their homes' (John 20.9 f.). 'The story appeared to them to be nonsense' (Luke 24.11 NEB; cf. also v. 21).

We note, too, if we read the reports in chronological order, an increasing emphasis on the materiality of the appearances. There is, further, a divergence among them as to where his appearances to the eleven took place; Matthew says Galilee; Luke Jerusalem; John Jerusalem and then (in the appendix to the Gospel) Galilee.

The debate among Christians as to what reportable events happened and what sort of events they were is obviously as old as our earliest records. It has been an intense debate in recent centuries; the rise of scientific inquiry and the later development of historical methods of research have brought it acutely before the minds of Christians and non-Christians alike. It is not likely to be concluded. For we are dealing with an event which is not a purely historical event. It is closely involved in the reality of Christian experience, not just another incident in the unfolding story. It was not the reports of what had happened to a limited number of witnesses that changed men's lives; it was the event itself. It was the revealing climax which made all the difference to the story. They could only say 'God raised him from death'.

The evidence suggests that in the few weeks following the death of Jesus some of his friends – some named, some not – had certain experiences of Jesus risen. Paul is careful to state that his own experience, which he lists with the others, fell outside this limited period. These special 'appearances' then ceased; the later experiences of the risen Christ, open to all who accepted him, were real but different. If we remember the uniqueness of this event (the resurrection of Jesus was not in the same category as other reported 'resurrections' of men; it was the defeat of death), these reports do not strike us, after the strictest historical scrutiny, as fictitious accounts that owe their existence to human imagination; they strike us as honest attempts to give some account of real experiences that defied all efforts to give a coherent account of them. Of their authenticity the early friends of Jesus had no doubt – their new experiences of God, their new fellowship with one another, their new understanding of human life and history were not something they had struggled to achieve; they were 'given'. The spirit of Jesus was present with them; they were not just imitating him. The final evidence for them that these reports were reports of what had actually happened – 'Christ was raised to life' – and not reports of queer hallucinations, was the reality of their new life and fellowship which was open to public scrutiny.

It was in the light of this transforming experience of Christ risen that later in the century the stories of Jesus' birth came to circulate. These are not historical accounts, but stories which sing the wonder and glory of Jesus. They are beautiful and profound stories which haunt the imagination – the coming of Jesus to humble shepherds and eastern astrologers. But the birth of Jesus is wrapped in mystery. Even the place of his birth is open to question. Most probably it was Bethlehem (he was a descendant of king David – as many others in Palestine at the time must have been), but some historians would say it was Nazareth. The nature of his birth is a matter of theology, not of history; Christians make different judgments. Our decisions on these matters are secondary to our decisions about the story of Jesus as a whole – the witness of his remembered ministry, what he did and said and how he died, and the witness of the resurrection and the Christian experience of God's love and all that this means in our living and thinking. The great claims made for Jesus – in the first century: 'God was in Christ reconciling the world to himself' (Paul), or in the twentieth century: 'Christ is the centre of life' (Bonhoeffer) – rest upon this broader foundation.

### *'Follow me !'*

No survey, such as we have attempted, of the whole ministry of Jesus – his life, his death, his resurrection – can be a mere historical inquiry. His story must be subjected to the strictest historical study; for us, as for the first friends of Jesus, it is a matter of utmost importance to be sure that what we claim happened really happened. Pious guesswork does him no service; too much is at stake. He invites our questions, and we are free to ask them and to seek, in the most rigorous way, the answers.

But we are not merely asking historical questions. Jesus pushes our questions back until we come to 'You – who do you say I am ?'. Any retelling of his story must bring us to this point, and leave us to answer it.

If we now stand back and look at the whole story, we find that it faces us with three questions.

*Isn't love the real human adventure ?* Men have looked in many directions for the fulfilling experience, the real adventure: to war, to self-enrichment, to wealth, to pleasure, to learning, to 'progress'. The brief story of Jesus puts a question mark against all our chosen ideals and ambitions, and faces us with this fundamental question.

*Isn't love the clue ?* From the beginning of history men have tried to make sense of our strange and tangled human story – the kind of sense which enables a man to live in its light – and to find some meaning in our frustrating human experience; or they have given up any hope of making sense of it at all. Jesus was no glib dogmatist; he came to his convictions the hard way. Is not all he said and all he lived – his death itself – summarized in this question ?

*Isn't love the end ?* Men have dreamed all kinds of dreams about the future of humanity as a common society in a common world. Our very inventions preclude any ultimate isolation from one another. We seek, in economics, in scientific research, in education, the clue to a common world. All these are important. But the story of Jesus forces us back to ask what kind of world we really want and how we expect to make it. He subjects all our common assumptions – as he subjected the common assumptions of his own time – to a critical scrutiny, and provokes us to a bolder inquiry. Isn't love 'the clue to history', its meaning and its end ?

It is important to get the questions right, but it is just as important to know how to go about finding the answers. Jesus' approach is summed up in his 'Follow me !' – the answers are to be found not only by hard thinking but also by bold living. Love is not a blueprint – it is a guide; its true meaning can only be found experimentally. God' world is a world in the making – to be explored, lived in, shared, enjoyed together. How this is to be done can only be found in the doing – 'Follow me !'

Jesus' own account of his work comes to us through the minds of his friends, often in their language and circumscribed by their horizons. But what he was and what he had to say has an originality and freshness which transcends them both. Perhaps it is the experimental note in word and deed that has enabled him to survive the great changes in human society of the last two thousand years, and to exercise his widest influence in the modern world.

Love is the great *human* experience, the attitude which is the precondition of finding the real answers to our human questions. Jesus was the pioneer; the trouble is that we follow him so far behind.

ALAN T. DALE

9. The Message of Jesus

## The needs of the first Christians

The Gospels in the form in which we possess them are church books. They were written in the second half of the first century AD to meet the needs of the early followers of Jesus gathered together out of a pagan environment in their Christian communities. These early churches were not, for the most part, Palestinian, and after AD 70 when the country had been laid waste and Jerusalem destroyed, Christians in Galilee and Judaea must have been few and unorganized. The growing churches were in the great cities of the Graeco-Roman world, Antioch in Syria, Ephesus in Asia Minor (now south-west Turkey), Corinth, Philippi and Thesslonica in Greece and in Rome. The members of these churches were Greeks, Romans, Syrians, Egyptians and Asiatics, though not a few Jews had also been converted to the new religion. These centres of Christianity and these church members were far away in distance from the world Jesus knew and very different from him in culture and upbringing.

The message of Jesus as it is presented to us in the four Gospels has three historical settings. Latest in time (c. AD 65-100) is the world of these established churches of the Roman empire; churches as far apart as Syrian Antioch in the east to Rome in the west, the world of the four Gospel makers, the men who compiled Mark, Matthew, Luke and John.

Earlier than this (c. AD 29-65) is the world of the first Christian communities. These were in Jerusalem, Samaria, Caesarea and other Palestinian cities and also, largely as the result of Paul's missionary activities, in Asia Minor, Greece and Rome. At this time the leaders of the new religion were mainly Jews and their understanding of the teaching of Jesus was partly coloured by their Jewish inheritance. These communities possessed no Gospels. Their knowledge came from oral traditions; from memories of what Jesus had said and done which were handed down by word of mouth in public addresses, instruction classes for converts, and, no doubt, also in private conversations. Some of the deeds and words of Jesus were probably written down quite early and the manuscript treasured in one of the local churches, but, for the most part, Christians at this time relied for their knowledge upon the shared memories of those who had known Jesus.

The third historical setting is Galilee and Judaea where Jesus lived, taught, died and triumphed over death: the brief period of time when the parables, the aphorisms and the proclamation of the kingdom of God were spoken for the first time.

It is necessary, therefore, to disentangle as far as possible the original message spoken by Jesus in Palestine from the meaning drawn out of it by Christian teachers and by the four evangelists. The Christian communities in both of the two later historical settings had a zeal for evangelism. They looked outward to a world which desperately needed the message of Jesus. They were missionary churches. Moreover, in the years *c*.AD 29–65 there was a particular reason why evangelism could not wait. The great decisive moment – the return to Jesus to earth in great power and glory – was, so they believed, imminent. To their disappointment the 'second coming' was delayed – in fact it never happened – but while they waited for the Day of Judgment and Reward the Christians evangelized fervently. An evangelist needs a message, and so the questions they asked were these: what did Jesus teach ? What message from him must I declare to the pagans in this city ? What promises and consolations, and what practical advice, did he speak for our help and comfort ?

The task of separating the original message of Jesus from the later additions and interpretations is difficult and often uncertain. Biblical scholars frequently disagree and an element of personal judgment is inevitable. There are, however, many instances which a teacher can use in the classroom where it is quite easy to see evangelists using 'the preachers' technique'. They begin with an incident, a saying, a parable, like preachers announcing their text, and then expound it to meet the needs of their audience.

This process can often be detected where a parable is told in more than one Gospel. For instance, the parable of the Good Shepherd in Luke 15.3–7 ends by declaring that when one sinner repents there is rejoicing in heaven. God is the Shepherd (a frequent Old Testament metaphor) who searches out those who are lost. In the Gospel of Matthew (18.12–14) the same parable is told in slightly different language. Then at v.15 the parable is used to point out a Christian's duty towards an offending brother-Christian. As the shepherd searches for a lost sheep, so 'if your brother sins against you, go and tell him his fault, between you and him alone. If he listens to you, you have gained your brother . . .' (vv.15–18).

Another example is the parable of the Empty House told both by Luke and Matthew in almost identical language. Here is Luke's version:

When the unclean spirit has gone out of a man, he passes through waterless places seeking rest; and finding none he says, 'I will return to my house from which I came.' And when he comes he finds it swept and put in order. Then he goes and brings seven other spirits more evil than himself, and they enter and dwell there; and the last state of that man becomes worse than the first (Luke 11.24–26).

Here in Luke's version the parable stands by itself, though it is preceded by the saying, 'If it is by the finger of God that I cast out demons, then the kingdom of God has come upon you', and by the parable of the Captured Castle. Since the story is about evil spirits we might say that it is an acute psychological analysis of the state of mind of people who, cured of mental hallucinations, slip back into their neurotic state because they can find nothing positive to live for. We could sharpen the interpretation by saying that Jesus himself must fill the house of life, if a man is to be creative and happy. The Gospel of Matthew adds its own interpretation: 'so shall it be also with this evil generation' (Matt. 12.45). The opponents of Jesus, the Pharisees and lawyers, are the houses inhabited by eight evil spirits, seven of whom are worse than the original occupier.

These are fairly simple examples. Our task, using the help which New Testament scholars provide, is to try to see, however imperfectly, Jesus the teacher as he was, and to understand his message.

## 'The greatest artist of us all'

This phrase from the painter van Gogh has been quoted by Alan T. Dale in the preceding article on the ministry of Jesus. He has written that 'Jesus was a poet holding his own with Dante and Shakespeare'. Here are some of the poems of Jesus in Dale's translation.

Everybody who listens to me
and then does something about it
is like a sensible builder.

He builds his house –
and he builds it on rock.

Then winter comes.
The rain pours down,
the mountain torrents come tumbling down
the hillside,
the great winds blow
and batter the house.
But it stands up to it all –
underneath it is rock (Matt.7.24 f.).

What did you go out on the moors to see ?
Grass blown by the wind ?
But what did you go out to see ?
Somebody clothed in silk ?
You must look in palaces for splendour and luxury !

But what did you go out to see ?
One of God's great men ?

Yes ! I tell you –
Somebody greater than God's great men of old (Matt.11.7–9).

To remember that Jesus was a poet with a poet's inward vision and a gift for handling words, using vivid images from everyday life, not abstract arguments, helps us in various ways to get to the heart of his teaching. For instance it is often a clue to those passages of the Gospels where someone has added an explanation of the words of Jesus. The parable of the Sower (Mark 4.3–9 = Matt.13.1–9) ends with the words, 'He who has ears to hear, let him hear', or as we might say, 'Now work out the meaning for yourself.' Then follows in both Gospels (vv. 10–20 in Mark; 10–23 in Matthew) a long and tedious explanation of the parable. Scholars can give their own reasons for saying that this is a later addition, but there is a sound common-sense reason as well. Poets do not explain their poems. They offer us their vision and leave us to discover the meaning.

If we take the teaching of Jesus as a whole we seem at first sight to be presented with deep-seated and irreconcilable differences. If the heart of his message is to be found in that collection of sayings which we call 'the Sermon on the Mount' (Matt.5–7 = Luke 6.20–49) then we shall think of him as an ethical teacher whose morality sprang from the imitation of God. 'You must be perfect, as your heavenly Father is perfect' (Matt. 5.48). If, on the other hand, the heart of his message is in Mark 13 then Jesus is a visionary whose eyes are fixed upon a dramatic future. The old order of the world will disappear and a new order will take its place:

And then they will see the Son of man coming in clouds with great power and glory. And then he will send out the angels, and gather his elect from the four winds, from the ends of the earth to the ends of heaven (Mark 13.26 f.).

Could one man have thought in two such different and apparently inconsistent ways ? Certainly it would be a defect in a systematic theologian, but Jesus was a poet. Think of

William Blake who wrote in *Songs of Innocence* such lines as:

Little Lamb, who made thee ?
Dost thou know who made thee ?
Gave thee life and bid thee feed
By the stream and o'er the mead.

and who also wrote at another time and in another context:

Bring me my bow of burning gold !
Bring me my arrows of desire !
Bring me my spear ! O clouds unfold !
Bring me my chariot of fire !

Poets are not usually interested in creating logical systems of thought in which each single parts fits into the whole. They speak or write about that which at a particular moment captures their imagination and stirs their soul. They sing as birds sing. The message of Jesus has no tidy outward shape, but it has an inner unity centred upon the proclamation of the kingdom of God.

## How did Jesus teach ?

We know from the Gospels that Jesus went regularly to synagogue on the sabbath and that sometimes he was invited to address the congregation (see Luke 4.16–30 and 13.10). Often, however, his teaching must have been his contribution to a conversation. He would stop to chat at the village well or in the market place, joining in ordinary friendly talk about fishing and farming, about housework and the care of children, and listening to wider talk about the taxes and the Roman overlords and the state of the nation. Presently he would drop into the conversation a remark of profound meaning. 'Look at those children over there squabbling at their play – some won't play at weddings and the others won't play at funerals; nothing

pleases them. And there are people in our nation whom nothing pleases. They don't like John the Baptist and they don't like me. But you'll see. God will be proved right' (see Luke 7.31–35 = Matt. 11.16–19).

Jesus frequently used a technique – well known to teachers – of making an inquirer answer his own question or puzzle out his own problem. 'What do you think about this ?' he said and went on to tell without comment the story of two sons; one promised to work in the vineyard and did not go; the other, who at first refused his father, later changed his mind and went to work. Which of these two did as his father wished ? (Matt.21.28–31). Again, when a Pharisee objected to a prostitute who knelt weeping at the feet of Jesus, and anointed them with myrrh, Jesus told a story about a money lender who wrote off the debts of two men, one for five hundred silver pieces, the other for fifty. Then came the challenging question: 'Which will love him most ?' (Luke 7.36–50). When a lawyer, wishing as lawyers do to justify himself, asked 'Who is my neighbour ?' Jesus told the parable of the Good Samaritan and said in effect to the lawyer, 'Now answer your own question' (Luke 10.25–37).

## The originality of Jesus

Jesus was a Jew brought up in an orthodox pious home, where religious festivals, the weekly sabbath and the yearly feasts were observed. We may safely assume that he learnt to read and write in the synagogue school at Nazareth. He spoke Aramaic and perhaps also Greek, but the language he learnt at school was Hebrew. His book was the Jewish Scriptures, the Old Testament.

Although the message of Jesus was continually illuminated by the faith and tradition of his nation, his thought was wider and owed much to his acute observation both of nature and of human behaviour. The background of his teaching was the daily life of men and women in Galilee, and it was also the needs and problems of his nation. He took sharp notice of what was happening in his world. We have not, for instance, fully grasped the significance of his temptations when we have traced back his three replies to the allurements of Satan to the book of Deuteronomy. The poverty – sometimes downright hunger – of some of his countrymen lies behind the temptation to turn stones into bread, and the problems of political power – the Roman grip upon the country and the mounting hatred and violence of the Zealots – is the background of his refusal to accept 'the kingdoms of the world and their glory' (see Matt.4.1–11 = Luke 4.1–13).

As we shall see later, many of the parables have their setting in actual events in the troubled life of Galilee, but one example may be given here:

> When a strong man, fully armed, guards his own palace, his goods are in peace; but when one stronger than he assails him and overcomes him, he takes away his armour in which he trusted and divides his spoil (Luke 11.21 f.).

The meaning seems to be that 'the strong man armed' represents the forces of evil which are overcome by Jesus who is stronger than the strong man in his castle, but what prompted the story and gave it immediate point for the listeners, may well have been one of the frequent Zealot raids on Roman garrison posts in order to capture weapons: 'he takes away his armour in which he trusted and divides his spoil.'

This realism was one reason why people said about Jesus that 'he speaks with authority – not like the lawyers' (Mark 1.22). It was an authority which he claimed explicitly. 'Years ago people said this and this, but I say to you', and the astonishing thing is that many people took this bold speaking without offence and approved of it.

Jesus was a Jew trained from childhood in the national religion and practising that religion throughout his life. Yet on certain issues he rejected the orthodox and accepted teaching of the Pharisees and lawyers. Mark, in the early part of his Gospel (2.15 to 3.6), has brought together four incidents in which Jesus defied the rules. First, at a supper party, he consorted with tax-gatherers, who either directly or indirectly were in the service of Rome, and also with 'sinners' – the outsiders of polite society whom the orthodox regarded as undesirable layabouts. In the second incident Jesus refused to fast as a sign of mourning for John the Baptist's imprisonment. In the third and fourth incidents he defied the strict regulations about working on the sabbath. He allowed his disciples to pluck ears of corn from a harvest field, to rub them in the palms of their hands in order to separate the kernel from the husk and to eat the kernels. This was not theft from the farmer's field, but technically it was working on the sabbath. Finally Jesus healed on the sabbath a man with a withered arm.

It is not necessary to suppose that these four incidents happened one after another at the same point in the ministry of Jesus. Mark grouped them together and put the spotlight upon them because they illustrate how Jesus consistently rejected the Pharisaic policy for Israel under the Roman occupation. That policy had its roots in Jewish theology, but the theology could hardly escape a political reference. Strict observance of the whole Law by the whole community was the only way to preserve Israel's distinctive and traditional way of life. Such observance made the sabbath and days of fasting into 'Independence Days'. So the Pharisees set up a barricade of rules and insisted that they should be kept. We can understand their reasons and respect their motives.

In place of the Pharisaic policy Jesus proclaimed a new way of life and a new kind of religion. He described himself as the bridegroom and his disciples as guests at the wedding. He likened his message to new wine and said that it would burst old wine-skins. When he was challenged about healing a man on the sabbath he forestalled hostile criticism by the direct question, 'Is it lawful to do good or evil on the sabbath, to save a life or to kill?' Mark ends this section of his Gospel by telling us that the Pharisees reacted by plotting with the partisans of Herod Antipas to destroy Jesus. This was a very odd alliance. The Pharisees had little use for a renegade like Herod who certainly did not practise strict obedience to the Mosaic Law. But they put their scruples in their pockets, as men will in a crisis, and began negotiations with Herod's supporters. At this moment, according to Mark, the shadow of Golgotha first fell across the pathway of Jesus.

To reject the policy of preserving national identity by strict obedience to the Law was, of course, only the negative side of the new religion. What was its positive message? To answer this question we must examine what Jesus said in parables and sayings and actions about God, about man's response to God, about the kingdom of God, about the fate of Israel; and what he said about himself.

## The parables

It is perhaps in the parables more than anywhere else in the Gospels that we realize the originality of Jesus. They are not, of course, unique. The Jewish Rabbis used parables and so did St Paul. But no other parables are comparable to those of Jesus in their terseness, their wit, their sharp observance of human behaviour and in their extraordinary power of conveying profound truth throughout a well-told story.

The background of the parables is the daily life of Palestine. The characters include farmers, fishermen, housewives and merchants; kings, landowners and judges; a woman searching for a lost silver piece; squabbling children, guests at a wedding and a family whose house had been burgled. Along with the parables are brief metaphors or similes which have no story line and which appeal to our imagination or our sense of humour. 'If one blind man guides another they will both fall into the ditch' (Matt.15.14 NEB). 'It is easier for a camel to pass through the eye of a needle than for a rich man to enter the kingdom of God' (Mark 10.25 NEB). 'Why do you look at the speck of sawdust in your brother's eye, with never a thought for the great plank in your own' (Matt.7.3 NEB)?

It is sometimes possible to detect an actual occurrence as the inspiration of the parable, though there must always be an element of uncertainty. For instance, in the parable of the burglar (Matt.24.43 = Luke 12.39) the past tenses suggest some recent burglary in the village which everybody was talking about. 'If the householder *had known* at what time of night the burglar was coming, he *would have* kept awake and *not have let* his house be broken into.'

It may be that we have another example in Luke's version of the parable of the Talents (19.11–27) which unlike Matthew's version (25.14–30) has, it seems, a double plot. The main part of the story as in Matthew tells how three servants were entrusted with differing sums of money while their master went on a journey. There is also a sub-plot which begins at Luke 19.12: 'A nobleman went into a far country to receive kingly power and then return.' At v. 27 the sub-plot reappears: 'But as for these enemies of mine, who did not want me to reign over them, bring them here and slay them before me.'

This sub-plot appears to be the beginning and ending of an entirely different story which became intermingled with that of the talents in the tradition used by Luke. It illustrates, however, how an event may have prompted a story. In the spring of the year 4 BC, Herod the Great died in Jericho. By his will his kingdom was divided among his three sons. Archelaus, the eldest, a young man of eighteen, was given Judaea and Samaria. Herod's will, however, had to be ratified in Rome by the emperor Augustus, and Archelaus left Palestine for Rome taking with him all the necessary documents and his father's signet ring – 'a nobleman went into a far country to receive kingly power'.

If Archelaus is the man of noble birth in the sub-plot it would throw light upon the closing verse (v.27) in Luke's version: 'but as for these enemies of mine who did not want me to be king, bring them here and slaughter them in my presence.' Archelaus proved himself to be a stupid, cruel and vain-glorious ruler who in AD 6 achieved the unique distinction of uniting Jews and Samaritans in a joint denunciation to Augustus. Archelaus was summoned to Rome and never returned.

For many centuries and up to recent times the church turned the parables into allegories in which every detail was given a moral or a theological meaning. The beginnings of this process can be seen in the use made of the parables by the early church. The additions to the original parable of the Sower in Mark 4.10–20 show clearly what happened. The seed sown by the farmer is 'the word'; the birds which ate the seed falling on the foot-path represent Satan; the young corn which had no proper roots is allegorized into those Christians who easily fall back from their faith. The seed which yields the abundant harvest represents the faithful, stalwart Christians.

Later interpretations carried this kind of interpretation to more extravagant lengths. For instance, in the parable of the Labourers in the Vineyard (Matt.20.1–16), the landowner at harvest time goes to the market place on five separate occasions in the course of a single day to hire labourers. Christian theologians in the second and third centuries saw great significance in these five summonses to work. For one of them, Irenaeus, they symbolized the periods in the history of redemption from Adam onwards. For Origen they held a different meaning. The five summonses to work in the vineyard represented the different stage of human life at which men become Christians. What the parable of the Labourers in the Vineyard means is discussed below. These fanciful interpretations are still sometimes heard in sermons but biblical scholars have long since abandoned them.

The parables, then, are vivid short stories rooted in everyday life. They are stories with meaning and many of the central themes of the message of Jesus are embodied in them. They were spoken by a poet, and their background and immediate reference is first-century Palestine. Yet, like all great art, they have a timeless quality and can illuminate modern issues.

### 1. *The wheat and the weeds* (Matt.13.24–30)
### *The drag-net* (Matt.13.47–50)

These two parables make the same point. Jesus says that at the time when he is speaking it is impossible to tell who is, and who is not, a member of God's kingdom. The weeds (darnel: a poisonous plant which is closely related to bearded wheat and in the early stages of growth hard to distinguish from it) cannot be rooted up until harvest time. Fishing with a seine or drag-net, usually slung between two boats, was normally done at night, and you cannot sort good fish from bad in the dark. It is when the net has been dragged ashore in daylight that the catch can be sorted. There is a time when you cannot tell wheat from weeds; good fish from bad, and the time has not yet come when a man can know who is shut in and who is shut out from God's kingdom.

Compare with this the story of the healing of the centurion's servant (Matt.8.5–13). There was no doubt considerable astonishment among those who witnessed the interview between Jesus and the centurion, that Jesus should even be willing to talk to, let alone befriend, a hated Roman. In v. 11 Jesus says in effect, 'Wait. Do not judge now. Many people like this Roman officer may find a place in God's kingdom, feasting with the great heroes of Jewish history, and many Jews, "born to the kingdom" will be shut out from it.' These parables are a warning against making hasty judgments about people, and they are a plea for toleration.

### 2. *The labourers in the vineyard* (Matt.20.1–15).
Note: v. 16 is a later addition.

Some early fanciful interpretations of this parable have already been rejected (see above p.136). One modern meaning imposed upon it may be swiftly dismissed. The story is not a blue-print for management in twentieth-century industry. Any employer of labour on a large scale who acted as did the owner of the vineyard would quickly find himself in trouble with the trade unions.

The parable is about the generosity of God: God who 'makes his sun rise on good and bad alike, and sends the rain on the honest and the dishonest' (Matt.5.45 NEB); God who gives not what we deserve but what we need. The labourers who have hung about the market place from early morning to late afternoon, need a full day's wage (the Roman *denarius* 'a penny a day' AV) if they and their families are not to go hungry. The owner of the vineyard knows this and pays his men according to their need. The nearest earthly parallel to the action of God is the way loving parents treat their children justly, but with special consideration and generosity towards any member of the family who is special need.

### 3. *The mustard seed* (Mark 4.30–32)
### *The yeast in the bread* (Matt.13.33)
### *The sower* (Mark 4.3–9)
### *The patient farmer* (Mark 4.26–29)

These four parables are grouped together because they are each in different ways 'parables of assurance'. They bid us have confidence in God. In each of them the kingdom of God is compared to what happens at the end of the process; the full grown mustard seed which by the lake of Galilee grows to a height of eight to ten feet; the tiny pinch of yeast which makes the bread to rise; the abundant harvest.

The people to whom Jesus told these stories

were not interested in the slow processes of growth as a modern botanist will be. Their minds worked like that of an amateur gardener who plants tulip bulbs in the autumn, forgets about them during the long winter, and then, one morning in May, is suddenly excited by signs of colour in the buds. The patient farmer sows the seed and then loses interest. He sleeps and gets up, and the seed sprouts and grows, 'and he doesn't know how'. Nor does he care (Mark 4.27). His interest is only quickened when the grain is ripe because this to him is the miracle. From a seemingly dead seed comes the harvest; from a pinch of yeast the daily bread. It is a miracle of resurrection; life springing out of death. From the same miraculous process, from a small band of disciples with Jesus at their head, the kingdom of God grows.

### 4. The pearl merchant (Matt.13.45)

A merchant with a fine collection of precious pearls, which is his joy and delight, searches for one pearl of matchless beauty and, having found it, he sells all that he possesses to buy the one pearl of great price. In this parable the emphasis falls upon the great joy which the merchant experiences when he has made his choice, sold all his possessions, finally committed himself and become the owner of the supremely lovely pearl. So is the joy of the man who enters the kingdom of God. (See a similar parable *Hidden Treasure* [Matt.13.44].)

### 5. The unforgiving servant (Matt.18.23–35)

The sum owed by the king's servant is enormous: 10,000 talents which was roughly equivalent to two and a half million pounds. Clearly the servant is not a bailiff on a private estate but the governor of a province; a pro-consul or procurator like Pontius Pilate.

One of the main responsibilities of so important an official was to collect the taxes and transmit them to the royal treasury. This pro-consul had evidently been feathering his own nest on a tremendous scale. Even so, the vast sum of the debt is deliberately exaggerated. The Jewish historian Josephus records that in 4 BC the annual taxes imposed upon the districts of Galilee and Perea amounted to only 200 talents – a fiftieth of the sum owed by the pro-consul in the parable.

There are other details which show that Jesus gave a Gentile setting to this parable. Under Jewish law the sale of a wife (v. 25) was forbidden. Again, although torture was frequently employed upon a defaulting governor of a district or a province to compel him to disclose where he had hidden the money it was forbidden under Jewish law (in v. 34 'jailors' in RSV means 'torturers' as in AV and NEB).

The parable ends with the phrase, 'forgive your brother from the heart'. It is the only kind of human forgiveness which is genuine in the sight of God. To say, 'I forgive you but I never want to see you again', is forgiveness only with the lips (see Matt.15.8 f. which is a quotation from Isa.29.13).

### Teaching about the kingdom

A large number of the parables, including most of those discussed in the preceding section, begin with the phrase, 'The kingdom of God (or 'of heaven' in Matthew) is like . . .'. The proclamation of God's kingdom is a dominant theme in the message of Jesus, but there is no clear-cut formal definition of its nature. Instead we are presented with a poet's rich confusion of similes and metaphors. What the kingdom is like and the evidence of its presence is conveyed in parables, short vivid phrases and sometimes in enigmatic sayings.

Those who first heard Jesus speak of the kingdom of God would not have found it an unfamiliar idea. The expectation that God's kingdom would come was a part of the Jewish faith. But the word 'kingdom' can mislead us. It suggests an area of territory like the 'United Kingdom', or the 'Kingdom of Norway' or 'the Hashemite Kingdom of Jordan'. 'God's kingship' brings us nearer to the meaning. What the Jews longed for and confidently expected was the vigorous and established power and activity of God in the world. In the time of Jesus, however, the world, from the point of view of the Jews, had long been a disordered place. Rome, in the persons of Pontius Pilate and the puppet kings of Galilee and Transjordan, was in command. Classical historians write about the Roman peace, Roman justice, Roman law and order, but to the Jews Roman domination was a usurpation of God's kingship. Yet it was a temporary seizure of power which rightly belonged to God. The Lord's throne was set in heaven; his kingship ruled over all the world.

God was king. His own people – the Jews who knew this unalterable truth – must wait, and waiting, be obedient to the will of their King which was enshrined in the Law. They had been waiting for many long years, but the time would come when God would take decisive action. He would assert his authority, destroy those who resisted his kingship and welcome into his kingdom the Jews who had steadfastly remained his loyal subjects.

How startling then was the proclamation with which Jesus began his ministry in Galilee.

The time is fulfilled and the kingdom of God is at hand; repent and believe in the Gospel (Mark 1.14).

This may be Mark's summary of the heart of the message preached by Jesus at the beginning of his public ministry, but there is no reason to doubt that it is an accurate summary. The phrase 'the kingdom of God is at hand' can be translated 'is upon you' as in NEB, but whichever translation is preferred the meaning is clear. God's kingship, Jesus declared, is a present reality here and now in Galilee. It has come or it is on the point of appearing like the rising sun coming up over the horizon.

Blessed are the eyes which see what you see! For I tell you that many prophets and kings desired to see what you see, and did not see it, and to hear what you hear, and did not hear it (Luke 10.23 f. = Matt.13.16 f.).

Prophets and kings had desired to see the triumph of God's purposes; the sovereign rule of God, and, said Jesus, 'you are seeing it now'.

Without doubt the announcement of the kingdom caused great excitement among the people of Galilee and to those who could believe it, it brought joyful expectancy and hope. 'After all these years of waiting,' they would say, 'it is going to happen in our time, before our very eyes.' We can sense this mounting excitement in the early chapters of the Gospel of Mark. 'The news spread rapidly.' 'Great crowds came to see him.' 'The large congregation (in the synagogue) were amazed.' But often the crowds must have been puzzled and some in the crowds were repelled. There was an element in the preaching of Jesus about the kingdom which seemed shocking and even blasphemous to the orthodox Jew. 'If it is by the finger of God that I cast our demons, then the kingdom of God has come upon you' (Luke 11.20; see Matt.12.28). The kingdom has come in the coming of Jesus. 'What ! This workman from Nazareth ?' He spoke, it is true, with conviction and authority, 'not like the lawyers'. He had magnetism and the gift of healing, but to men who expected that a king of the line of David, or a heavenly representative of God, would come to inaugurate the kingdom, the proclamation of this Galilean was, to say the least, perplexing. So, as Jesus himself recognized, his proclamation divided men. 'A man's foes will be those of his own household' (see Matt.10.34–39; 8.21 f.).

There was something else disturbing about this preaching of the kingdom. It was the sense of urgency. There was, said Jesus, a crisis and the crisis had been created by his own coming. Men must make a decision and act now, but his hearers were slow to recognize the immediacy of the crisis. 'The kingdom is upon you,' said Jesus. 'All the signs of its appearing are before your eyes !'

When you see a cloud rising in the west, you say at once, 'a shower is coming'; and so it happens. And when you see the south wind blowing, you say, 'There will be scorching heat'; and it happens. You hypocrites ! You know how to interpret the appearance of earth and sky; but why do you not know how to interpret the present time ?' (Luke 12.54–56).

Yet in other parables and sayings the time scale is somewhat different. The crisis is building up but the decisive moment has not yet come.

I have come to set fire to the earth and how I wish it were already kindled (Luke 12.49 NEB).

Remember, if the householder had known what time the burglar was coming he would not have let his house be broken into. Hold yourselves ready, then, because the Son of man is coming at the time you least expect him (Luke 12.39 f. NEB).

Be ready for action, with belts fastened and lamps alight. Be like men who wait for their master's return from a wedding-party, ready to let him in the moment he arrives and knocks. Happy are those servants whom the master finds on the alert when he comes (Luke 12.35–36a NEB).

In these stories the crisis though imminent has not yet come upon men. The master has not yet come home.

What is life like when God reigns ? In the Gospels there is a rich profusion of metaphors, but we can separate out four main ideas.

1. The coming of the kingdom is compared to natural processes of growth. This is not a contradiction of the sense of urgency and crisis for the point is not slowness of growth but the small beginnings and the assurance of an abundant harvest. Jesus and his small band of followers must have seemed pitifully weak in contrast with the political and religious forces ranged against them, and the inertia of the ordinary man. Yet, like the tiny mustard seed which grows into a large bush or the pinch of yeast which makes the bread to rise, the kingdom grows and spreads and works in society.

2. When God reigns men receive what they need and not what they deserve (see above, The Labourers in the Vineyard, Matt.20.1–15, p.137 f). There will be justice but above all generosity, for God 'makes his sun rise on good and bad alike, and sends the rain on the honest and the dishonest' (Matt.5.45 NEB).

3. When God reigns, forgiveness will be the paramount social virtue, and for those who have already recognized the coming of the kingdom, and have accepted God's rule it is the permanent moral obligation. 'Forgive us . . . as we have forgiven' (Matt.6.12 NEB).

4. When God inaugurates his reign there will be a time of separation. The wheat will be harvested and the weeds burned (Matt. 13.24–30. See pp. 137 f.). There will be – to use a favourite metaphor of Jesus – a great feast to which some who are invited will refuse to come, and the poor, the crippled, the blind and the lame, and the homeless who sleep along the hedgerows, will come to the banquet (Luke 14.16–24 = Matt.22.1–14). There will be a great Day of Judgment when the sheep will be separated from the goats; when the hard-hearted will be rejected and the compassionate will enter and possess the kingdom (Matt.25.31–36).

## Teaching about God

When we speak about God today we face two problems. How do we know there is a God? There is, of course, no proof in the sense of a logical watertight progression of argument to an inescapable conclusion. There *are* reasons, some intellectual, some moral, some born of personal experiences, but probably no one single reason can withstand the corrosive acids of modern disbelief. Faith in God is like a rope in a gymnasium: it is made up of many different strands twisted together. No one single strand will bear the weight; only the rope will hold.

This problem did not confront Jesus in his teaching. No one in his day would ever have dreamed of asking the question, 'How do you know that there is a God?' It was as self-evident to Jesus and his contemporaries that God is, as it was self-evident that sun, moon and stars are.

The second problem is to make the word 'God' sound real, so that instead of being an emotive noise it conveys a mental picture with a clear outline and sharply defined details. This was a challenge to Jesus as it is to us, and he answered it in two ways.

1. All his preaching of the kingdom was, as we have seen, a declaration of God's universal power and of his purpose for the world.

2. He gave a rich meaning to the phrase 'God is Father'. In the Old Testament God is frequently spoken of as 'Father'.

As a father pities his children,
So the Lord pities those who fear him (Ps.103.13).

The Jewish Rabbis used the metaphor. 'Be strong as a leopard', one of them wrote, 'and swift as an eagle and fleet as a gazelle and brave as a lion to do the will of thy Father who is in heaven.'

Jesus himself did not use the word 'Father' as often as is sometimes thought. In the developed theology of the Fourth Gospel the word occurs 107 times, often in the phrase 'my Father', but in the Synoptic Gospels it occurs much less frequently: only four times in Mark, six in Luke, eight or nine in the 'Q' passages and twenty-three in Matthew. What is original in the teaching of Jesus and gave such clarity to the word 'Father' was the way he used it in his sayings and parables.

Is there a man among you who will offer his son a stone when he asks for bread, or a snake when he asks for fish? If you, then, bad as you are, know how to give your children what is good for them, how much more will your heavenly Father give good things to those who ask him? (Matt.7.9–11 NEB. See Luke 11.11–13).

It is surprising that in a patriarchal society in which the authority of the father over his family was unquestioned, the emphasis in the teaching of Jesus falls not upon God's arbitrary power, but upon his watchful, loving care of men and women. This heavenly Father, whose name is to be used with reverence and whose will men must strive to do, is like a shepherd searching for a lost sheep, or a housewife looking for a lost coin, or an anxious father longing for his son's return (Luke 15).

In the narrative of Jesus' agony in Gethsemane (Mark 14.32–42) we catch a glimpse of his attitude towards God his Father. Here was a real struggle to maintain his faith and to keep to his purpose, but when the conflict was over he was back on the rock on which he had always stood; his absolute trust and unswerving obedience. For the sake of his Father's purpose he would endure physical torment and mental and spiritual suffering.

## Teaching about prayer

In the thought of Jesus religion was not ostentatious observance and prayer was the very opposite of a lengthy monologue (Matt.6.1–8). Sincerity was everything (Luke 18.10–14). The brevity of the prayer which Jesus taught to his disciples is significant. It is enough to acknowledge the holiness of God ('hallowed be thy name'), to desire his kingly rule on earth ('they kingdom come'), to pray for everyday needs and for forgiveness, and for deliverance in every fiery trial (Matt.6.9–13).

There are two parables about prayer which can easily be misinterpreted. Both appear on the surface to emphasize that prayer consists of persistent begging. In the parable of the Friend at Midnight (Luke 11.5–9) a man knocks up his neighbour at night to borrow three loaves of bread. At once he gets a blunt refusal. 'Don't bother me. The door is locked, and we are all in bed.' But the man outside goes on hammering at the door until 'because of the very shamelessness of his request' (v. 8 NEB) he gets his three loaves of bread.

The clue to resolving the difficulty presented by this parable lies in the way we translate the opening words; 'Which of you . . . ?' (AV). The New English Bible has 'Suppose one of you . . .'. The three Greek words thus translated regularly introduce questions which expect emphatic replies, such as 'No one !', 'Impossible !', or 'Everybody, of course'. So the parable begins, 'Can you imagine that if a friend came to you at midnight to borrow three loaves of bread, you would answer, "Go away. We're all in bed"?' The answer to this rhetorical question would be, 'Impossible ! Of course I'd get up for a friend in need.' And can you imagine God not answering your cry for help ? 'No ! Of course not. It's unthinkable.'

The second parable, that of the Unjust Judge (Luke 18.2–8a), teaches the same lesson and should be interpreted along the same lines. A widow brings her case before a single judge, not before a tribunal, which suggests a dispute about money: a debt, a pledge, money due to her as her inheritance is being withheld and she seeks justice. She persists until the judge finally yields 'so that she will stop pestering me'. The meaning is in v. 7. God listens to the cries of the poor and the oppressed and suddenly he acts to befriend and rescue them. Perhaps those to whom Jesus told this parable were men who thought of the poor and the weak as 'outsiders', and assumed that God also had no time for them.

## Teaching about man

### 1. Dependence upon God

'Blessed are the poor in spirit, for theirs is the

kingdom of heaven' (Matt.5.3). Luke's version of the first beatitude reads, 'Blessed are you poor' (6.20). There has been much argument as to which of these versions is the more original, but whichever we choose makes little difference to the meaning. 'Poor in spirit' does not mean 'poor-spirited', like a race horse that will not run; 'poor' has a wider connotation than material poverty. In Jewish thought the 'poor in spirit' and the 'poor' were those people who were much too wise to imagine that they were 'self-made'; isolated and entirely independent. They were those who recognized and lived by their dependence upon God – and this is not often the attitude of mind of very wealthy people. We catch a glimpse of the 'poor in spirit' in the first two chapters of Luke.

My soul magnifies the Lord
and my spirit rejoices in God my Saviour,
for he has regarded the low estate of his handmaiden (Luke 1.46 f.).

According to the teaching of Jesus man is a dependent creature (see Matt.6.25–34). It is the reason why he said, 'Unless you become as children, you will never enter the kingdom of heaven' (Matt.18.3). Children are not innocent but they are dependent, and they have a great capacity for trusting others.

From this fundamental premiss about our human condition flow all the attitudes of the truly unaggressive person which are set out in the beatitudes – mercy, purity, peaceableness and so on. Such people are 'the salt of the earth' and 'the light of the world' (Matt.5.13 f.).

### 2. The inward springs of action

In the collection of sayings which is known as 'The Sermon on the Mount' the emphasis falls not so much upon outward acts as upon inward desires and emotions; lust which leads to adultery, anger which may end in murder (Matt.5.21 and 27). Jesus speaks in other places in the Gospels of the contrast between outward observance and inward sincerity. Mark 7 begins with an explanation of a Jewish custom for non-Jewish readers. A strict Jew tried to avoid all social contact with Gentiles even to the extent of touching anything which had been handled by a Roman, a Greek or a Syrian. At the market a Jew might brush accidentally against a non-Jew, or handle a bunch of grapes which a Gentile had fingered. With the taint of the Gentile still on his hand he might touch a cup or a table when he returned home. That was why his wife was always washing the cups and pots. Jesus dismissed all this as nonsense. It is not outward contacts which defile a man but inward thoughts and desires (see vv. 1–8, 14–23).

It was this inward sincerity which Jesus commended in the generosity of the widow who put two small copper coins into a collecting bowl at the temple (Mark 12.41–44) and in the act of a woman who anointed his feet with precious ointment (Mark 14.3–9). It is commended also in the parable of the Lowest Seats at the Feast (Luke 14.7–11). Generosity and humility and gratitude, issuing in good manners, are marks of those who are poor in spirit and know their dependence upon God.

### 3. Reconciliation

Jesus was profoundly troubled and indeed alarmed by the deep divisions within the nation. The political and social climate of Galilee and Judaea in his day was one of hatred, suspicion and resentment. There was the fierce anger of the Zealots (and of many more who did not belong to that party) against the Roman occupying forces. There was the centuries-old smouldering resentment against the Samaritans, and the social antagonism between the 'respectable' and 'not respectable'; between the Pharisees and lawyers on the one hand and the 'publicans and sinners' on the other. Jesus resisted this quarrelsomeness with all the force at his command. His parable of the *Good* Samaritan must have angered many who heard it, and his willingness to befriend a Roman centurion and tax-gatherers like Matthew who worked for Herod Antipas, that puppet ruler of Rome, brought him no popularity. 'Love your enemies,' he said, 'and pray for those who persecute you' (Matt.5.44). 'Pass no judgment and you will not be judged' (Matt.7.1 NEB).

Jesus pressed upon individuals, and especially upon his disciples, the need to offer forgiveness. 'How often am I to forgive my brother if he goes on wronging me,' asked Peter, 'as many as seven times?' 'Seventy times seven' was the answer, leaving Peter with a mathematical problem on his hands which he probably could not work out (Matt.18.21 f.). 'If when you are bringing your gift to the altar, you suddenly remember that your brother has a grievance against you, leave your gift where it is before the altar. First go and make your peace with your brother and then come back and offer your gift' (Matt.5.23 f. NEB). The only altars in first-century Israel were in the temple at Jerusalem. Suppose (as is most likely) that this saying was spoken in Galilee. Was the man expected to leave his gift unoffered in Jerusalem and to travel post-haste back to Nazareth or Capernaum? With such vivid and challenging statements Jesus proclaimed the necessity for reconciliation.

### 4. *Renunciation*

According to the Fourth Gospel Jesus said, 'I have come that men may have life and may have it in all its fullness' (John 10.10 NEB). There are many places in the Gospels which give the impression that Jesus was happy in the abundant, creative life which he led. Yet at the heart of his teaching lies the stern demand for renunciation. Broadly speaking, the demand takes two forms.

### (a) *Worldly possessions*

There is a romantic picture of the child born in poverty in a stable; but there is no evidence as to whether the family was poor, or whether Jesus himself had sufficient resources for his simple needs. In his teaching there is no idealistic praise of a life of complete poverty, but there is a demand that his followers should sit lightly towards the standards and values of the world. 'Do not lay up for yourselves treasures on earth . . . but lay up for yourselves treasures in heaven' (Matt.6.19). 'Beware of all covetousness,' he said in reply to a request to settle a property dispute, 'for a man's life does not consist in the abundance of his possessions.' And then he told the parable of the Rich Fool (Luke 12.13–21).

Jesus spoke of the way in which great wealth threatens a man's true and creative life, using the well-known simile of the camel and the eye of a needle. At the end of this discourse there is a difficult saying. Peter said, 'We have left everything and followed you' to which Jesus, according to the Gospel of Mark, gave this long reply:

Truly I say to you, there is no one who has left house or brothers or sisters or mother or father or children or lands, for my sake and for the gospel, who will not receive a hundredfold now in this time, houses and brothers and sisters and mothers and children and lands, with persecutions, and in the age to come eternal life (Mark 10.28–30).

Any interpretation of this enigmatic reply is bound to be uncertain. Many scholars regard it as an addition, in whole or in part, by the early church which looked beyond persecutions, to its reward. The long list of benefits, 'houses, lands, brothers, sisters, mothers and children' may reflect the intimate fellowship of the first Christians and the ideal of sharing possessions and having all things in common. If the passage in any form is an authentic saying of Jesus, it may be that he was gently laughing at blundering Peter. 'What about us ?', says Peter, 'We've given up everything.' 'Do you want your reward, Peter ?', Jesus replies, 'Would you like a hundred houses; a hundred mothers, brothers and sisters ? Well you can have them.' And then the sting in the tail – 'with persecutions !'

(b) *'Take up the cross'*

The story of a man who ran up to Jesus and asked what he must do to win eternal life is reported in all three Synoptic Gospels (Matt.19.16–22; Mark 10.17–22; Luke 18.18–23). It is Matthew who tells us that the man was young and rich, and Luke who describes him as 'a man of the ruling class': hence the familiar title of the incident 'the Rich Young Ruler'. Jesus loved this young man at sight and laid upon him the heaviest demand: to give away to the poor everything he possessed and to follow Jesus – which surely means to become one of the small intimate band of disciples.

When James and John asked for prominent places in the coming kingdom, what they were promised was a cup of sorrow and a baptism of death (Mark 10.35–40 = Matt.20.20–23). In a public utterance to the people as well as to the disciples Jesus said, 'Anyone who wishes to be a follower of mine must leave self behind; he must take up his cross and come with me' (Mark 8.34 = Matt.16.24 = Luke 9.23). Clearly 'taking up the cross' meant different things for different individuals both in the lifetime of Jesus and afterwards. For some it led to sufferings and hardship, for some martyrdom and for many others faithful, unspectacular service. There is a saying of Jesus which, then and now, unites all who follow him in obedience:

> You know that in the world the recognized rulers lord it over their subjects, and their great men make them feel the weight of authority. That is not the way with you; among you whoever wants to be great must be the willing slave of all. For even the Son of man did not come to be served but to serve, and to surrender his life as a ransom for many (Mark 10.42–45 NEB).

## Time present and time future

This section deals with a perplexing and controversial aspect of the message of Jesus. Much of his teaching was directed to the immediate needs and problems of the men and women to whom he talked in small groups in the market place, or in large crowds gathered to listen to him. This teaching was concerned with 'time present'. On the other hand, in all the Gospels there is teaching which seems on the face of it to refer to dramatic and even cataclysmic events in the future. The thoughts of Jesus moved not only in 'time present' but also in 'time future'.

### 1. Time present

Alan Dale in the preceding article has written of Jesus as a man 'making a costly and dangerous attempt to ask real questions about a real world'. Jesus was not a visionary nor a spectator of life's scene: he did not dwell in an ivory tower. The backcloth of his message was the Roman occupation and the revolutionary movement directed against it. It was also the deep division between the Jewish hierarchy – the priests and Sadducees – and the ordinary people led by the Pharisees. The 'setting in life' of his teaching was the daily round and constant worries of farmers and fishermen, shopkeepers and merchants, housewives and their children. 'Don't be anxious,' he said constantly, 'and don't be afraid' (Matt.6.25 f.). He urged men to be generous towards each other as God is generous (Matt.5.43 f.), and to make courageous gestures of friendship even towards traditional enemies (Luke 10.29–37).

As Jesus spoke of men's daily needs and preached generosity, compassion and forgiveness there was always in his mind the reality of God's kingship. Don't be anxious or afraid; your heavenly Father knows what you need. 'Seek first his kingdom and his righteousness and all these things shall be yours as well' (Matt.6.31–33). As we have seen in many parables and sayings, Jesus proclaimed that God's kingship was a present reality. It had come or it was very near, now in Galilee in the early years of the first century AD.

In Luke 17.21 there is a saying of Jesus which reads in the Authorized Version, 'the kingdom of God is *within you*'. Modern versions give the translation, '*in the midst of you*' (RSV) or '*is among you*' (NEB). Taken by itself the saying refers to 'time present'. The kingdom of God is actually here now. Luke, however, or the source which Luke used, placed this saying in a context which prophesies future events. The time of the Son of man will come and it will be a time of catastrophe and terror. 'Like the lightning-flash that lights up the earth from end to end, will the Son of man be when his day comes' (17.24 NEB). The arrangement of these verses in Luke is no doubt the work of someone in the early church, but it illustrates an important point about the teaching of Jesus. His thought moved easily from 'time present' to 'time future'.

## 2. *Time future*

In the Gospels there are predictions; forecasts concerning the future. In Matt.23.37–39 = Luke 13.34–35 there is the well-known lament over the Holy City. 'O Jerusalem, Jerusalem . . . behold your house is forsaken and desolate.' Luke, however, included in his Gospel another and very different lament.

When he came in sight of the city, he wept over it and said, 'If only you had known, on this great day, the way that leads to peace ! But no; it is hidden from your sight. For a time will come upon you, when your enemies will set up siege-works against you; they will encircle you and hem you in at every point; they will bring you to the ground, you and your children within your walls, and not leave you one stone standing on another, because you did not recognize God's moment when it came, (Luke 19.41–44 NEB).

This is a terse and vivid prediction of the siege and destruction of Jerusalem which began in May and ended in September of the year AD 70. Since this event took place some forty years after the time of Jesus, it is often argued that such a description of the great catastrophe must have arisen within the early church. This supposition can be neither proved nor disproved, but it seems unnecessarily pedantic. The prediction does not describe in detail the actual siege of Jerusalem, as the Jewish historian Josephus reported it many years later. The words of Jesus describe a typical siege; a city encircled, siege engines battering at the wall and so on. Moreover, to one who like Jesus took a close interest in the political clamour and unrest of the Jews, and yet, standing apart from it, was not blinded by partisan emotions, it needed no special insight to realize that if the revolutionary elements continued to oppose the government by violent acts, the Romans would reinforce their troops in the country and drive straight towards Jerusalem.

There are other passages in the Gospels which may reflect the horrors of the war which began in AD 66, though scholars hold different views on the point. Mark 13 is clearly a collection of sayings which Mark himself may have put together, or which may already have been in existence as a separate document. It is probable that genuine sayings of Jesus are embedded in it, and some of these seem to be predictions of the great war between the Jews and the Romans. Here, for instance, is a prediction of the plight of war refugees. The editor's hand is evident in the opening phrases.

When you see 'the abomination of desolation' usurping a place which is not his (let the reader understand), then those who are in Judaea must take to the hills. If a man is on the roof, he must not come down into the house to fetch anything out; if in the field he must not turn back for his cloak. Alas for women with child in those days, and for those who have children at the breast! (Mark 13.14–18 NEB).

## The future of Israel

Did Jesus predict the rejection of Israel as the chosen instrument of God's purpose? It is clear that this view was held at least in some quarters in the early church. The part played by the Jewish authorities in the death of Jesus; the hostility displayed by some Jews towards the new Christian communities, both played their part in shaping the belief that the 'Old Israel' had been rejected and the 'New Israel' – the Christian church – had taken its place. This belief has certainly left its mark upon the form in which some of the sayings and parables of Jesus have come down to us.

In Matt.23 we have a sustained and bitter condemnation of the Pharisees and lawyers. This was certainly put together in its present form by an editor. It has a clear literary shape: an introduction (vv. 1–12); the seven accusations against the lawyers and Pharisees, each beginning, 'Woe to you' (vv. 13–36); and in conclusion a lament over Jerusalem, the centre of unfaithfulness, 'killing the prophets and stoning those who are sent to you' (vv. 37 f.). How far this stylized chapter truly reflects the teaching of Jesus is a difficult question to answer, but the evidence of the Gospels as a whole makes clear that he did attack the religious leaders of Israel and declare that they and the kind of religion for which they stood would be rejected. But did Jesus predict the rejection of Israel as the chosen people of God? The answer we give to this question depends largely upon the way we interpret two parables: the Vineyard (Mark 12.1–11 = Matt.21.33–43 = Luke 20.9–18), and the Marriage Feast (Matt.22.1–14 = Luke 14.16–24).

The vineyard is let by an absentee landlord to tenants. On three separate occasions at harvest time he sends a servant to receive the rent in kind, and each of the servants is shamefully treated and sent away empty-handed. Finally the landlord sends 'his beloved son', and the tenants seize him, kill him and throw him out of the vineyard. The parable ends with the question, 'What will the landlord do ?', and the answer is that he will destroy the tenants and give the vineyard to others.

The parable of the Marriage Feast, which is a parable of the Kingdom, tells a similar story. The invited guests make various trivial excuses and refuse to attend the banquet, and their places are taken by people 'both bad and good' collected at random by the king's servants.

The parable of the Vineyard is unusual because unlike most of the parables each detail has a meaning. The vineyard stands for Israel, the owner for God, the tenants are the Jewish authorities, the servants are Old Testament prophets who had been despised and rejected, the 'beloved son' is Jesus. Mark's version ends with the words, 'and they (the Jewish authorities) tried to arrest Jesus . . . for they perceived that he spoke this parable against them'. The vineyard is given to others just as in the parable of the Marriage Feast the ordinary citizens take the place of the invited guests. 'The publicans and harlots,' said Jesus on another occasion, 'go into the kingdom of Heaven before you' (Matt.21.31). It seems clear that it is not the nation as a whole which is rejected but the religious leaders, the lawyers and the Pharisees.

## The Day of Judgment

Another controversial question concerning 'time future' is this: did Jesus predict that he would come again in glory; that there would be a final Day of Judgment and the end of the world ? This, as we have seen, was a belief strongly held by Christians during the early years of the first century (see I Thess.5.1–11; II Thess. 1.5–12). The belief waned as the years went by and the risen Christ did not appear in glory, but in mediaeval times it gained great popularity and was a favourite subject for artists. The belief finds expression in Mark 13 and is expanded in Matt.24–25 and in Luke 21.5–36. Here the predicted events are dramatic and terrifying – wars, earthquakes, famine and persecution, the rise of bogus messiahs and false prophets precede the appearance of Christ as judge of the world. There is a different picture in Luke 17.22–37 which comes from the source 'Q'. Men and women are going about their daily routine, eating, drinking, sleeping, trading, marrying and then, suddenly like a flash of lightning the Day of the Son of man is upon them.

The teaching which we have quoted from the Gospels and the Epistles has a technical name: *eschatology*. The language in which it is expressed is *eschatological language*. It is alien to our way of thinking. Many Christians quietly ignore this element in the New Testament and some biblical scholars deny that Jesus ever thought in these terms, or expected his own second coming. What are we to make of it all ?

1. Eschatological thinking arises when there is a contradiction between the harsh realities of life and man's faith in God's power and justice. In this kind of situation the religious man says with Paul that 'the sufferings of this present time are not worthy to be compared with the glory that is to be revealed to us' (Rom 8.18). Eschatological teaching brings hope to men, and when present sufferings are severe then the hope of a glorious future is often expressed in imaginative pictures. Sometimes the language is poetic and pastoral:

The cow and the bear shall feed;
  their young shall lie down together; and the

lion shall eat straw like the ox (Isa.11.7).

Sometimes it is dramatic, 'technicoloured' language to match the drama of the moment. In the dark days of the second century BC when the Jews were engaged in a desperate struggle with the Seleucid rulers, this was written:

Behold, with the clouds of heaven
    there came one like a son of man,
and he came to the Ancient of Days
    and was presented before him.
And to him was given dominion
    and glory and kingdom,
that all peoples, nations and languages
    should serve him;
his dominion is an everlasting dominion,
    which shall not pass away,
and his kingdom one
    that shall not be destroyed (Dan.7.13 f.).

It was natural that the first Christians, often isolated from the rest of their fellow citizens because of their faith, usually under suspicion, taunted for worshipping a crucified Saviour, and at times persecuted, should rest their hopes on Christ's return in power and glory. They believed that this hope was founded upon the teaching of Jesus, and they made collections of sayings which supported their faith and included them in their church books–the Gospels.

2. Jesus faced opposition, slander and resentment, and seems to have known – at least in the final months of his life – that his enemies would turn the full force of their power against him. But more than this; he was alarmed and sorrowful at the political situation of his nation. He knew that armed rebellion could only end in national disaster. Yet his faith in the purposes of God and in the realities of God's kingship did not waver. He, too, was a man of hope, and it

should not surprise us that sometimes he expressed this hope in vivid and dramatic language. He was, we have said, a poet, 'the greatest artist of us all', and poets dream dreams and see visions.

3. Whether or not Jesus believed in his own 'second coming', he knew that he had been chosen by God to fulfil a particular rôle in history. The sayings and parables which he used when he thought about the future were his way of expressing his confident faith in God's undefeated purpose.

### Who was Jesus of Nazareth ?

A modern biographer, writing the life of a public or semi-public figure, can usually draw upon other material for his portrayal of character than the known facts of his subject's career. There may be family letters and documents, reminiscences of friends, published articles, newspaper cuttings and even, with luck, a personal diary kept over the years of public life. With such materials at hand the biographer can explore the inner life and private thoughts of the man or woman of whom he is writing. He can trace the development of ideas and convictions and often he can discern not only what his subject thought about public affairs and private concerns, but also what he thought about himself.

Such a biography cannot be written of Jesus of Nazareth. The materials just are not there. In the nineteenth and early twentieth centuries devout and scholarly authors often included in their books a chapter on 'the self-consciousness of Jesus'. But there are no private letters, and no diary and no published articles. There are reminiscences of friends and followers, but these, as we have them in the Gospels, have been interpreted to meet the needs of the early Christians (see pp. 130 f.). Moreover, in the Synoptic Gospels Jesus displays a marked reluctance to speak about himself or to disclose his identity. For instance, when the disciples of John the Baptist were sent to ask, 'Are you he who is come or shall we look for another?' Jesus turned the question aside. 'Are you the Promised One: God's Messiah?' asked John's disciples, and Jesus replied obliquely by pointing to his ministry of healing and preaching (Matt.11.2–6 = Luke 8.17–22).

Many scholars of the present day, therefore, say that we cannot answer the question, 'Who was Jesus of Nazareth?'. We know nothing for certain of his inner life and private thoughts. We cannot explore his 'self-consciousness' or know what he believed to be the truth about himself.

On the other hand, some New Testament scholars have recently re-opened the question of what Jesus believed about himself. Their studies are concentrated upon a fresh examination of three titles which occur in the Gospels: 'Christ', 'Son of man' and 'Son of God'. In this section the evidence provided by these designations is briefly reviewed.

### 1. *Christ*

This title is of course the Greek form of the Hebrew 'Messiah': in both languages it means 'the Anointed One'. It occurs several times in the Synoptic Gospels, two of the references being of particular importance. The first of these is in Mark 8.27–33 = Matt.16.13–20 = Luke 9.18–22.

> And he asked them (the disciples), 'But who do you say that I am?' Peter answered him, 'You are the Christ.' And he charged them to tell no man about him (Mark 8.29 f.).

Luke's version is identical with Mark's except that Peter's reply reads 'the Christ of God'. In Matthew's version, which is surely an extended version of the early tradition, Peter replies, 'You are the Christ, the Son of the living God', and this is followed by an enthusiastic response from Jesus. 'Blessed are you, Simon son of Jonah. Flesh and blood has not revealed this to you but my Father who is in heaven.' This is followed again by the promise that 'on this rock' Jesus will build his church and that to Peter, or to all his disciples, will be given 'the keys of the kingdom of heaven'.

In the early church the title 'Messiah' or 'Christ' became the corner-stone of the new faith. Jesus was the Anointed One, the long promised Deliverer, but what does the reply of Peter, 'You are the Christ', tell us about the convictions of Jesus concerning himself? He does not take the title upon his own lips and in Mark and Luke he sharply commands secrecy and begins immediately to speak of his approaching sufferings and death. As with the question asked by John's disciples, Jesus seems to turn aside an awkward situation by speaking of the present realities of his life. 'The Son of man must suffer many things.'

The second key passage is Mark 14.61 f. = Matt.26.63 f. = Luke 22.66 f. The scene is the examination of Jesus before the Jewish High Council. Caiaphas the high priest askes Jesus, 'Are you the Christ, the Son of the Blessed?' According to Mark Jesus replied 'I am'; Matthew reports that he answered, 'You have said so', and in Luke he replies, 'If I tell you you will not believe.' What is significant, however, is that all three Gospels agree that Jesus went on immediately to speak of himself as the 'Son of man', as if the title 'Christ' was of little importance to him. On this evidence we may well hesitate before asserting that Jesus claimed for himself the title 'Messiah'.

### 2. *Son of man*

In the two incidents discussed in the previous paragraphs Jesus, when named by others as the Christ, seems immediately to have substituted the designation 'Son of man'. It is a title which occurs frequently in the Synoptic Gospels, and only on the lips of Jesus. Apart from the Fourth Gospel, where it occurs nearly as often as in Mark, it is only found once in the rest of the New Testament (Acts 7.56). To some scholars this title is the clue to the hidden thoughts of Jesus concerning his own identity. Others reject most of the texts in which it occurs as later interpolations. It is a puzzling title which appears to carry different meanings in different sayings. There are, for instance, sayings in which it is uncertain whether Jesus is speaking of himself, of his future return in glory, or of some other One who is yet to appear. 'When the Son of man comes will he find faith on the earth ?' (Luke 18.8). One writer who attaches considerable importance to this designation and examines it at length has written, 'Here all is obscure and hotly debated.'

In the Old Testament 'Son of man' usually means simply 'man'. In the book of Ezekiel, for instance, it is constantly used whenever God speaks to the prophet. 'Son of man, stand upon your feet and I will speak with you' (Ezek.2.1). This seems to be the usage in such a saying of Jesus as, 'Foxes have holes, and birds of the air have nests, but the Son of man has nowhere to lay his head' (Matt.8.20 = Luke 9.58). 'I have nowhere to lay my head.'

There are, however, sayings in which Jesus claims the title and gives it greater significance. Consider first the story told in Mark 2.1–12.

Jesus has before him a paralytic lying on a mattress, and says to him, 'My son, your sins are forgiven.' A group of lawyers who witness the scene declare that this is blasphemous talk. Jesus then heals the paralytic man saying that he does so 'that you may know that the Son of man has authority on earth to forgive sins'. Again at Mark 2.28 Jesus declares that 'the Son of Man is lord of ('sovereign over' NEB) even the sabbath'. In these two narratives, if they truly represent what happened, Jesus in taking the title Son of man claims in the first instance authority from God and in the second sovereignty over a sacred institution.

Perhaps the most significant occasion on which Jesus appears to have claimed the title Son of man is one which has already been mentioned, namely the examination before the Jewish High Council after his arrest in Gethsemane. Having replied to the high priest's question, 'Are you the Christ, the Son of the Blessed ?' Jesus added, 'You will see the Son of man sitting at the right hand of power and coming with the clouds of heaven' (Mark 14.62 = Matt.26.64 = Luke 22.69). Clearly the reference is to the prophecy in the book of Daniel which has already been quoted (see above, p. 149).

Behold, with the clouds of heaven
there came one like a son of man.

The title 'Son of man' appears in the Gospels in three contexts: the earthly ministry of Jesus, his sufferings and his future glory. What remains uncertain is whether all three uses of the term are authentic, or whether the church, looking back upon the past events of the cross and resurrection, gave its own meaning – a messianic meaning – to the title so that it became almost a synonym for 'Messiah'.

### 3. *Son of God*

There is a saying preserved by Matthew and Luke which is highly characteristic of the Fourth Gospel but unique in the Synoptics.

All things have been delivered to me by my Father; and no one knows the Son except the Father and no one knows the Father except the Son and anyone to whom the Son chooses to reveal him (Matt.11.27 = Luke 10.22).

Apart from this the title 'Son of God' is only spoken by supernatural voices at the baptism of Jesus (Mark 1.11 = Matt.3.17 = Luke 3.22) and at his transfiguration (Mark 9.7 = Matt.17.5 = Luke 9.35); it is also spoken by demons before their defeat at the hands of Jesus (see, for instance, Mark 5.6 f.). Jesus, of course, spoke of God as his Father, but on the evidence of the Synoptic Gospels it would be hazardous to assert that he thought of himself as 'the Son of God' in the sense in which the early church proclaimed him.

The questions discussed in this final section are difficult and complicated. The issues have been simplified, and for a fuller discussion reference should be made to the commentaries and other books suggested in the bibliography.

This discussion of the evidence has raised questions but has not provided answers. If now we extend our thought and look again at the central message of Jesus the three titles come into a different focus and we can make a more positive statement.

Jesus, as we have seen, proclaimed that the kingdom of God had come. God's kingship was already exercising sway in Galilee and Judaea. The kingdom was not yet come in all the fullness of its power. The disciples must still pray 'Thy kingdom come', but a new power and authority and benevolence had arisen to give new hope to the people of Palestine.

The evidence for this new assertion of God's kingship was Jesus himself. One of his most significant sayings was spoken after he had, to use the words of the Gospel, 'cast out a demon that was dumb'. 'If,' said Jesus, 'it is by the finger of God that I cast out demons, then the kingdom of God has come upon you' (Luke 11.14–20). 'By the finger of God . . . by the power of God himself I do my work . . . and God's sovereignty is established.' By the will of God he was at the centre of this new movement in history. The world had turned upon a new course and would never be the same again because he had come. Whether or not he, in the depths of his own mind, expressed this fact by thinking of himself as 'Messiah', or 'Son of man' or 'Son of God', for those who believed on him in Palestine and for those who in the wider world entered the Christian fellowship, these titles expressed the new reality which they had come to know in Jesus.

ROBERT C. WALTON

10 Paul and his World

## The Graeco-Roman world

When a reader of the Bible turns from the Gospels to the other books of the New Testament, one thing that cannot fail to strike him is the sudden enlargement of the stage of action. The events of the Gospel story have hardly taken him beyond the narrow confines of Judaea and Galilee (and area comparable with, shall we say, Yorkshire). But turn the page, and the scene changes. The action shifts rapidly over a great part of the Near and Middle East, and as far west as the Adriatic. Over this wide area travellers move freely by land or water, untroubled by national frontiers or language difficulties. This is the Hellenistic world; that is to say, that part of the world which, embracing many different nationalities, was bound together by the use of the Greek language, serving as a vehicle for Greek thought and Greek social and political ideals. It was largely the outcome of the conquests of Alexander the Great, whose deliberate policy it was to permeate the conquered territories with the Greek spirit. The cultural unity which he promoted survived the break-up of Alexander's empire, but the kingdoms formed out of the fragments gradually sank into decline, until a great part of the region presented the spectacle of a society in dissolution.

Then Rome came on the scene. Appearing first as one more competitor in the scramble for power, and a brutal and ruthless one, it ended by imposing peace and good order on the Hellenistic world, and adding to its cultural unity a political cohesion which it had lacked. It now becomes appropriate to speak of the 'Graeco-Roman' world. The transformation of a predatory and aggressive power into the presiding genius of a highly civilized international society was in large measure the work of the emperor Augustus, whose reign covers the transition from BC to AD. The imperial rule was accepted willingly enough by most of its eastern subjects. No doubt there were pockets of discontent (Jewish Palestine was one), but with inherited memories of prolonged anarchy and misrule to which the strong arm of Rome had put an end, most of them knew when they were well off.

## The empire: political and social structure

Augustus had emerged from the civil wars as undisputed master of the whole Hellenistic world as far east as the Euphrates. Within the imperial frontier a few puppet principalities were allowed to survive, as a useful 'buffer' or an administrative convenience, but the greater part of the annexed territories was given a provincial organization which amounted to a business-like and efficient bureaucracy. Frontier provinces were placed under military governors in command of legionary troops, with the title 'legate'. They were appointed directly by the emperor and were under his personal supervision. Peaceful provinces away from the frontiers had civilian governors with the title 'proconsul'. They were appointed, nominally, by the Roman Senate, but the emperor had them well in hand. Minor provinces (like Judaea) might be administered by governors of inferior rank appointed by the emperor, with the title 'prefect' or 'procurator'.

Within his province the governor was invested with all the authority of the empire, subject only to remote control by the emperor in Rome. He was responsible for every aspect of administration, but most particularly for the administration of justice, which he exercised by holding regular assizes at the principal cities of his province in turn. Roman rule, however, was not so severely centralized as to leave no room for a measure of local government. Throughout the eastern provinces there were numerous partly self-governing cities. They might be ancient Greek city-states, like Athens or Ephesus, or cities founded after their pattern by Hellenistic monarchs, like Antioch-on-the-Orontes, the capital of the province of Syria. Or they might be Roman colonies, like Philippi in Macedonia. The original colonists had been time-expired legionaries, who were given grants of land in the conquered territories by way of pension. Their institutions were closely modelled on those of the mother-city, and they took pride in their Roman citizenship (see, e.g., Acts 16.21). All these cities continued to be administered by their own magistrates and senates, who were allowed to exercise a certain degree of autonomy. It was no more than a shadow of the sovereign independence of the Greek cities in their prime, and it shrank with the years. But in the New Testament period the cities could still feel a justified pride in their civic liberties.

In most cities there were colonies of Jews. The Hellenistic monarchs had encouraged them as valuable settlers, and the emperors continued to accord them favourable treatment. Among the populace in general there was at most times an undercurrent of anti-Semitism, sometimes breaking out in violence. On the other hand there was widespread interest in some aspects of the Jewish religion, and its influence on Hellenistic thought was by no means negligible.

The Greek cities and the Roman colonies alike had a democratic element written into their constitutions. In the New Testament period the popular assembly, or town's meeting, still had an active, even if a restricted, part to play. But democracy was not a plant to flourish in the climate of the empire. Municipal communities tended more and more to reproduce the rigidly stratified structure of imperial society as a whole. At its head was the Roman nobility, wealthy and amply privileged, with exclusive access to the highest offices of state. At its base was the slave class, upon whose labour the economic structure ultimately rested.

The lot of slaves was inevitably harsh, especially of those employed in industry or agriculture, though Roman law now gave some protection against the extremes of brutality which in former times had often provoked large-scale insurrections. Domestic slavery had its alleviations. Some masters were considerate, and treated their slaves as subordinate members of the family. Besides, a slave who was well educated, as many were, or qualified by native talent or acquired skill for some specialized employment, was too valuable a property to be handled recklessly. It was possible for a slave to earn and save enough to purchase his freedom, or he might hope for emancipation by testament on his master's death. A steady stream of emancipated slaves passed into the free community. Many were employed in (what we should call) the imperial civil service. Many were 'rising men'.

For the humbler orders of the free population, with little or no share in civic privileges, there were voluntary associations (*collegia*). Such voluntary associations, or clubs, had abounded among all classes in Greek and Roman society, but the emperors looked on them with a suspicious eye, and disallowed them except in so far as their activities could be directed into obviously harmless channels. Associations of tradesmen were permitted, under supervision, and poor men's 'friendly societies' were treated indulgently. They functioned as burial clubs, and could assure other benefits to their members, beside providing for social intercourse, especially on such occasions as the festivals of the deities which a club might have adopted as patrons. The 'friendly societies' included in their membership both slaves and free men of the poorest sort, and they must have done something to humanize the lot of a rootless proletariate. They seem to have provided in part the model on which the earliest Christian churches were organized. Their open membership, their regularly appointed officials, the common fund maintained by members' contributions, and their social meals with a religious complexion, are all features that reappear in adapted forms.

## Philosophy and religion

In the eastern provinces of the empire, with their strongly Hellenic heritage, intellectual life was vigorous. The lively interchange of correspondence, attested by papyri, among business men, farmers, soldiers, and all manner of ordinary folk, reveals a large literate public. Such a public, even if not highly educated, was open to the spread of ideas. It is characteristic of the period that philosophy was no longer the preserve of academics or gentlemen of leisure, but came out into the market place. The 'street-corner' philosopher became a familiar figure. Some acquaintance, however superficial, with philosophical ideas must have been widespread. The school of philosophy with the widest appeal was Stoicism. It was on the one side an elaborate and deeply thought system of logic and metaphysics, which incorporated the most advanced natural science of the time. It was not, however, on this side that it made its widest popular impact, but in its ethical teaching. However little the austere Stoic code might be honoured in the observance, at any rate it did much to inform a 'conscience' (the word itself is a Stoic coinage) in a society which had been notably without moral anchorage.

In earlier times Greek philosophy had been critical of popular religion and in general sceptical about belief in gods. It now came to terms with the return to religion which was a marked feature of the time. It has been described as a 'failure of nerve', shaking the old Greek confidence in reason under stress of the fearful insecurity which had long overshadowed Hellenistic society. It might more fairly be described as an awakening to the reality of dark forces in man and his world, not amenable to pure reason, which Greek rationality had tried to keep out of sight – never, indeed, with complete success. Men began to feel the need for redemption from the dark forces, however these might be conceived. This need was not met by the ancient gods of Greece and Rome, though their time-honoured and imposing ceremonies retained their appeal, and were a matter of pride and emulation among the cities. But the Hellenistic world was open to contacts with religions of another type, particularly those of Egypt, Iran, and the Semitic East, including Judaism. From such sources, often in a confused mixture, strange cults emerged. Many of them offered initiation into a 'mystery', which in one way or another assured to the initiate deliverance from the evils he most feared. The new popularity of these cults reminded the Greeks that they had their own ancestral 'mysteries', and these now acquired a new prestige – and acquired also meanings which might have surprised the ancestors.

Of these 'religions of redemption', we know little in detail; the secret of the mysteries was well kept. But it seems possible to draw some broad outlines. There were, it appears, commonly two main elements: the ritual action, or drama, and the tale, or 'myth', which underlay the action. The myth might recount, for example, how the god or hero who was the lord of the cult had died and come to life, or had penetrated into the dark underworld and won his way out into the light. The ritual action was designed to reproduce in dramatic symbolism – often, it seems, elaborate and spectacular – the plot of the myth, and this made the initiate partaker in the experience of his lord, and guaranteed him a blessed immortality. What proportion of the population of the empire received initiation into these cults we cannot know; it was probably a very small minority; but the influence of this type of religion on the thought and ethos of the time is unmistakable.

Where popular philosophy and popular religion met, there emerged a widely diffused way of thinking which, with great variety, shows some constant features. It held that this world is a realm of darkness and death in which the soul of man is imprisoned. He can, however, escape into the world of light and life through the attainment of 'knowledge'. But this was not the rational or scientific knowledge that ancient Greek philosophy had valued. It was more like revelation, or esoteric vision; and here the influence of the 'mysteries' is evident. At its highest it might take the form of a 'mystical' experience of oneness with 'The Real', or with 'The All'–which was often spoken of as 'knowledge of God'. At its lowest it might be nothing better than abracadabra. Popular religion and popular philosophy alike were deeply infected with the enervating belief in the dominance of the stars over human destiny, and astrology flourished.

## Christianity in the Graeco-Roman world

All this went to constitute the climate of thought and feeling in which people of the Graeco-Roman world lived. It is at any rate an index to the kind of spiritual need of which they were conscious. And these were the people to whom the early Christian missionaries made their approach. They brought a religion of redemption. It took seriously the reality and power of the dark forces that menace the human spirit, but it brought also a buoyant confidence in the victory gained over them once and for all by Christ, and now open to be shared by all who would put their faith in him. It had, like the 'mysteries', its rites of dramatic symbolism, but its rite of initiation was a simple washing in water, and the drama of its central 'mystery' was no more than the sharing of bread and wine in memory of the Lord. These rites had behind them a tale, or 'myth'; but the 'myth' was a true story of a real man who had lived not so long ago. The death-and-resurrection of which it told was an event that had occurred within living memory. Yet in the two symbolic rites, or sacraments – baptism and the eucharist, or Lord's supper – what was past became present, and the believer shared the virtue of the death and resurrection of the Lord, and entered into union with him. So the Christian gospel affirmed.

This reference to a Lord whose person, character and teaching were well attested gave a specific ethical stamp to the Christian religion of redemption. Social ethics had, so far as can be judged, little place in the popular religions. The new religion had behind it the strong Jewish tradition of ethical monotheism inherited from the Hebrew prophets. Its Founder countersigned that tradition, and yet by what he taught, and through his own action, liberated it from the limitations of the existing Jewish system, and offered the possibility of life under a 'law of liberty'. Here Christianity met the aspirations of Stoicism at its best, along with the assurance (which Stoicism lacked) of divine assistance towards the attainment of its ideals. Much of the ethical teaching of the New Testament would be recognized by any Stoic. And yet in the end the Christian ethic came out very differently. The Stoic ideal, lofty and austere as it was, remained essentially self-centred, and there was about it a certain coldness and hardness, however attractive the character of some of its exponents. Christianity, following the teaching and example of Christ, placed the centre of the ethical life in a warm regard for others, using for it the almost untranslatable term *agape*, which has to be rendered into English as 'charity', or 'love'. Here was a deeper basis for genuine human fellowship than other associations in the Graeco-Roman world could offer, and it was certainly one reason for the strong appeal that the church made to those who hungered for

true community and had failed to find it.

## Paul: Jew and Roman citizen

The pioneer leader in the Christian approach to the Graeco-Roman public was the apostle Paul. The fortunate preservation of a number of his letters has put us in a position to know him better than we can know most personages of the ancient world. The information they give can be supplemented from the account of his career given in the Acts of the Apostles. It is true that there are points where it is not easy to bring the two sources of our knowledge into complete harmony, and there are critical questions about the Acts which are still open. But in the parts of the book with which we are more particularly concerned – those which deal with the extended missionary tours undertaken by Paul – there is good reason to believe that the author was well-informed. In the later chapters the narrative is sometimes in the first person plural. It appears that the author has incorporated extracts from something like a travel diary – his own diary, likely enough. If so, then we are reading an account which emanates from one of Paul's travelling companions, who was at times an eyewitness of what he records. The 'diarist' is with much probability taken to be Luke, the Greek doctor whom we know from the letters to have been a close associate of the apostle (Col.4.14; II Tim.4.11; Philemon 24). His work may be used – so far as it goes, for there are large gaps –as an historical frame in which to set the letters, which are Paul's own account of himself.

Paul was born at Tarsus in Cilicia (Acts 21.39), an ancient Greek city, and now a strong centre of Hellenistic culture. His parents belonged to the Jewish colony there. They were orthodox and brought up their son in the Pharisaic persuasion (Acts 23.6; 26.5; Phil.3.5). At the same time, the father possessed the coveted status of Roman citizen, which meant that the family had a superior standing in the local community. The son was a Roman citizen by birthright (Acts 22.25–29). At home he was Saul, named after the first king of Israel; outside he was Paulus, citizen of Tarsus, citizen of Rome. He was bilingual, equally conversant with Aramaic and Greek. More exactly, he was trilingual, for he could read the Hebrew Scriptures in the original. Thus his mind had the freedom of two worlds of thought. Though it does not appear that he was deeply versed in Greek literature or philosophy, he had perhaps rather more than the educated man's general acquaintance with ideas that were in the air. His language quite often carries echoes of Stoicism. On the other hand his formal education seems to have been entirely within the native Jewish tradition. He was sent to study in Jerusalem, under Gamaliel (Acts 22.3), the most disting- uished Rabbi of his time. The fruit of his education is everywhere apparent in his minute acquaintance with the Scriptures of the Old Testament, and the Rabbinic methods of inter- preting them (which for his modern readers sometimes make difficulties). He was thus exceptionally equipped for the task to which in the end his life was devoted, that of mediating to the Hellenistic public a religion rooted in Judaism.

Saul the Pharisee and Paul the Roman, it seems, did not live in complete harmony inside the same skin. There are signs of psychological tension. In early life the Pharisee was upper- most. He recites with pride the privileges of the chosen people: 'They are Israelites; they were made God's sons; theirs is the splendour of the divine presence, theirs the covenants, the law, the temple worship, and the promises' (Rom.9.4. In this article biblical quotations in general follow the translation in the NEB). And not only was he proud of his people (as is right and proper); he was also proud beyond meas- ure of his own standing as a Jew: 'Israelite by race, of the tribe of Benjamin, a Hebrew born and bred: in my attitude to the law a Pharisee, in pious zeal a persecutor of the church, in legal rectitude faultless ' (Phil.3.5–6). In another retrospect on his early life he adds a significant phrase: 'In the practice of our national religion I was *outstripping many of my Jewish contemporaries* in my boundless devotion to the traditions of my ancestors' (Gal.1.14). That tells us some- thing important about the man; he had an irresistible urge to excel, to be distinguished. It was necessary to his self-respect that he should see himself as the perfect Pharisee: 'in legal rectitude faultless' (Phil.3.5–6). In another for something extravagant or abnormal which some Jewish readers have found in Paul's account of his pre-Christian phase.) But the time came when he was forced to confess to himself that this was fantasy and not reality. He was not faultless, and his efforts to be so were self-defeating. 'When I want to do the right, only the wrong is within my reach. In my inmost self I delight in the law of God, but I perceive that there is in my bodily members a different law, fighting against the law that my reason approves' (Rom.7.21 f.).

It is a recognized fact of psychology that when an inward conflict becomes unendurable, the subject may seek relief by externalizing the conflict, and projecting the hatred he feels for something in himself upon some object outside himself. This is what Paul did, and it was this that made him a persecutor. His first contact with the new sect of the 'Nazarenes', it appears, was through one of its most radical and aggressive representatives, a Hellenistic Jew (like Paul himself) named Stephen, who was reported to be 'forever saying things against the holy place and the law', saying, indeed, 'that Jesus of Nazareth will destroy this place (the temple) and alter the customs handed down to us by Moses' (Acts 6.13 f.). This was to impugn the most sacred pledges of Israel's status as God's chosen people. And when it appeared that these sectaries hailed Jesus of Nazareth as God's Messiah, this was sheer blasphemy. Did not the Law say, 'cursed is everyone who is hanged on a gibbet' (Gal.3.13) ? These people were dragging the glory of Israel in the mire: they were enemies of the temple and the Law, enemies of Israel, enemies of Israel's God. All the hatred (and fear ?) that Saul felt for that in himself which was 'fighting against the Law' could now be directed upon overt enemies. Stephen was stoned to death, with Saul as an accessory. This was only a beginning. With characteristic energy and initiative – and, it may be added, with characteristic determination to outstrip everyone else in zeal for the Law – he obtained from the high priest a commission to hunt the heretics down wherever they might be found (Acts 9.1 f.).

## The conversion of Paul

It was in the pursuit of this grim mission, on the road to Damascus, that he met with that which changed the current of his life. There are three accounts of it in Acts (Acts 9.3–9; 22.4–11; 26.12–18); but it is little that any narrative of events can tell us about spiritual experience. It can only hint at what took place in the depths of the soul under the form of describing objective occurrences. We are told of a light and a voice. The voice identified itself: 'I am Jesus whom you are persecuting'. Paul never doubted that he had actually met with Jesus, risen from the dead. When he calls the roll of witnesses to the resurrection he adds, 'In the end he appeared even to me' (I Cor.15.8); and when his credentials were called in question he retorted, 'Did I not see Jesus our Lord ?' (I Cor.9.1) – as if that settled the question. This is the kind of certainty it is useless to argue with; it does not abide our question. What the meeting meant to Paul himself we have to gather from occasional allusions in his letter, where he partly breaks through his customary reticence on the subject. Perhaps he comes nearest to letting the secret out when he speaks of 'the revelation of the glory of God in the face of Jesus Christ' (II Cor.4.6).

The effects, however, of the experience in his career and in the passage of history in which he played his part are open to our observation. It is evident that it brought the solution of his personal problem. The attempt to solve it by externalizing the inward conflict had proved to be no solution at all. The new solution he now found did bring real reconciliation of the contending forces in his own soul, in reconciling him also to the enemies he was pursuing with a pious hatred. He threw in his lot with the persecuted, that is, with 'Jesus whom he was persecuting'. But to throw in his lot with Jesus meant standing in with one who was under the 'curse' of the Law: it was to become an 'outlaw'. 'I have been crucified with Christ,' he wrote (Gal.2.20). It was the most complete break possible with his past self. It took all meaning out of the desperate struggle to see himself 'in legal rectitude faultless'. He could accept himself as he was, aware of his weaknesses, but willing, such as he was, to stand at the disposal of his new Master. 'We make it our ambition,' he wrote, 'to be acceptable to him' (II Cor.5.9). This was a different kind of 'ambition' from that which had spurred him on to 'outstrip his Jewish contemporaries'. It was the displacement of self from the centre. And that proved to be the removal of a crushing burden. Above all it was a liberating experience: 'Christ set us free, to be free men' (Gal.5.1).

It shows itself in an expansion of the range of his interests and energies, no longer restricted by Jewish nationalism and orthodoxy. For an orthodox Jew who lived the life of a great Greek city the problem of relations with Gentiles must always have been difficult. With the lines of his temperament and character before us in his letter, we cannot doubt that Paul was repressing his natural instincts in maintaining the degree of separation from his Gentile fellow-citizens which 'legal rectitude' seemed to require. Now he could give those instincts free rein. From the moment of his meeting with Jesus on the Damascus road he knew that the 'dividing wall' (as he called it) was broken down, and that he must 'go to the Gentiles'. Thus the main direction of his new mission was decided from the outset, though it may have been some years before the required strategy was worked out.

About Paul's earlier years as a Christian we are scantily informed. The skeleton outline in the Acts tells us little, and the little it tells is not easily correlated with what Paul himself records – also in mere skeleton outline. Looking back upon his career after many years, he recalls some of the unpleasant situations into which his missionary activities had brought him: 'Five times the Jews have given me the thirty-nine

strokes; three times I have been beaten with (Roman) rods; once I was stoned; three times I have been shipwrecked, and for twenty-four hours I was adrift on the open sea' (II Cor.11.23–33) – and so forth; and very few of these find a place in the narrative of Acts. There is much that we do not know.

By Paul's own account, it was not until three years after his conversion that he returned to Jerusalem (Gal.1.17–19). At that time he stayed for a fortnight with Peter (or Cephas, as he calls him, using his Aramaic name), and met also James 'the Lord's brother'. These two would be able to tell him much at first-hand about Jesus. His stay in Jerusalem, however, seems to have been cut short, and he then spent a period which can hardly have been less than twelve years in 'the regions of Cilicia and Syria' (Gal.1.21). We should gladly have heard more about his activities during that period. Perhaps some of the unrecorded adventures he recalls belong to those hidden years. But we do not know. The Acts records only his arrival at Tarsus, in Cilicia (Acts 9.30), and his removal to Antioch, in Syria (Acts 11.25 f.). It is with his arrival at the Syrian capital that the story of Paul's missionary career really begins.

### The first missionary journey

In that important and populous city believers in Christ were already prominent enough in the public eye to be given a nickname – for that is what 'Christian' really was (Acts 11.26). The community included a substantial proportion of non-Jewish converts from paganism. The introduction of this Gentile element had no doubt acted as a stimulant, and it is not surprising to be told that they soon felt themselves impelled – indeed divinely inspired

– to reach out to a still wider public in the Graeco-Roman world. For this enterprise they selected a Cypriot Jew named Barnabas (Acts 4.36 f.; 11.22–24; 13.2), and an obvious choice for his companion was Paul, whom Barnabas himself had first introduced to the Antiochene church (Acts 11.25 f.). The junior colleague soon slipped into the leading role for which his vigour and decision marked him out.

Thus began what is commonly referred to as Paul's 'First Missionary Journey'. It brought the two first to Cyprus (Acts 13.4–12) and then as far as the interior of Asia Minor, and in particular to a group of towns in the southern corner of the province of Galatia (Acts 13.14,51; 14.6 f.). In the light of what happened afterwards, it can be seen to have disclosed a pattern of events which was to recur with almost monotonous frequency. The author of Acts has depicted it in a full-length description of what happened at the first of these towns, Antioch-towards-Pisidia, a description which he no doubt intended to be taken as typical (Acts 13.15–50). It began with an address in the synagogue, to a congregation which included both Jews and 'Gentile worshippers'. The latter is an almost technical term for a class of persons, fairly numerous in many Hellenistic cities, who were attracted by the Jewish religion and liked attending the synagogue services, without becoming regular 'proselytes' and members of the 'commonwealth of Israel'. The 'Gentile worshippers' showed a lively interest, which spread in circles without previous association with the synagogue. The kind of approach that Paul made to these people implied (as we can gather from his letters) that Gentiles could become full members of the people of God without submitting to the Jewish Law, by joining the Christian church. As this implication became clear, it provoked a violent reaction among the stricter Jews. Thereupon the missionaries put out a statement of policy: 'It was necessary that the word of God should be declared to you first, but since you reject it . . . we now turn to the Gentiles' (Acts 13.46). It was the principle that guided Paul's procedure all through: 'To the Jew first, and also to the Greek' (Rom.1.16, 2.9 f.), as he expresses it more than once in his letters. In his Letter to the Romans he has provided a theological justification for it (Rom. 11.1–27). The outcome of this tour was, on the one hand, the foundation of several communities, largely Gentile in membership, and, on the other hand, the unleashing of a Jewish hostility to Paul's mission which was to follow him wherever he went, and finally to bring his active career to an end.

The missionaries now returned to the church which had commissioned them, at Antioch-on-the-Orontes (Acts 14.25–28). The measure of success they were able to report made it evident that the initiative must be followed up (Acts 15.36). Plans for a further tour included a change of partners. Barnabas chose to return to his native Cyprus (Acts 15.39). Paul, who was evidently raising his sights, took as his new colleague Silas (or, in Latin, as Paul's letters have it, Silvanus). He was a member of the church at Jerusalem (Acts 15.22 f.), but, from his name, a Hellenistic Jew, and, just possibly, a Roman citizen, like Paul himself (Acts 16.37).

## The second missionary journey

The 'Second Missionary Journey' was to be marked by a momentous new departure, not, it would appear, premeditated. It began unadventurously enough, with a return visit to the young churches founded on the previous tour (Acts 15.40–16.5). After this the missionaries pursued a curiously devious and uncertain course, without, so far as we are told, finding any opening for work, until they reached the shore of the Aegean at Troas, not far south of the Dardanelles (Acts 16.6–8). It is at this point that we come upon the first extract from the 'travel diary' incorporated in Acts: 'We at once set about getting a passage to Macedonia, concluding that God had called us to bring them the good news' (Acts 16.10). The decision to cross from Asia into Europe proved a turning point, opening a new period in Paul's career, during which he may be said to have really found himself. It is a period, too, illuminated for us by the letters he wrote during it.

A comparatively short sea passage brought the party to the nearest port on the European side, and they made their way through Macedonia towards the province of Achaia, or Greece. Several churches were founded, though the tour was chequered, as usual, with opposition. At Philippi it came from pagans, not without overtones of anti-Semitism (Acts 16.19–24). At Thessalonica and Beroea the old pattern reasserted itself: the Jewish opposition made mischief with the civil authorities, and Paul was obliged to move on, leaving his companions behind (Acts 17.1–14). He arrived at Athens alone (Acts 17.15), in great disquiet (as he tells us in letters to Thessalonica written about this time) about the new converts whom he had been compelled by police pressure to leave prematurely (I Thess.2.13–35; II Thess.3.6–16). For this and perhaps other reasons he was, as he tells us in retrospect (I Cor.2.3), in low spirits as he left Athens for Corinth, which was, as it turned out, to be the scene of his greatest success so far.

Corinth had been one of the most important of the old Greek city states. After its destruction by the Romans it was refounded by Julius Caesar, and became the capital of the province of Achaia. Situated on the isthmus which separated the Aegean from the Adriatic – and the eastern half of the empire from the western – it had become an immensely busy and prosperous emporium of trade, with a large and mixed population. It had the unsavoury reputation which cosmopolitan seaport towns seem to attract.

Here Paul, now reunited with his companions, spent not far short of two years, maintaining himself by working at his trade of tent-making (Acts 18.3, 11, 18). It was his longest stay anywhere since he had started on his travels. The inevitable breach with the orthodox Jews set him free for independent action. He left the synagogue, taking with him one of its office-bearers, and set up his headquarters – defiantly perhaps, rather than tactfully – in a house next door belonging to a 'Gentile worshipper' (Acts 18.5–8). The opposition, as so often, tried to embroil him with the civil authorities, but the proconsul refused to entertain the charges they brought, as being no more than 'some bickering about words and names and your Jewish law'. The case was dismissed, and this must have considerably strengthened Paul's position (Acts 18.12–17). He succeeded in building up a numerous and active, if somewhat turbulent, Christian community, predominantly Gentile in membership, before he left to return to Jerusalem and Antioch (Acts 18.18, 22), making a brief call on the way at Ephesus (Acts 18.19–21), which he had already marked out as his next centre of work.

## The third missionary journey

About all this the narrative in Acts is singularly reticent. We may take it that the 'diarist' was not of the party at this stage. The 'Third Missionary Journey', through the interior of Asia Minor, is also given the most cursory treatment (Acts 18.23; 19.1). The author seems to be in a hurry, as Paul himself probably was, to reach Ephesus. It is evident that he had formed definite ideas about the most effective way of conducting his mission. It was, not to cover ground by moving rapidly from place to place, but to settle (as he had done at Corinth) at a suitable centre from which he could reach a whole province. Ephesus was to be such a centre. It was one of the principal cities of the province of Asia, with excellent communications by land and sea. Settled by Greeks in remote antiquity, but always with something oriental about it, it had been a meeting place of East and West long before the conquests of Alexander had inaugurated the Hellenistic age. Its world-famous temple was dedicated to the native Anatolian fertility-goddess whom the Greeks chose to call Artemis (Diana to the Romans) (Acts 19.27, 34 f.), though she had little in common with the virgin huntress of the classical pantheon. From ancient time a seat of Greek philosophical thought, Ephesus was also hospitable to all manner of superstitions, and in Paul's time it was notorious as a centre of the 'black arts' of magic (Acts 19.18 f.).

Such was the place which for the next three years or so was to be Paul's headquarters (Acts 20.31). There are evident signs of a planned strategy. As usual, he first made contact with the synagogue. When his position there became impossible, he was fully prepared with a plan. He formally 'withdrew his converts', and estab-lished himself on neutral territory in a lecture-hall in the city. Here he held daily conferences, open to all comers, which attracted numbers of residents and visitors to the city (Acts 19.8–10). But this was not all. By this time Paul had built up an efficient 'staff'. Their names keep recurring in his letters – Timothy (Rom.16.21; I Cor.4.17; 16.10; Phil.2.19–23, etc.,), Titus (II Cor.7.6, 13; 8.6–17, 23, etc.), Luke, Tychicus (Eph.6.21; Col.4.7; II Tim.4.12; Titus 3.12), and several others (Silas has now faded out). They were available either for work by his side at headquarters, or to be sent where they could be useful in keeping touch with churches already founded or in breaking new ground. It was in this way that Paul's mission spread in the province of Asia. We happen to learn from his letters the names of three up-country towns where churches were founded without any visit from the apostle – Colossae, Laodicea, and Hierapolis (Col.1.7; 2.1; 4.13–16) – and there were certainly others. The author of Acts says, perhaps with pardonable exaggeration, that 'the whole population of the province of Asia, both Jews and pagans, heard the word of the Lord' (Acts 19.10).

Meanwhile, however, trouble was brewing. There was furious opposition from the Jews (Acts 20.19), and some from pagan quarters (Acts 19.23–27), though we hear also of 'some of the dignitaries of the province who were friendly towards him' (Acts 19.31). Of the opposition we have some record both in Acts and in the letters (e.g., I Cor.15.32; II Cor.1.8). From the latter we also learn, what the author of Acts has not told us, that Paul was at this time driven almost to distraction by disorders in the church at Corinth. He sent members of his staff to deal with them (II Cor.12.17 f.), but he found it necessary to interrupt his work and cross the Aegean himself (II Cor.12.14). There are two letters to the Corinthians in the New Testament, but these contain clear indications that the correspondence they represent was more extensive. They illustrate vividly the problems that arose when people of widely differing national origin, religious background, education, and social position were being welded into a community by the power of a common faith, while at the same time they had to come to terms with the secular society to which also they owed allegiance. These problems were threatening to split the church into fragments. It may have been about the same time that the very serious trouble broke out which provoked Paul to write his fiercely controversial Letter to the Galatians. The date of the letter is uncertain, as is also its precise destination, but if this is the time to which it belongs (as seems most probable) there would be a sharp point in Paul's *cri de coeur* in the Second Letter to the Corinthians:'There is the responsibility that weighs on me every day, my anxious concern for all our congregations' (II Cor.11.28).

The difficulties at Corinth were eventually resolved, and Paul, having wound up his work at Ephesus, was able to re-visit a church now fully reconciled. It is at this point that he wrote the longest and most weighty of all his surviving letters, that addressed to the Romans. In this letter he takes a brief retrospect on the work that lay behind him, and sketches a plan for the future. He has now covered the eastern provinces of the empire, 'from Jerusalem as far round as Illyricum,' as he expresses it. 'Now,' he adds, 'I have no further scope in these parts,' and 'it is my ambition to bring the gospel to places where the very name of Christ has not been heard.' Accordingly, he is planning to open up work in the west, with Spain as his objective. On the way he will visit Rome, and hopes to find there support for his enterprise (Rom.15.19–29). He had to tread somewhat delicately. The church of Rome was not of his foundation, nor within his 'sphere of influence'. He knew there was some prejudice against him, and before presenting himself in Rome he sends a considered and comprehensive statement of his theological position, which should disarm prejudice and establish his standing as a Christian teacher.

### The Judaistic controversy

The visit to Rome, however, was not pending immediately. First he must go to Jerusalem. Significantly, he implores the Roman Christians to 'pray to God for me that I may be saved from unbelievers in Judaea and that my errand to Jerusalem may find acceptance with God's people' (i.e., the church) (Rom.15.31). He therefore not only apprehended danger from Jewish opposition, but also felt some doubt how far he would be welcome to his fellow Christians at Jerusalem. To understand this we need to look at the situation which had developed as a result of his startling success in building, all over the eastern empire, a close-knit Christian community which was fully supra-national, multi-racial, with no distinction (as he wrote) between 'Greek and Jew, circumcised and uncircumcised, barbarian, Scythian, slave and free man' (Col.3.11). This inevitably antagonized those who adhered to a stiff, nationally orientated type of Judaism – those, in fact, who stood where Paul himself had stood before his conversion. He had 'ratted' on them, and that could not be forgiven or forgotten.

But there were many Jews within the church

itself who were uneasy about Paul's missionary policy. Admit Gentiles to the church, by all means, but why do away with the salutary restraints of the Law ? The first demand of this party was that Gentile converts should submit to the rite of circumcision, which brought a man within the 'covenant' guaranteeing the privileges, and the obligations, of God's people (Acts 15.2). In other words, a man must become a Jew before he could be recognized as fully Christian. This matter was satisfactorily arranged – or at least Paul thought so – at a fairly early stage. He went up to Jerusalem, he tells us, and conferred with the leaders of the church there. There emerged a kind of concordat between Paul and Barnabas of the one part and Peter, James and John of the other part. It was agreed that they should respect each other's independence of action. Peter and his colleagues would be responsible for missions to Jews, Paul and Barnabas for missions to Gentiles. It was clearly understood that circumcision should not be imposed on Gentile converts, and Paul at least took the view that this carried with it freedom for Gentile Christians from the 'bondage' of the Jewish Law (Gal.2.1–9). In Acts we have another account of a conference in Jerusalem, which may be the same, viewed from a different angle, or may be a different one (Acts 15.4–29). According to this account also Gentile converts were dispensed from the need for circumcision, and from demands of the Law apart from certain minimum requirements about which there is some measure of ambiguity (Acts 15.28 f.); in any case, to judge from Paul's correspondence, they remained more or less a dead letter.

The controversy was by no means settled. It dragged on for years, and brought in various side-issues, such as that of Paul's own status as an apostle, about which he was sensitive. But in the main it seems to have been accepted that Gentile Christians were not obliged to conform to the Law, but that Jewish Christians should be expected to do so. This would appear to be the position of James, 'the Lord's brother', who had become head of the Jerusalem church, and was regarded as the leader of all law-abiding Jewish Christians, amounting (so he claimed) to 'many thousands' (Acts 21.20). Paul could hardly take exception to this in principle. He himself, he tells us, conformed to the Law when he was moving among Jews (I Cor.9.20). But such a position was essentially unstable. The majority of the churches of Paul's foundation had a mixed membership of Jews and Gentiles. Could they really live together while following different codes of conduct ? The centre of Christian fellowship lay in the communal meals in which they joined. Could Jewish Christians in practice keep their Law, with all its dietary regulations, while eating in common with fellow-Christians who did not observe it ? Was 'inter-communion' possible without hurt to somebody's conscience on the one side or the other (Gal.2.11–13) ? In his letters Paul is seen to deal with difficulties of this kind with conspicuous tact and consideration, but on the main issue he was adamant. The church could not be allowed to become a Jewish institution with Gentile Christians tolerated as second-class citizens. 'There is no distinction,' he repeated (Rom.3.22; 10.12). If he had been finally defeated, the church might have had as little impact on the great world as any other of the numerous Jewish sects. He was not defeated, but neither could he be said to have gained a decisive victory in his life-time. Advocates of the narrower view dogged his steps to the end, and sought to win over his converts. No doubt they were honest and conscientious men, who stood obstinately by their principles, as he did. But they were wrong. He speaks of them in his letters with a passionate indignation, for the issue was to him vital.

## *Jerusalem and Rome*

And yet the journey which he was planning when he wrote to the Romans was essentially a peace-making mission. When the Jerusalem concordat was made, the leaders of the church there had stipulated – and as Paul understood the matter it was the only stipulation – that the Gentile churches should take some responsibility for the support of the poverty-stricken Jewish Christians of Jerusalem. Paul responded eagerly to this request (Gal.2.10). The leaders in Jerusalem may have had in mind something like an equivalent for the contributions which Jews living abroad made to the temple at Jerusalem. But for Paul (as we know from his letters) it was an opportunity to demonstrate the true fraternal unity of Christians, bridging any divisions that arose among them. He set on foot a large-scale relief fund, to be raised by voluntary subscription from members of the churches he had founded; he recommended a system of regular weekly contributions (Rom.15.25–28; I Cor.16.1–4; II Cor.8.1–9,15). The raising of the fund went on for a considerable time and there was now a substantial sum in hand to be conveyed to Jerusalem. He was to be accompanied by a deputation carefully composed, it appears, so as to represent the several provinces (I Cor.16.3 f.; Acts 20.4). The handing over of the relief fund was to be both an act of true Christian charity and also a formal embassy from the Gentile churches affirming their fellowship with Jewish

Christians in the one church (Rom.15.27).

The goodwill mission miscarried. Paul's reception by the leaders of the church at Jerusalem, if not unfriendly, was cool. James was thoroughly frightened of the effect his presence in the city might have on both Christian and non-Christian Jews, in view of his reputation as a critic of Jewish 'legalism'. He urged Paul to prove his personal loyalty to the Law by carrying out certain ceremonies in the temple (Acts 21.20–24). Paul was quite willing. 'To Jews,' he had written, 'I became like a Jew, to win Jews; as they are subject to the law of Moses, I put myself under that law' (I Cor.9.20). Unfortunately he was recognized in the temple by some of his inveterate enemies, the Jews of Asia, who raised a cry that he was introducing Gentiles into the sacred precinct (Acts 21.27–29). This was a high misdemeanour. There ran across the temple court a barrier with an inscription (which can still be read) threatening with death any foreigner who should trespass beyond it. There was no truth in the charge, but it was enough to rouse the rabble, and Paul was in danger of being lynched. He was rescued by the Roman security forces, and put under arrest. Having identified himself as a Roman citizen, he came under the protection of the imperial authorities (Acts 21.30–39), and was ultimately transferred for safe custody to the governor's headquarters at Caesarea (Acts 23.23–33). There were wearisome wrangles over jurisdiction between the Jewish Council and two successive Roman governors, Paul meanwhile being kept in confinement. In the end, seeing the possibility that he might after all be sent back to Jerusalem and fall into the hands of his enemies, he exercised his citizen's right and appealed to the emperor (Acts 25.1–12). Accordingly he was put on board a ship sailing for Rome. The account in Acts of the voyage, with the shipwreck off Malta, is reputed one of the finest sea-pieces in Greek literature (Acts 27.1–28.15).

And so Paul fulfilled his cherished plan of a visit to Rome, but as a prisoner. He was placed under something like house-arrest. He occupied his own private lodging, with a soldier constantly on guard (Acts 28.16) but with liberty to receive visitors, while awaiting trial, which was still continually delayed. It is probable, though not certain, that the Letters to the Philippians, Colossians and Philemon, all of which refer to the writer as being in prison at the time of writing, belong to this period of confinement – as also Ephesians, if this is indeed from Paul's hand. They show him actively at work, even under these difficult conditions, keeping in touch with his churches by letter, receiving and dispatching messengers.

The period of house-arrest lasted, we are informed, for two years (Acts 28.30). Then the curtain comes down. We may presume that the case eventually came up before the imperial tribunal, but whether it resulted in acquittal and a further period of freedom to travel, or ended in condemnation and execution, we have no means of knowing. The Letters to Timothy and Titus have been thought to refer to a second imprisonment in Rome, but the evidence is at best ambiguous, and it is unlikely that these letters, in the form in which we have them, come from Paul's own hand. That he ultimately suffered martyrdom may be taken as certain, and there is no good reason to doubt the Roman tradition that he was beheaded at the spot on the road to Ostia known as Three Fountains, and buried on the site now occupied by the noble church of St Paul-without-the-Walls.

## A note on chronology

The chronology of Paul's career cannot be fixed precisely, but fortunately we have one precise date to start from. The proconsul before whom Paul was cited at Corinth was Junius Annaeus Gallio, who is known to have held the appointment from July AD 51 to June AD 52. On the showing of Acts, therefore, Paul was in Corinth from early in 50 to late in 51. From this fixed point we can calculate backwards and forwards, making the best of such indications of time as are supplied in Paul's own letters or in the Acts. The results will inevitably be in part conjectural, but the possible margin of error anywhere can hardly be more than three or four years.

If Paul reached Corinth early in 50, then his 'Second Missionary Journey' must have begun in 49, and the visit to Jerusalem which preceded it, when he came to an understanding with the leaders of the church there, would presumably fall in 48. Paul dates his earlier visit to Jerusalem fourteen years before this. As he may be assumed to use the inclusive reckoning then customary, this probably points to AD 35. This was three years (or on our reckoning 2-plus) after his conversion, which may therefore be tentatively dated to AD 33.

Returning to our starting-point in AD 50–51, and working forwards, we have first a condensed summary of protracted journeys, including stays of unspecified length at various places, without any notes of time, until we find Paul established at Ephesus for three full years. At what date this three-year period is conceived to have begun we can only conjecture. All things considered, it seems more likely to fall in AD 54–57 than any earlier. If so, then he can hardly have arrived in Jerusalem before 59. He was then arrested, and spent two years in prison, ending in 61. At that point the governor Antonius Felix was succeeded by Porcius Festus. On the reckoning we have followed this would be in 61, and in fact this seems the probable date for the succession, on the (somewhat ambiguous) evidence of non-biblical sources. Accordingly, Paul will have started for Rome in autumn 61, wintered in Malta, and arrived in Rome early in 62. His two years of house-arrest would then bring us to AD 64. Beyond that we cannot go, but it may be significant that it was in the winter of 64–65 that the emperor Nero made his savage attack on the Christians of Rome.

C.H. DODD

11 The Thought of Paul

## Paul and his letters

For the thought of Paul we naturally turn to his letters. Although the Acts gives a very fair account of his life and work, and a general idea of what he stood for, it is in the letters that his mind is revealed.

In the New Testament there are thirteen letters which mention Paul as the writer. A fourteenth, the Letter to Hebrews, is by long custom included with them, but it is in fact an anonymous work; in the early church it was admitted that no one knew who wrote it. Of the thirteen it is not certain that all are directly from the apostle's hand. In his time it was not unusual for the disciples of an outstanding teacher to compose books to propagate his teaching as they understood it, and to publish them under his name; nor was the practice considered discreditable. There are reasons for thinking that some of the 'Pauline' letters may have originated in some such way. The strongest reasons apply to the Letters to Timothy and Titus. On the other hand, the four Letters to the Romans, Corinthians and Galatians, to which we might add the short note to Philemon, carry the stamp of Paul's style and personality on every page. There is no question that he composed them. Most scholars, probably, would say as much for Philippians and the First (and perhaps also the Second) Letter to the Thessalonians. About the Letter to the Colossians there is more doubt, but the balance of probability seems to fall in favour of Paul's authorship, possibly with some collaboration.

Whether the Letter to the Ephesians should be included is debatable. In some ways its style is curiously 'un-Pauline'. Yet if it was written by a disciple he must have been one with an almost uncanny insight into the apostle's mind, and whether or not it comes from his own hand we cannot go far wrong in using it to fill out our picture of his thought in its maturest form.

The letters were almost all called forth by some particular occasion, and none of them, unless it be the Letter to the Romans, makes any attempt to present the writer's thought in a systematic way. Written at intervals in the midst of an extremely busy life, they are the product of a powerful intelligence responding to the challenge of urgent situations; it may be the challenge of practical problems of Christian living in a pagan environment, as in the Corinthian correspondence, or of subtle propaganda which seemed to him subversive of the truth, as in Galatians and Colossians. We have to gather his teaching by combining what he says in different places.

Any man's thought is necessarily formed in part by his background and environment, as well as by his personal experience. With Paul we have to take account of his Jewish upbringing and of what he owed to the primitive Christian community which he joined at an early stage in its history.

## The Jewish heritage

Among religions of the ancient world the Judaism of the first century was unique in being strictly monotheistic. Its fundamental tenets were that there is, and can be, only one God; that he is good – good in the same plain sense in which he requires men to be good, that is, just, merciful, true and the like – and that he is a 'living God' who reveals himself in history through action, in which he is working out his purpose for his world. Such was the faith which Judaism had inherited from the prophets of Israel. In this faith Paul was brought up.

But there was a certain contradiction deeply embedded in this monotheistic faith. The one God is God of the whole world, Maker and Ruler of all mankind. Yet in a special sense he is the God of Israel, the nation bound to him in an 'everlasting covenant'. The charter of this covenant was the Law, believed to have been dictated by the Almighty himself to Moses on Mount Sinai. It was held to be the perfect embodiment of the righteousness of the one God and the righteousness he requires of men. As such it was necessarily absolute and universal. And yet it was primarily Israel's law; no other nation knew it. Paul himself has given eloquent expression to the pride which the Jew felt in this unique privilege: 'You rely upon the Law and are proud of your God; you know his will; instructed by the Law you know right from wrong; you are confident that . . . in the Law you see the very shape of knowledge and truth' (Rom.2.17–20. In this article biblical quotations in general follow the translation in the NEB). The possession of the Law marked Israel out as God's chosen people. It was to this people that God had revealed himself in 'mighty acts', and through it his purpose went forward to fulfilment. This was the central motive of its history and the key to its destiny. Thus the highest moral idealism was wedded to an assertive nationalism.

## Judaism and the nations

In this perspective, what is the status and the destiny of 'the nations that know not God'? To this question the answers were various and uncertain. Some of them show a finely humane spirit which will go as far as possible –without prejudice to Israel's prior claim – in generosity to the Gentile. Others must seem to us to approach the limit of nationalist arrogance. But there was in first-century Judaism a strong 'missionary' movement towards the pagan world. On one level it was content to propagate the monotheistic idea and certain fundamental moral principles, but its ulterior aim was to bring Gentiles within the scope of the divine mercy by incorporation in the chosen people. The 'proselyte' submitted himself to the Law of God – that is, to the Jewish Law; he became a Jew.

On the other side the question arose, what is the status and the destiny of Jews who, knowing the Law, do not in practice observe its precepts? Here again the answers were uncertain and various. The Law itself pronounced a 'curse' on 'all who do not preserve in doing everything that is written in the Book of Law' (Gal.3.10), and prophets and Rabbis alike use language of the utmost severity in castigating offenders. Yet there is a notable reluctance to admit that in the last resort any 'son of Abraham' could be rejected by God; 'for the sake of the fathers' he would come through in the end. For Paul, who looked at the matter with a wider knowledge of the outside world, this was not realistic; moreover, it was inconsistent with the principle of monotheism. 'Do you suppose,' he writes, 'God is the God of the Jews alone? Is he not the God of Gentiles also? Certainly, of Gentiles also, *if it is true that God is one'* (Rom.3.29). The conclusion is unavoidable: 'God has no favourites; those who have sinned outside the pale of the Law of Moses will perish outside its pale, and all who have sinned under the Law will be judged by the Law'(Rom.2.11f.)

But while this clears the ground by setting aside any idea of preferential treatment, it is a negative assessment of the human predicament. 'There is no distinction; all have sinned' (Rom.3.22). While allowing that there may be some good Jews who keep God's Law (Rom.2.29), and good Gentiles who 'carry out its precepts by the light of nature' (Rom.2.14), Paul holds that in principle human society is in breach of the Law of God, and is therefore headed for disaster. It is subject, as he puts it, to 'the law of sin and death' (Rom.8.2). This universal human condition enters the experience of the individual in the desperate moral struggle which Paul has depicted with such psychological insight in the seventh chapter of Romans: 'When I want to do the right, only the wrong is within my reach' (Rom.7.21). (A Roman poet, some half-century earlier, had put it in similar terms: 'I see the better and approve it; I pursue the worse' – *Video meliora proboque; deteriora sequor*.) The problem which started as a domestic concern within Judaism has turned out to be a broadly human one. That is why Paul's controversy with his Jewish opponents, which at first sight looks like an antiquated and parochial dispute, has permanent significance.

### The divine initiative

The problem is acute in any religion of ethical monotheism which takes itself with full seriousness. The more nobly the goodness of God is conceived, the stronger is the sense of man's moral distance from him, and, at the same time,

the stronger the conviction that in communion with such a God lies man's highest good. It is this that lends poignancy to Paul's account of the moral deadlock in which he felt himself, and mankind in general, to be trapped. The only possible solution he could contemplate was a fresh initiative from the divine end, parallel, he might have said, to the initiative God had taken when he established the 'covenant' with Israel at Sinai. Such a new initiative he now saw to have been taken when Christ entered history: 'What the law could not do because our lower nature robbed it of all potency, God has done – by sending his Son' (Rom.8.3). This divine initiative is an entirely free and self-originated act of God, conditioned only by his love for the human race 'while we were yet sinners' (Rom.5.8). This is what Paul describes as the 'grace' of God. The response that is asked for from men is 'faith', or better – since the word 'faith' has accumulated a variety of meanings, not all of them true to Paul's thought – it is simply that they should trust God and let him have his way with them.

In speaking of the effect of this divine initiative in human experience Paul uses a variety of expressions. The most general expression is 'salvation'. In common Greek usage the word had a wide range of meaning. It could mean safety or security; it could mean escape from calamity, actual or threatened; or it could mean simply good health or well-being. In effect the word stood for a condition in which 'all is well', and the particular way in which all is well depends on the context in which it is used. In Paul, as in New Testament writers in general, 'salvation' stands for a condition in which 'all is well' in the absolute sense; a condition in which we are secure from all evils that afflict, or menace, the human spirit, here or hereafter. Thus the expression, while strongly emotive, is hardly capable of telling us what precisely, as Paul sees it, God does for us in Christ. More illuminating are some of the metaphorical expressions he uses. Three of these have played so large a part in the development of Christian doctrine that they need to be looked at carefully.

First, there is the legal, or forensic, metaphor of 'justification' (Rom.3.24,26; Gal.2.15 f., etc.). Sin is here conceived as an offence against law. The sinner stands at the bar. No one but a judge with competent authority can condemn or acquit. Before the divine tribunal the defendant is unquestionably guilty. But 'God acquits (justifies) the guilty' (Rom.4.5). Of course it is a violent paradox, and Paul was quite aware that it was so. He is putting in the most challenging terms his conviction that God takes a man as he is, 'with all his imperfections on his head' (as in the Gospels Jesus received the 'publicans and sinners'), and gives him a fresh start. He can now undertake his moral task relieved of the crippling sense of guilt.

Secondly there is the metaphor of 'redemption' (Rom.3.24; I Cor.1.30; Eph.1.7; Col.1.14). The Greek word was used of the process by which a slave acquired his freedom; it means 'release', 'emancipation', or 'liberation' (and is translated accordingly in the NEB). For Paul, the condition of a man caught in the moral dilemma he has described is a state of slavery, since he is unable to do what he wishes to do. (An almost contemporary Stoic philosopher said much the same: 'No sinner is a free man.') But God, exercising his supreme authority, declares the slave free, and free he is. All that Christ did – his entry into the human condition, his life of service, his suffering and death – may be regarded (still in terms of the metaphor) as the price God pays for the emancipation of the slave. 'Christ set us free, to be free men' (Gal.5.1): this exultant note of liberation sounds all through the letters. It was, unmistakably, Paul's own experience.

Thirdly there is the ritual metaphor of sacrifice. Sin can be regarded not only as a crime against the law, bringing a sense of guilt, or as a state of slavery, bringing a sense of impotence, but also as 'defilement', which makes a man feel ashamed and disgusted with himself. In ancient religions defilement could be incurred in all sorts of ways, many of them having nothing to do with morals. The defilement (it was assumed) could be removed by the performance of the proper ritual, most commonly, and perhaps most efficaciously, by the sacrifice of a victim. This was called 'expiation' (less accurately, 'atonement'). The metaphor of expiation, drawn from a world of thought quite alien to us, was ready to hand for anyone, like Paul, who was familiar with the elaborate ritual of sacrifice laid down in the Law of Moses, and in his time still practised in the temple at Jerusalem – or indeed for anyone acquainted with the religious rituals of the Greek states. This is the background of what he says about the work of Christ: 'God designed him to be the means of expiating sin by his sacrificial death' (Rom.3.25; literally, 'by his blood'; when Paul speaks of the 'blood' of Christ, he is using a kind of shorthand for the idea of sacrifice). There is no suggestion, here or elsewhere, that Christ offered himself as a sacrifice to 'propitiate' an offended deity. In using the metaphor of sacrifice Paul is declaring his conviction that the self-sacrifice of Christ meant the release of moral power which penetrates to the deepest recesses of the human spirit, acting (if one may put it so) as a kind of moral disinfectant.

These are the metaphors which have most captured the imagination of Paul's readers. His thought has sometimes been obscured through taking one or another of them – justification, redemption, or expiation (atonement) – by itself, and then forgetting that it is after all a metaphor. What he is saying all the time is that in Christ God has done for us what we could never do for ourselves. The criminal could not pronounce his own acquittal, nor the slave set himself free, and God alone could 'expiate' the defilement we have brought upon ourselves.

In the course of a passage (II Cor.5.18 f.) which is perhaps the clearest and most succinct statement of his teaching on this theme Paul writes: 'From first to last this is the work of God. He has reconciled us men to himself through Christ ... What I mean is that God was in Christ reconciling the world to himself, no longer holding their misdeeds against them.' In the idea of 'reconciliation' his thought has passed out of the realm of mere metaphor and adopted the language of actual personal relations. Many people know something of what it means to be 'alienated', or 'estranged' – perhaps from their environment or their fellow-men, perhaps from the standards of their society, perhaps, indeed, from themselves. The deepest alienation is from the true end of our being, and that means estrangement from our Maker, out of which comes a distortion of all relationships. The great thing that Paul had to say to the alienated is that God, from his side of the gulf that has opened, has put an end to the estrangement; he has reconciled us to himself. Nowhere does he suggest that God needed to be reconciled to us. His attitude towards his creatures is, and always was, one of unqualified goodwill (as Jesus said, he is 'kind to the unthankful and wicked'). Out of that goodwill he has provided the way to reconciliation.

## God in Christ

The whole process turns upon the action of God in Christ, and that action took place in history – in that historical episode which is the life and teaching, the death and resurrection, of Jesus Christ. About his life the letters have comparatively little to say. There was little occasion for it; they were all addressed to Christian readers, who might be presumed to know the salient facts. That Paul had a definite conception of his character is clear enough (see below, p. 184). His sayings are seldom quoted directly, but many echoes and reminiscences of them, as they are known to us in the Gospels, can be recognized by the attentive reader. (And how many sayings which never found their way into the Gospels may have left their mark ? Acts 20.35 is suggestive.) In short, behind the theology of the Pauline letters stands firmly the figure of the 'Jesus of history'.

Of outstanding significance are the circumstances of the death of Jesus: the facts that he gave his life willingly for the sake of others, and that he died under the 'curse' of the law on a Roman cross (Gal.3.13). That meant a decisive breach with the old order. All that followed was to be understood as the breaking-in of something new. Christ died, but he rose again, and thus inaugurated a new order of life. To establish the fact of his resurrection Paul calls a whole series of witnesses, including some of those who had known Jesus most intimately, besides adding that he could corroborate their testimony out of his own experience. The fact of the resurrection gave him the clue to the meaning of the whole historical episode.

It was entirely in harmony with the prophetic

valuation of history as the field of the 'mighty acts' of God that Paul should see the life, death and resurrection of Jesus Christ as one more 'mighty act', the 'fulfilment' of all that God had purposed and promised in the whole history of Israel. In common Jewish belief the symbol of that fulfilment was the expected 'Messiah'. After his conversion Paul accepted what the followers of Jesus were saying, that in him the Messiah had come. But what Paul meant by 'Messiah' was something different from any of the variant forms of Jewish messianic expectation. The messianic idea had to be re-thought in the light of a new set of facts.

One invariable trait of the Messiah in Jewish expectation was that he should be the agent of God's final victory over his enemies. On the popular level that meant, quite crudely, victory over the pagan empires which from time to time oppressed the chosen people. In Paul's thinking the idea of the messianic victory is completely 'sublimated'. It is the 'cosmic powers and authorities' that Christ 'led as captives in his triumphal procession' (Col.2.15). Paul is here drawing upon a mythology which in one form or another belonged to the mental furniture of most men of his time. Man as part of the visible universe was conceived as subject to 'phantom intelligences' (to borrow a term from Thomas Hardy) which limit his freedom and thwart his purposes. (Paul has an extensive and varied vocabulary to describe them; see Rom.8.38; Gal.4.3; Eph.6.12; Col.2.8,15 etc.) We do not readily think in that way. But the mythology stood for something real in human experience: the sense that there are unexplained factors working behind the scenes, whether in the world or in our own 'unconscious', frustrating our best intentions and turning our good to evil (for example, perhaps, perverting the achieve-ments of science into the menace of racial destruction). As Paul saw it, Jesus was in his lifetime in conflict, not only with his ostensible opponents, but with dark forces lurking in the background. To all appearance he was worsted by them. It was, Paul says, 'the (superhuman) powers that rule the world' that crucified him (I Cor.2.8), perverting intended good to evil ends (for neither Pilate nor the priests and Pharisees, at bottom, meant ill, any more than we do). But in the outcome Christ was not defeated. Unclouded goodness prevailed. His resurrection was the pledge of victory over all enemies of the human spirit, for it was victory over death, which Paul personifies as 'the last enemy' (I Cor.15.26); and appropriately enough, since death is the final frustration of all human designs – if that were indeed the end. But we now live in a world where victory has been won in a decisive engagement. 'God be praised !' Paul exclaims. 'He gives us the victory through our Lord Jesus Christ' (I Cor.15.57).

How Christ's victory is also ours will become plainer at the next stage of our inquiry. But for the present we note that the victory was won on the field of history, on which our own 'battle of life' must be fought out. It is for Paul of high significance that Christ lived a truly human life, 'born of a woman, born under the Law' (Gal.4.4 – in other words, he was a man and a Jew). But that does not mean that he is just one more individual thrown up by the historical process. On the contrary, his coming into the world can be seen as a fresh incursion of the Creator into his creation. God, who at the beginning said 'Let there be light', has now given 'the light of the revelation of the glory of God in the face of Jesus Christ' (II Cor.4.6). In the act of creating, according to an influential school of Jewish thinking, it was the (half-personified) divine 'wisdom' that was at work; and Christ himself, Paul says, was 'the wisdom of God' visibly in action among men (I Cor.1.24). The wisdom manifest in creation, said the Jewish thinkers, is 'the flawless mirror of the active power of God and the image of his goodness' (Wisdom of Solomon 7.26); and so Christ, Paul says, is 'the image of the invisible God' (Col.1.15). Indeed, 'in him the complete being of God, by God's own choice, came to dwell' (Col.1.19). In such terms, employing, and indeed straining, the resources of traditional and contemporary language, Paul seeks to bring out the meaning of a new and unprecedented fact – that fact of Christ. Here, then, is one line along which the idea of messiahship is developing into something new. We shall presently observe another such line.

### The people of God

Paul had first encountered Christ in the community of his followers. The voice he heard at his conversion had announced the identity of Jesus with the persecuted church (Acts 9.5; 22.8; 26.14). It is therefore not surprising that he was led from the first to understand the work of Christ, and of God in him, in terms of the community which had arisen out of that work. This was a new historical phenomenon, to be brought into relation with the history of Israel as the field within which the purpose of God was working itself out. The formative motive of that history was the calling into existence of a 'people of God' – a divine commonwealth, we might say – in and through which the will of God might be done on earth, an 'Israel' worth the name. The distinguishing mark of such an 'Israel' Paul found (not without some warrant in the best prophetic teaching) in the promise said to have been made to Abraham, the founder of the Hebrew race, that in his posterity 'all nations shall find blessing' (Gal.3.8). This ideal had never yet been realized, though in successive periods there had been some who had it in them to become such a people, the 'remnant' of which prophets spoke (Rom.9.27; 11.5). In the emergent church of Christ Paul saw the divine commonwealth coming into active existence. 'If you belong to Christ,' he writes, 'you are the issue of Abraham' (Gal.3.29), i.e., you are the true Israel in whom 'all the nations shall find blessing'. Here we have a pointer to one reason, at least, why Paul set such store by his mission to the Gentiles. Thus the church was the consummation of a long, divinely directed, history. It is a theme to which he returns again and again (particularly in the long and intricate discussion in Rom.9–11).

The new, supra-national Israel was constituted solely on the basis of 'belonging to Christ', and not any longer through racial descent or attachment to a particular legal system. 'There is no such thing as Jew and Greek, freeman, slave, male and female; for you are all one person *in Christ Jesus*' (Gal.3.28). That expression 'in Christ' is one which recurs with remarkable frequency throughout the letters of Paul. The doctrine for which it stands is a highly original product of his fertile mind. But the reality of it was present in the church from the beginning. It found its expression in the two rites, or sacraments, of baptism and the 'breaking of bread'. These were practised in the church before ever Paul became a Christian, but he found in them a hitherto unexplored range and depth of meaning.

It was through baptism that a person was incorporated into the community of Christ's followers. In its suggestive ritual, in which the convert was 'buried' by immersion in water, and came out cleansed and renewed, Paul saw a symbolical re-enactment of the death and resurrection of Christ: 'by baptism we were buried with him and lay dead, in order that as Christ was raised from the dead in the splendour of the Father, so also we might set our feet on the new path of life' (Rom.6.4). Baptism therefore affirmed the solidarity of all members of the church with Christ.

So, even more clearly and emphatically, did the other primitive sacrament of the church. From the first, its fellowship had been centred in the solemn 'breaking of bread' at a communal meal. As the bread was broken, they recalled the mysterious words which Jesus had spoken when he broke bread for his disciples at his last supper: 'This is my body' (I Cor.11.23 f.). Reflecting on these words, Paul observed, first, that in sharing bread the company established a corporate unity among themselves: 'We, many as we are, are one body, for it is one loaf of which we all partake' (I Cor.10.17). But not only so; Christ himself had said, 'This is *my* body.' Consequently, 'when we break the bread, it is a means of sharing in the body *of Christ*' (I Cor.10.16). The church therefore is itself the body of Christ; 'he is the head, and on him the whole body depends' (Eph.4.16). It is in this way that the new people of God is constituted, 'in Christ'.

## Life in Christ

In all forms of Jewish messianic belief it was common ground that the Messiah is, in some sense, representative of Israel in its divine calling and destiny. This idea of representation Paul presses further. Those who adhere to Christ in sincere faith are identified with him in a peculiarly intimate way, as if they were indeed included in his own being. He is the *inclusive* representative of the emergent people of God. Another way of putting it is to say that Christ is the 'Adam' of a new humanity, of which the church is the spearhead. In the Jewish schools where Paul had his training there was much speculation about the 'First Adam' (the name is simply the Hebrew word for 'man'), and about the way in which all men, as 'sons of Adam', are involved in his fortunes as depicted mythologically in Genesis. Paul takes up this idea: mankind is incorporate 'in Adam'; an emergent new humanity is incorporate 'in Christ'. 'As in Adam all men die, so in Christ all will be brought to life' (I Cor.15.22, see Rom.5.12–14). Once again we see a fresh expansion of the messianic idea.

This line of thought points to the way in which Paul would understand the whole work of Christ. His action is our action; we are involved in it. 'One man died for all, and therefore all mankind has died. His purpose in dying was that men, while still in life, should cease to live for themselves, and should live for him who for their sake died and was raised to life' (II Cor.5.14 f.). In other words, the displacement of self from the centre is indeed a kind of death, but a death which leads into a new kind of life; and this displacement is already effected when a man adheres to Christ by faith. For he is then identified with him in his living and dying, and the reality and power of Christ's moral achievement are communicated to him: 'In dying as he died, he died to sin, once for all, and in living as he lives, he lives to God. In the same way you must regard yourselves as dead to sin and alive to God' (Rom.6.10 f.). What this meant to Paul person-

179

ally we may learn from some words he wrote to the Galatians: 'The life I now live is not my life, but the life that Christ lives in me; and my present bodily life is lived by faith in the Son of God who loved me and gave himself up for me' (Gal.2.20). The deep feeling that comes out in this and other similar passages should satisfy us that all he says about the solidarity of the church with Christ is not mere theological theory-spinning. He is speaking about what he knows in himself with immediate certainty.

### Problems of the church

On one side, then, life 'in Christ' is a deeply personal and inward experience. But Paul also drew from it principles of fruitful application to the church as a society living in the world. The period during which his letters were written saw an immense expansion of the Christian community. Largely through his own enterprise it spread, geographically, over a remarkably large area, at a surprisingly rapid pace. The very rapidity of the advance brought him problems.

The enthusiasm which his mission aroused had sometimes disconcerting effects. It acted as a stimulant to the innate individualism of the Greek genius, and led to rivalry and competition. Parties were formed, each party boasting the eminence of its chosen leader and depreciating his rivals (I Cor.1.10–12). The unity of the church was seriously threatened. To anyone acquainted with the history of the ancient Greek city-states it is all sadly familiar. They had been torn with chronic faction, which in the end cost them their independence. Paul saw the Christian community in a like danger. That the church, as the new 'Israel of God', is in its essential nature one was for Paul axiomatic, and

this unity, he held, should be reflected in the life of each of its local congregations. He was dismayed to see it being disrupted.

Apart from the tendency to factiousness endemic in Greek society, there were two problems special to the church as such. The first resulted from the persisting influence, in the minds of converts, of ideas and practices – they might be Jewish or they might be pagan – which they had so recently disavowed. Some grew out of them quickly, others more hesitantly, with the result that different levels of opinion and practice became marked. The other problem was incidental to the fact that the community had as yet no agreed body of belief or doctrine, beyond a few very simple and fundamental convictions. Yet the new way of life demanded intellectual expression adequate to its real significance. Adventurous minds experimented with ideas, with an intellectual agility which again is typically Greek. In itself this was healthy enough; it was the way in which a Christian philosophy was hammered out over the years. Paul's own mind was as adventurous as anybody's. But for Christians of less maturity, extravagance and eccentricity lay in wait. Here again was a threat to the unity of the church.

In so far as the problem was an intellectual one, he attacked it positively by developing the implications of faith in Christ along lines which met the questions that were actually being agitated. It is indeed largely in reaction to what he regarded as unfortunate experiments in answering such questions that his own theology was built up. Some of the practical problems he attacked in detail and *ad hoc*. He discusses, for example, divergences among Christians about the continued observance of Jewish holy days and food regulations (Rom.14), and, on the other side, about the extent to which they might share in the social life of their pagan neighbours without sacrifice of principle (I Cor. 8.1–13; 10.18–33).

But apart from such special discussions Paul sought to undercut the whole threat to unity by insisting on the idea of the church as a body, analogous to a living organism, in which the parts, while endlessly various, are interdependent and subordinate to one another, and each makes its indispensable contribution to the well-being of the whole. There is a passage in his First Letter to the Corinthians (12.14–27) which is a classical statement of the idea of the social organism. The idea in itself was no novelty in Greek thinking. But in Paul's hands it takes an original turn, because he develops it in relation to his governing conception of the church as the body *of Christ*. In all its members, however various their endowments and functions, it is Christ who is at work, and God in Christ, through his Spirit pervading the body. 'There are varieties of gifts, but the same Spirit. There are varieties of service, but the same Lord. There are many forms of work, but all of them, in all men, are the work of the same God' (I Cor.12.4–11). So he writes, and there follows a list of such 'services' and 'forms of work' – a list which can be supplemented out of similar lists in other letters (Rom.12.6–8; Eph.4.11 f.). We can see how manifold and complex the activities of the Christian society had already become. If its unity was to be preserved, the various talents thus brought out must be accepted as the means by which Christ's members were equipped to be the channels of his own life in his body, and the temptation must be resisted of regarding them as claims to distinction for those who possessed them.

## The Spirit in the church

It is in this setting that Paul develops his doctrine of the Spirit, which again is one of his most original contributions to Christian thought. It was indeed an innovation, and one of considerable consequence, but it was an innovation rooted in what he had taken over from his Jewish background and from the first Christians. In some forms of Jewish messianic expectation it was held that in 'the days of the Messiah', or in 'the age to come', the divine Spirit, which was believed to have animated the prophets and heroes of Israel's remoter past, would be 'poured out' afresh, and in larger measure (Acts 2.16–18). The early followers of Jesus, when the realization broke upon them that he had risen from the dead, experienced an almost intoxicating sense of new life and power. It was accompanied, as often happens in times of religious 'revival', by abnormal psychical phenomena – visions, the hearing of voices, ecstatic utterance ('speaking with tongues'), and the like. The early Christians valued these as evident signs that God was at work among them through his Spirit.

These abnormal phenomena reproduced themselves in the new Christian communities which sprang from Paul's mission to the Gentiles, and here they created an excited atmosphere which he saw to be full of danger. The situation needed delicate handling. Paul did not wish to damp down the enthusiasm of which these strange powers were one expression (I Thess.5.19–21). Nor indeed did he wish to deny that they could be the outcome of genuine inspiration. He knew what it was himself to have visions and hear voices (II Cor.12.1–4), and he could (so he tells his correspondents) 'speak with tongues' (I

Cor.14.18). But there were other 'gifts of the Spirit', less showy, but in the end far more important to the community, such as wisdom, insight, powers of leadership, the teacher's gift, a gift for administration, and even such apparently humdrum qualities as those which enable a person to give effective assistance to others who are in need or distress (see Rom.12.6–8; I Cor.12.28). These are gifts which 'build up' the community (I Cor.14.12; the old translation, 'edify', here and in many similar places, is now misleading, for 'edification' in current speech means something different from what Paul had in mind). Paul has thus diverted attention from the abnormal and exceptional to such moral and intellectual endowments as any society would wish to find among its members. It is the devotion of such endowments to the common good that gives them real value.

The principle thus established is obviously of wide application. Paul's congregations were not unique as communities threatened with disruption because individuals exploited their abilities and privileges for their personal advancement. But in applying it within the Christian church he had a powerful leverage for attacking the evil. Those to whom he wrote were right at least in attributing the powers or abilities of which they were conscious to the work of God through his Spirit. They were in no sense achievements of their own. They were, strictly, 'gifts' (the word Paul uses is a strong one, meaning something like 'grace-and-favour gifts', the sheer, unmerited bounty of the Creator). Give this full value, and it goes very far towards correcting the false attitude to which these people were inclined. 'What do you possess,' he asks, 'which was not given you ? If then you really received it all as a gift, why take credit to yourselves ?' (I Cor.4.7).

But Paul was able to take the matter a good deal further than that. If, as he holds, the church is truly the body of Christ, then it follows that all the various activities by which the body is built up are the work of Christ himself in his 'members' (the limbs and organs of his body). Any gifts which they are able to devote to that end are indeed gifts of the Spirit, and they are the work of God, but, more immediately, they are the gifts of Christ to his church (this is set forth at length in Eph.4.4–16; note especially vv. 7, 11 f., 16). The expressions, 'Spirit of God', 'Spirit of Christ', 'Christ dwelling in you', can be used as if they were, for practical purposes, equivalent (Rom.8.9 f.; a similar equivalence is implied in I Cor.12.4–6).

This meant a re-thinking of the whole idea of the Spirit and 'gifts of the Spirit'. The Spirit is no longer to be thought of as some kind of impersonal force acting on a man to produce astonishing effects. It is now to be recognized as the mode in which Christ himself is personally present in his church, inspiring and directing his members and shaping the whole body to his own pattern.

## The law of the Spirit

This truly original concept of the Spirit as the mode of Christ's own presence in his church opens up a new approach to ethics. Here Paul found himself obliged to meet a formidable challenge to his whole position. It was central to his message that the Christian man is free from the 'bondage' of the law, since Christ 'annulled the law with its rules and regulations' (Eph.2.15). This kind of language ran the risk of being misunderstood. His Jewish critics, outside and inside the church, suspected that in sweeping away the discipline of the Mosaic Law he was leaving his Gentile converts without moral anchorage in a licentious environment. Paul perhaps scarcely realized at first how open to misconstruction his language was. He soon discovered that he was widely understood to be advocating a purely 'permissive' morality, which was in fact far from his intention. People were saying, 'We are free to do anything' (I Cor.6.12; 10.23), in the belief that they were echoing his own sentiments. And the trouble was that he could not flatly deny what they were saying. He could point out that there were some obvious limitations on freedom: '"We are free to do anything," you say. Yes, but not everything is for our good. "We are free to do anything," you say; but does everything help to build up the community' (I Cor.10.23)? And again, 'You were called to be free men, only do not turn your liberty to licence for your lower nature' (Gal.5.13). But the matter called for more radical treatment.

On the central point he made no concession: Christian morality is not conformity to an external code; it springs from an inward source. 'Let your minds be remade,' he writes, 'and your whole nature transformed; then you will be able to discern the will of God, and to know what is good, acceptable, and perfect' (Rom.12.2). This transformation is effected by the work of the Spirit within, and here is the true source of Christian character and action: 'The *harvest* of the Spirit is love, joy, peace, patience, kindness, goodness, fidelity, and self-control. There is no law dealing with such things as these' (Gal.5.22 f.). The church is under a 'new covenant', which is not, like the 'old covenant', guaranteed by a code of commands and prohibitions 'engraved letter by letter upon stone' (II Cor.3.7), but by the Spirit animating the whole body of the church.

Then is the Spirit simply an 'inner light', and, if so, how am I to distinguish the promptings of the Holy Spirit from the promptings of my own spirit, which may be far from holy? Paul's answer to this question is found by drawing the full logical consequences of his doctrine that the Spirit of the church is the Spirit *of Christ* working in the members of his body. 'Christ dwelling within you' is no other than the Christ who lived and taught, died and rose again. Christians who have received the Gospel and the teaching that went with it are in a position to know what is 'Christlike' in character and conduct, and this is an objective standard by which all inner promptings may be brought to the test. It may even be described as 'the law of Christ' (Gal.6.2; I Cor.9.21). Paul is indeed cautious of using such quasi-legal language; he would not like to be thought to be introducing a kind of new Christian legalism. But he does mean that the norm of what is 'Christlike' is no less objective, and no less binding, than any written code could be. The 'law of Christ', and the 'life-giving law of the Spirit' (Rom.8.2) are not two things but one; apprehended inwardly, but essentially *given* by an authority beyond ourselves. To 'let your minds be remade' (Rom.12.2) is, ultimately, to 'possess the mind of Christ' (I Cor.2.16). Sometimes Paul speaks as if this reshaping of the mind took place all at once when a man became a Christian, but there are sufficient passages in his letters to show him fully aware that the process might be a gradual, and a long one (e.g., Gal.4.19; Eph.4.13, and, reflecting directly his own experience, I Cor. 9.26 f.), a process, even, possibly never completed in this life (Phil.3.12–14). But when once the process is genuinely afoot, a man is 'under the law of Christ', and Christ himself – not the man's own ideas or ideals, not even in the end, his conscience – is the judge to whom he defers in all his actions (I Cor.4.3 f.).

## The law of Christ

The law of Christ, then, is no other than Christ himself working through his Spirit in the church to give ethical direction. And it is *all* that we know of Christ that comes into it – his teaching, the example of his actions, and the impact of his death and resurrection. To illustrate this, it will be worthwhile to look rather closely at one passage where Paul is dealing in a practical way with delicate questions on which there were acute differences within the church – the long discussion in Rom.14.1–15.6 about the observance of holy days and dietary rules. First, the careful reader will be reminded time and again of sayings of Jesus known to us from the Gospels, though none are quoted verbally. They may be listed as follows:

|  | *Romans* | *Gospels* |
| --- | --- | --- |
| on judging others | 14.4, 10, 13a | Matt.7.1 f. |
| on 'stumbling-blocks' | 14.13b, 21 | Mark 9.42, see Matt.18.7 |
| on 'clean' and 'unclean' | 14.14 | Mark 7.15,19 |

What is important here is not the verbal echoes, but the way in which the teaching of Jesus has lodged so deeply in Paul's mind as to establish a standard and a point of view which has become truly his own. Secondly, he appeals to the *example* of Christ: 'Each of us must consider his neighbour and think what is for his good . . . for Christ did not consider himself' (Rom. 15.2 f.). There is no Gospel text that could be cited for this, but it seizes upon what was clearly central to the whole ministry of Jesus as the Gospels present it. And indeed the entire discussion, which is an application of the principle that the Christian should 'receive', or 'accept', people whom he might be tempted to reject, 'as Christ accepted us' (Rom.14.1; 15.7), recaptures the theme which is so prominent in the Gospels: how Jesus received 'little ones' (children, of course, in the Gospels, but to Paul it suggested the spiritually immature), and, still more, how he received 'publicans and sinners'. And finally, he appeals to the meaning and effect of Christ's death and resurrection: 'No one of us lives, and equally no one of us dies, for himself alone . . . Whether we live or die we belong to the Lord. That is why Christ died and came to life again' (Rom.14.7–9; the connection of thought may be illuminated from II Cor.5.14 f.). In sum, then, the teaching of Jesus, the example of his life, the impact of his death, have acted as influences on Paul's thought, not as from outside, but creatively from within. His ethical judgments are informed by the Spirit of Christ, and yet are intimately his own. That is why the law of Christ, while it commands him absolutely, can never be felt as a 'bondage', like the old law 'with its rules and regulations', but 'where the Spirit of the Lord is, there is liberty' (II Cor.3.17).

From this point of view, Paul's ethical teaching is the application, to actual situations, of what it means to be 'Christlike'. He himself, he says, follows the example of Christ in 'regarding not my own good but the good of the many' (I Cor.10.33–11.1), and he would have his converts do the same. They are to imitate the 'gentleness and magnanimity of Christ' (II Cor.10.1), his 'steadfastness' (II Thess.3.5), his readiness to forgive (Eph.4.32; Col.3.13), his humility and his unreserved 'obedience' to the will of God (Rom.5.19, etc.), even at the cost of his life (Phil.2.8). His death is the commanding example of self-sacrifice for the sake of others (Gal.2.20; Eph.5.2, 25), and it was the expression of his limitless love for men (Rom.8.34 f.; Gal.2.20; Eph.3.18 f., etc.).

It is this quality of love, above all, that Paul holds up as the essence of what it means to be 'Christlike', and as the basic and all-inclusive principle of Christian living (Rom.13.8–10; Gal.5.14; Col.3.14; Eph.1.4, etc.). The word he uses is the almost untranslatable Greek *agape*, a word first brought into common use in a Christian setting. We can hardly do other than translate it 'love' (unless we follow the older rendering 'charity'), but in doing so we have to think away the flavour of sentiment or facile emotion that tends to cling to the word in our common usage. *Agape* certainly includes feelings of affection (Rom.12.9 f.), but basically it is an energy of goodwill going out towards other people, regardless of their merit, or worthiness, or attractiveness. The eloquent passage in I Cor.13, which has the aspect of a hymn in praise of *agape*, contains pointers to the kind of attitude and behaviour it inspires, and in this context it is presented as the highest of all 'gifts of the Spirit' (I Cor.12.31; 14.1). Once again, the 'law of the Spirit' and the 'law of Christ' are indistinguishable.

## Social ethics

*Agape*, then, is the source of the distinctively Christian virtues and graces of character. It is also the constructive principle in society: 'It is love that builds' (I Cor.8.1). Thus the ideas of the building of the body and the centrality of love imply one another, and form the effective basis for Paul's teaching on social ethics. The whole of Christian behaviour can be summed up in the maxim, 'Love one another as Christ loved you' (Eph.5.1; see also Gal.5.13 f.; I Thess.4.9; Col.3.14).

This does not, however, mean that Paul is content to say, 'Love and do as you please.' Nor, on the other hand, does he undertake to show how detailed rules of behaviour could be derived deductively from a single master-principle (which was the method favoured by Greek moralists). Ethical behaviour is essentially a man's response to actual situations in which he finds himself in day-to-day living as a member of society. Paul envisages his readers in their actual situation, not in just any society, but in this particular society in which their daily life must be lived, namely the Graeco-Roman world, which Paul knew so well, with its specific institutions, political, legal and economic and the rest, and within that world the young Christian communities with their distinctive ethos and their special problems. He casts his eye over the scene and indicates, by way of selected examples rather than exhaustively, and always in concrete terms, how this whole network of relations may be permeated with the Christian quality of living.

On one side of it, indeed, he sees pagan society as so deeply corrupted that the Christian can do nothing but repudiate it root and branch. Of this side he has drawn a sombre picture, possibly with some rhetorical over-emphasis, in Rom.1.18–32 (see also Gal.5.19–21; Eph.5.3–5; Col.3.5, etc.). How close these immature Christians stood to the corruptions of paganism, and how easily they could relapse into them, we can gather from some startling remarks which he lets fall about his converts (e.g., I Cor.5.1 f., 11; 6.8–10; Col.3.5–7; I Thess.4.3–8), as well as from the passion with which he insists that there must be a complete and final break with the past (Col.3.5–10). So alarmed was he at the possibility of infection that he sometimes speaks as if the only way of safety was for the church to turn in upon itself and withdraw from pagan society altogether (II Cor.6.14–18); but he had to explain that this was not his real intention: the idea that Christians should avoid dangerous contacts by 'getting right out of the world' he dismisses as absurd (I Cor.5.9–13); and in fact it is clear that he contemplated Christians living on terms of normal social intercourse with their pagan neighbours (I Cor.10.27 f.). Their task is the more difficult one of living as full members of the society in which their lot is cast, while firmly renouncing its corruptions.

There was in truth another side to Graeco-Roman civilization. Deeply corrupted it might be, but nevertheless it was not without moral ideals. A certain standard of what was 'fitting' was widely accepted, at least in theory. The Stoics spoke of it as 'the general feeling of mankind' (*communis sensus hominum*). And up to a point there was a genuine desire to see this standard observed in corporate life. Paul was well aware of this, as he shows when he enjoins his readers, 'Let your aims be such as *all* men count honourable' (Rom.12.17). Even after his fierce castigation of pagan vices at the beginning of his Letter to the Romans he goes on to say that the good pagan may do God's will 'by the light of nature'; his conscience bears true witness (Rom.2.14 f.). And there is a broad universality about what he writes to the Philippians: 'All that is true, all that is noble, all that is just and pure, all that is lovable and gracious, whatever is excellent and admirable – fill all your thoughts with these things' (Phil.4.8). The language would seem to be deliberately chosen to suggest that such worthy themes for contemplation are to be sought and found over the widest field possible, in the church or out of it.

It is thus not surprising that Paul is content to work out his sketch (it is hardly more) of Christian behaviour within the framework of Graeco-Roman society as it actually existed. The empire itself is for him part of the divinely given setting for a Christian's life in the world, and he will be following the law of Christ in obeying the Roman law, respecting the magistrates, and paying his taxes. This is 'an obligation imposed not merely by fear of retribution but by conscience'. In fact, fulfilment of such obligations is an application of the maxim, 'Love your neighbour as yourself' (Rom.13.1–10).

Similarly, in dealing with family life he takes over a general scheme current among moralists at the time (it is found especially in Stoic writers), which assumes the existing structure of the Graeco-Roman household, with the *paterfamilias* as the responsible head, and the other members, including the slaves, having their respective obligations (Eph.5.21–6.9; Col.3.18–4.1), and indicates how within this general structure Christian principles can be applied and Christian motives find scope.

His earliest treatment of family life and its obligations in I Cor.7, is largely tentative. He is feeling his way through a tangle of discordant views and practices, and 'giving his judgment' as best he can (I Cor.7.25). The whole discussion is biased by the belief he then entertained that 'the time we live in will not last long' (I Cor.7.29); everything therefore is provisional. In spite of this, we can see how Christian principles and motives are beginning to remould the pattern. That marriage is indissoluble for Christians he knows because there is a saying of the Lord to that effect (I Cor.7.10 f.; see Mark 10.2–9). Beyond that he can only give his honest opinion, guided, as he believes, by the Spirit (I Cor.7.12, 25, 40). In Christ there is neither male nor female (Gal.3.28), and therefore, although the husband is inevitably the head of the household, the marriage relation itself must be completely mutual as between husband and wife: 'The wife cannot claim her body as her own; it is her husband's. Equally, the husband cannot claim his body as his own; it is his wife's' (I Cor.7.4). So sacred is the bond that in a mixed marriage the heathen husband is 'holy', i.e., belongs to God, through his Christian wife, and the heathen wife through her Christian husband, and the children of such a marriage are 'holy', i.e., 'belong to God' (I Cor.7.14). The implication is that the natural ties of family relationship are valid within the Christian fellowship which is 'the body of Christ'. Thus, although Paul feels that 'in a time of stress like the present' married life is strictly an irrelevance (I Cor.7.26–29), the idea of the Christian family is beginning to push through. By the time he wrote to the Colossians he had fully accepted the principle that the family should be a part of life 'in Christ', though the brief hints given here of its distinctive character are meagre enough (Col.3.18–21). In the Letter to the Ephesians (if we may take that as representing his mature thought), he sets forth a high Christian ideal of marriage in which a man's love for his wife is an image of the sacrificial love of Christ, who 'loved the church and gave himself up for it' (Eph.5.25–33).

The Graeco-Roman household included the slaves, and here again we can see Christian principles and motives making their way. It is fundamental that in Christ there is neither slave nor free man (Gal.3.28; Col.3.11). Accordingly, there is a level on which their status is equal: 'The man who as a slave received the call to be a Christian is the Lord's freedman, and, equally, the free man who received the call is a slave in the service of Christ' (I Cor.7.22). In writing to the Colossians he urges slaves to give their service 'as if you were doing it for the Lord and not for men ... Christ is the Master whose slaves you must be'; and then he adds, 'Masters, be fair and just to your slaves, knowing that you too have a Master in heaven' (Col.3.23 f.; 4.1; see also Eph.6.5–9). The ideal of free mutual service transcends the legal relations of master and slave. As it happens, we have a letter, the short note addressed to Philemon, in which Paul deals with a particular case. Philemon's slave Onesimus had run away, having, apparently, helped himself from his master's cash-box. Somehow or other Paul came across him, and he was converted to the Christian faith. What was Paul to do? Under Roman law anyone harbouring a fugitive slave was liable to severe penalties, and a runaway recovered by his master could expect no mercy. Paul decided to send Onesimus back to his master, gambling everything on Philemon's readiness to take a fully Christian view of the matter. 'Perhaps this is why you lost him for a time,' he writes, 'that you might have him back for good, no longer as a slave, but as more than a slave, as a dear brother' (Philemon 12–16). The 'law of Christ', without disrupting the civil order, is transforming it from within.

## Christ, the church, and the future

The permeation of the church, and ultimately of society, with the Christian quality of life gives actuality to Paul's doctrine of the indwelling of Christ, through the Spirit, in the body of his followers. This is seen to be no longer a bare theory, or, on the other hand, merely the inward experience of an individual. It is a force working in history. But if Christ is thus present in the church, then he is to be known not only through his historical life, supremely important as that is, but also in what he is doing in and through the church in the present, and in the future into which the present dissolves at every moment. His brief career on earth had ended, so far as the world in general could see, in failure. His disciples knew better. But how was the world to know ? For many early Christians a sufficient answer to this question was that very shortly he would 'come again', and then 'every eye shall see him' (Rev.1.7). Paul began by sharing this belief. At the time when he wrote his earliest surviving letters (as they probably are), those to the Thessalonians, although he was concerned to damp down exaggerated expectations of an *immediate* 'second advent' (II Thess.2.1–3), he seems to have had no doubt that he and most Christians would live to see it (I Thess.4.15). Even when he wrote his First Letter to the Corinthians he was still assured that 'we shall not *all* die' (I Cor.15.51). Before he wrote the Second Letter there was an occasion when his life was despaired of (II Cor.1.9), and it may be that for the first time he faced the likelihood that he would die before the Day, and in that way 'go to live with the Lord' (II Cor.5.8). At any rate, from this time we hear little more of the urgent, even impatient, expectation of earlier years.

He came to be less preoccupied with a supposedly imminent 'second advent', as he explored the range of Christ's *present* activity in the church. He saw the church expanding its influence abroad, and developing internally the complexity that marks the evolution of a living organism. If all this raised some problems, it was all part of the growth of the body – of Christ's body – and it was Christ's own work. 'It is from the Head that the whole body, with all its joints and ligaments, receives its supplies, and thus knit together grows according to God's design' (Col.2.19, cf. Eph.4.16). This, as he now saw it, is the way in which Christ is revealed to the whole universe (Eph.3.10). Nor is there any limit to this growth, 'until we all at last attain to the unity inherent in our faith' (Eph.4.13). In the church Paul saw men actually being drawn into unity across the barriers erected by differences of race or national tradition, language, culture, or social status. Naturally enough (since he had been personally involved) he was most powerfully impressed by the reconciliation of Jew and Gentile in the fellowship of the church (Eph.2.11–22). In this, as his horizons widened, he saw the promise of a larger unity, embracing all mankind (Rom.11.25–32). In this unity of mankind, moreover, he finds the sign and pledge of God's purpose for his whole creation. In a passage which has much of the visionary quality of poetry or prophecy, he pictures the whole universe waiting 'in eager expectation' for the day when it shall 'enter upon the liberty and splendour of the children of God' (Rom. 8.19–21). In the church, therefore, can be discerned God's ultimate design 'to reconcile the whole universe to himself . . . to reconcile all things, whether on earth or in heaven, through Christ alone' (Col.1.20, cf. Eph.1.10). Such is the vision of the future which in the end Paul bequeathed to the church for its inspiration.

C.H. DODD

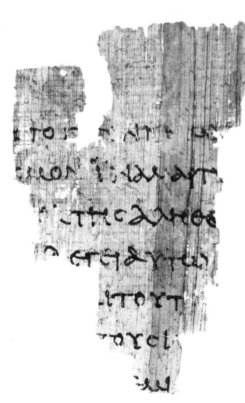

# 12  The Gospel According to John

There is far more to the Gospel of John than appears at first sight. Its simplicity of expression, its short sentences and limited vocabulary are deceptive. To penetrate its thought a certain sophistication is needed, and an appreciation of the symbolic use of language. Thus the mighty works of Jesus (miracles such as the feeding of the five thousand or the healing of a blind man) are here signs embodying spiritual truths. Much of the Gospel consists of discourses attributed to Jesus, and the movement of a discourse can depend upon the deliberate use of a phrase with a double meaning: in the conversation with Nicodemus, 'born afresh' or 'born from above' (3.3); to the woman of Samaria, 'running water' or 'living water' (4.10); speaking of his own destiny, 'elevated vertically from the earth (on the cross)' or 'exalted from earth (to heaven)' (12.32 f.). The surprising fact that this Gospel does not contain a single parable of the Synoptic type probably means that the evangelist regarded all Jesus' utterances as parabolic (16.25). Moreover, he can write on more levels than one at the same time. For instance, is the reconstituted temple (2.19 ff.) the risen body of Jesus, or the body of Christ the church, or both ?

The Gospel of John also demands to be taken as a whole and in its own right; it is not to be used piecemeal to supplement, or to fill up supposed gaps in a Synoptic narrative. For, although the discourses may each have been constructed separately and then brought together (and perhaps added to by a later

hand), and although certain breaks in the narrative have led some scholars to the view that there are sections which are not in their original order, the Gospel even as it now stands is a far more unified structure than any of the Synoptic Gospels, and it must be allowed to tell its own story in its own way. The form-critical method of separating out originally independent paragraphs, and then considering them on the background of the oral tradition of the church through which they came to the evangelists, works for this Gospel only to a limited degree and with limited results. Thus, here, the feeding of the five thousand is no longer a separate episode standing on its own feet, but is the occasion for a discourse upon the bread of life. Even such a Synoptic-sounding and probably originally independent saying as 'He who loves his life shall lose it' (12.25) is now part and parcel of a discourse for the Greeks on the death of Jesus, and is inseparable from that context. The immediate background of this Gospel is not the oral tradition, but the highly distinctive type of Christianity reflected in the Epistles of John (whether or not these are by the same author as the Gospel), and Jesus utters throughout the thought and language of that type of Christianity. This gives the Gospel its unity and coherence, even at times its monotony, as does also the 'cyclic' method of writing characteristic of I John. The author introduces a subject, develops it, moves around it, and in doing so picks up something from a previous subject. For instance, the raising of Lazarus (11.1 ff.), with its climax, 'Lazarus, come forth', refers back to the saying in 5.25: 'The hour is coming, and now is, when the dead shall hear the voice of the Son of God, and those who hear shall live.'

## Authorship and date

Where the Gospel and its author are to be located in the spectrum of early Christianity, and at what place and date it was written are questions which do not admit of definite answers. The origin of the ascription of the work to a 'John' is unknown. There is evidence to suggest that the author may have stood closer than was later thought desirable to some form of that spiritual movement of 'salvation through knowledge' called Gnosticism with which the churches were in conflict in the second century. Thus it is in Gnostic circles that we first know of the Gospel being used. The first commentator on it was a Gnostic named Heracleon (*c*.160). In the second century there were some 'orthodox' who bitterly attacked it and rejected it.

It is the theologian Irenaeus (*c*.185) who makes the identification of the author with the beloved disciple, the apostle John, the son of Zebedee, resident at Ephesus to old age. This identification, while never proved to be impossible, is now generally rejected, chiefly on the grounds that apostolic authorship conflicts with, rather than illuminates, the particular character of this Gospel, and that it is hardly consistent with the early opposition to it in the church. The mysterious, unnamed 'disciple whom Jesus loved' is said to be the author in a note appended by a later hand (21.24), but in 19.35 he is referred to by the author as someone other than himself. In view of these and other difficulties most modern scholars

have abandoned the search for the author's identity, and prefer to concentrate on the Gospel itself as indicating what kind of person he was. Ephesus as the place of origin rests on the same evidence of Irenaeus; other suggestions have been Alexandria, in view of the character of the Gospel's thought, and Syria, in view of similarities to that thought in writers like Ignatius of Antioch. Papyrus fragments of the Gospel belonging to the early part of the second century fix the latest time for composition at about the turn of the first century; there are no indications of a more precise date.

## The structure of the Gospel

While there is plenty of room for dispute over details there would seem to be a general plan, which might perhaps be compared to that of a great cathedral.

1. The approach to the cathedral through west front and portico is by way of a double introduction; first the religio-philosophical prologue (1.1–18), and then a prologue of a more traditional kind (1.19–51).

2. This opens into the nave with its pillars, which is the public ministry of signs and discourses, marked at one end by, 'This, the first of his signs . . .' (2.11), and at the other by, 'Though he had done so many signs before them, yet they did not believe in him' (12.37), and by quotations from Isaiah to characterize this ministry as one of rejection.

3. This is followed by the choir narrowing towards the sanctuary, which consists of a single discourse of Jesus in private to 'his own' issuing in a prayer of Jesus to the Father in their presence (13.1–16.33; 17).

4. This in turn leads into the sanctuary proper, which is the narratives of the passion

191

and resurrection (chs. 18–21).

### 1. *The prologue (1.1–18)*

Unique in the New Testament in form and to some extent in content is a rhythmical composition, either from the author's own hand or taken over by him and interpolated by him with the two prose passages (1.6 f., 15) which are designed to underline the subordinate position of John the Baptist and his function as witness. While the key title 'the Logos' (Word) does not recur outside the prologue, the predicates of the Logos in the prologue – life, light, flesh, glory, only-begotten (Son) – provide principal terms for the portrayal of Jesus in the rest of the Gospel. The two divisions of the Gospel, at chs. 2–12 and chs. 13–17, may be said to be explications of two statements in the prologue, 'He came to his own home, and his own people received him not' (1.11), and 'But to all who received him, who believed in his name, he gave power to become children of God' (1.12). Thus the prologue is an overture, which in pregnant language places the works and words of Jesus in their widest cosmic setting as the revelation in action of the eternal relationship between the Father and the Son, between God and the creative Word. The second prologue (1.19–51) also emphasizes the subordinate position of John the Baptist – here and elsewhere the evangelist may be opposing claims of John's disciples current in his own day. John the Baptist bears witness both negatively by what he says that he is not, and positively by what he says Jesus is, namely the Lamb of God. This leads to a gathering by Jesus of personal followers, two being from among John the Baptist's disciples, and these make various (inadequate) professions of faith in terms of 'Rabbi', 'Messiah', 'Son of God', 'King of Israel', the climax being reached when Jesus refers to himself in terms of 'the Son of man' who spans heaven and earth.

### 2. *The public ministry (2.11–12.37)*

The public ministry is made up largely of signs and discourses. C. H. Dodd calls it the 'Book of Signs'. Rudolf Bultmann detects two separate sources, a 'Signs'-source and a 'Discourse-source', but the two elements appear to be too closely connected for that. The signs may be reckoned as six in number, three located in Galilee (water into wine, the nobleman's son, the feeding of the five thousand), and three in or near Jerusalem (the lame man, the blind man, the raising of Lazarus). Only the former are specifically called 'signs', but the latter also establish the reputation of Jesus as a performer of signs (9.16). By the use of the word 'sign', and by the way he uses the signs, the author indicates that he has made a selection of those actions which for him were the most significant because in their outward and physical circumstances they served as the clearest pointers to what in Christian experience believers had come to see Jesus to be and his gifts to be. This is evident when a sign gives rise to an interpretative discourse. For instance, the healing of the lame man on a sabbath day (5.1–47) signifies that Jesus is the Son who shares with the Father his continuing sabbath 'work', and who exercises by delegation the divine prerogatives of conferring eternal life on men and of judging them. Again the feeding of the multitude (6.1–65) signifies that Jesus as the Son of man both gives and is himself the heavenly manna, the living bread of God. So also the cure of the blind man (9.1–41) signifies that Jesus is the light of the world which both illuminates human life and exposes it for what it is. But sign and discourse can be related in a different way. Thus the first sign at Cana and the cleansing of the temple which follows (2.1–22) stand on their own, but they presage symbolically the new order of existence in the Christian gospel over against the Jewish dispensation, and these are themes which are taken up in the discourse with Nicodemus (3.1–21), a representative of Judaism, on the new birth of the Spirit to which the heavenly Son of man on earth testifies, and in the discourse with the heretical Samaritan woman (4.1–42) on the true and spiritual worship of God which is imminent through the Messiah who is the Saviour of the world.

How the discourses, which are without real parallel in the Synoptic Gospels, came into being is a difficult question to answer. They fall roughly into two classes.

(a) *Dialogues with individuals or a group*

In these dialogues Jesus introduces a theme by a paradoxical statement which is misunderstood by being taken literally; he then repeats the essence of the statement and elaborates the theme until it comes to rest in what he gives and who he is (chs. 3; 4; 6; 11). Sometimes the other persons fade into the background, and the dialogue becomes a monologue.

(b) *Dialogues with the Jews and their official representatives*

These (chs. 5; 7–10) can also contain a misunderstood saying, but more often they are bitter controversies over the claims and status of Jesus arising out of his actions and words. They concern Jewish themes such as the sabbath, the Messiah, etc., and can include arguments which assume a Rabbinic method of interpreting Old Testament texts (7.23; 8.17; 10.34). It is these discourses which are principally responsible for the strong anti-Jewish flavour of this Gospel, in which 'the Jews' are constantly referred to without further discrimination as a single body and as the stock opponents both of Jesus and of the church (chs. 9–10).

What also orientates the Gospel in a Jewish direction is that the notes of time are largely provided by references to the feasts of the Jewish calendar (Passover, 2.13; 6.4; 11.55; an unnamed feast, 5.1; Tabernacles, 7.2; Dedication, 10.22). In some cases (e.g., chs. 6; 7; 10) part of the subject matter of the discourse corresponds with the special theme or commemoration belonging to the feast. Aileen Guilding has argued that this arises out of the special Old Testament lections prescribed for the feast. The discourses may thus be the results of a process of preaching, teaching and homily within that type of Christianity which the evangelist represents, and have been designed to present Christ as the fulfilment of the Jewish religion in its inner and deepest sense. In this way various themes are worked out. The 'glory' of Jesus as the revelation of the Father is displayed; the light is shown shining in the darkness and rejected but not overcome by it; the actions, words and person of Jesus give rise to belief or unbelief, and his ministry is the occasion of *krisis* in its double meaning of judgment and sifting by decision.

### 3. *The private discourse (13.1 to 16.33 and ch. 17)*

The foot-washing, which is both a powerful symbol of the death and resurrection of Jesus on behalf of his disciples and also a lesson to them of service, introduces a single esoteric discourse to an inner circle. This is distinctive in tone and content even in this Gospel, and it may have been shaped more by Greek models of the intercourse between a great teacher and his intimates. Speaking in full knowledge of his origin and destiny (13.1 ff.), and as it were from the further side of his death and resurrection, Jesus unfolds their inner meaning and their consequences for the believers. The fact that some of the themes occur first in chs. 13–14 and then recur in chs. 15–16 – e.g., the commandment of love, the necessity of abiding in Jesus as Jesus abides in the Father and of observing his commandments, prayer, the Paraclete, 'a little while', the defeat of the prince of this world, peace, the denial of Jesus by disciples – has led to the suggestion that two versions of the same discourse have been combined. Some of the subjects treated – e.g., warnings of persecution, of Jesus' departure, promises of divine assistance, the mission to the world – are in some measure parallel to what is found in the Synoptic Gospels, especially in the farewell speech in Mark 13, but they have been transposed into the Johannine idiom. What in the Synoptics belongs to the imminent future end of the age is here drawn into the present state of the indwelling of Jesus in the disciples through the Paraclete by virtue of his departure to the Father. The principal theme is that of love. This is all summed up in a last will and testament in the form of prayer, which is part declaratory of what Jesus has accomplished, and is part a petition in that he prays that the disciples and their converts may be maintained and perfected in the divine unity and truth through the efficacy of his own perfected work and self-consecration.

### 4. *Passion and resurrection (chs. 18–21)*

Though inevitably covering some of the same ground as the Synoptics, the passion narrative is distinctive, and is highly dramatic. It is the first 'passion play'. It has a scenario in the form of the praetorium, with Jesus inside, the Jews outside, and Pilate as go-between. With dramatic irony the characters other than Jesus are made to speak better than they know, as when Pilate, ruler and judge, in two dramatic presentations of Jesus to those outside testifies that it is he who is 'the Man' (i.e., the Son of man, and hence judge, 19.5) and 'the King' (19.14); or when the Jews in demanding the Roman punishment of crucifixion unwittingly bring about the fulfilment of Jesus' own prophecy that he would die by being 'lifted up' (18.32; cf. 12.33) – cf. also 11.49 ff., where Caiaphas without knowing it utters prophetic words which to the believer describe the nature of Jesus' death. The Jewish aspect of the story has almost disappeared, being reduced to the perfunctory statement that the high priest interrogated Jesus about his disciples and his teaching (18.19). This is because in this Gospel the Jewish people has already passed judgment of death by the end of the public ministry (11.45–53). The whole weight falls on the Roman aspect. The Romans, a whole cohort of them, are introduced at the beginning to make the arrest, and the 'trial' takes the form of interviews between Pilate and Jesus on the nature of authority and kingship. Jesus is mocked in charade as a dummy king, and Pilate bears further witness by having the title over the cross written in three languages and by refusing to alter the wording. The choice is not, as in the Synoptics, between two individuals, Jesus and Barabbas, but a choice belonging to the evangelist's own time of Christ or Caesar, the one the king in the heavenly kingdom of truth and the other the representative of a this-worldly salvation. Jesus is condemned at the moment when the Jews turn their backs on

Israel's vocation to testify that it is 'the Most High who rules in the kingdoms of men' and commit spiritual suicide with the cry 'We have no king but Caesar' (19.15). Jesus is represented as being in control throughout. From the cross he makes disposition for his family (19.25–27), brings about the fulfilment of Scripture (19.28), and announces the completion of his work (19.30), and from his completed death there flows symbolically the two sacraments (19.34).

After the presentation of the death of Jesus as itself his 'exaltation' and 'glorification', the resurrection comes as something of a surprise in this Gospel. The appearances of the risen Lord in ch. 20, like those in Luke, are confined to Jerusalem, but are distinctive and highly theological. In the first appearance Mary knows the Lord when, as the Good Shepherd, he calls her by name (20.16; cf. 10.3), and the message to be conveyed is that the resurrection is a stage not, as in Mark, on the way to Galilee, but on the way to the Father. In the second appearance in Jerusalem Jesus inaugurates the second creation by breathing on the disciples as God had breathed on Adam, and gives them the Spirit and power over sin for their universal mission. In the third appearance Thomas in face of the reality of the risen Lord utters the highest confession of faith, comparable with the opening words of the prologue, as the basis of the faith of future believers. What is probably an addition by a later hand (ch. 21) reflects the Galilean tradition of the resurrection in Mark and Matthew. Disciples whose work has been fruitless until the Lord appears make a perfect catch of fish under his direction – clearly a symbol of the Apostolic mission to the world – and after a threefold interrogation corresponding to his threefold denial Peter is charged with

the care of Christ's flock. A correction is made about 'the beloved disciple', a figure who makes his appearance in the Gospel at the passion narrative as companion and to some extent rival of Peter.

## The background of the Gospel

What factors of religious thought and environment have contributed to the construction of the Gospel ? This is seldom an easy question to answer about any writing of the ancient world, since the surviving documentation from which to reconstruct that world is so limited. It is even less easy in the case of this Gospel, as the evangelist seems to be able to move easily in more than one realm of thought without being completely captured by any. Thus he is clearly at home in Judaism, though, so far as we can check it, this would appear to be the somewhat later Judaism of the Rabbis after AD 70, and so his book has been called 'the most Jewish book in the New Testament except Revelation'. On the other hand, some of his language is characteristic of the religious world of Hellenism, and his book has been called 'The Gospel of the Hellenists'. Moreover, except in the highly individual case of the Jewish philosopher Philo, we are insufficiently informed as to the extent to which, and the manner in which, these two types of religious thought, the Jewish and the Hellenistic, had already intermingled with each other before the evangelist's own time. There is further the question of his relation to the Christian tradition before him and contemporary with him. Was he a relatively isolated figure, and his type of Christianity a relatively isolated type ?

### 1. Synoptic Gospels

Whether he wrote in knowledge of any of the

Synoptic Gospels is still debated. The common view has been that he certainly knew Mark and probably knew Luke. This view is supported by C.K. Barrett in his commentary on the ground of similarities not only of wording but of the order in which some groupings of events are narrated, and differences are accounted for by John's theological motives. On the other hand P. Gardner-Smith (*St John and the Synoptic Gospels*) concluded that John was ignorant of the Synoptic Gospels; the similarities, which are not sufficient to offset the great dissimilarities, are to be put down to the stereotyping effect of oral tradition. C.H. Dodd (*Historical Tradition in the Fourth Gospel*) has argued convincingly that behind this Gospel lies an historical tradition, including a passion narrative, which is independent of the Synoptists and which stems from southern Palestine, though this applies to only part of the material and hardly affects the discourses. It is noteworthy that in some instances where scholars are undecided on this matter they nevertheless frequently find themselves expounding a passage in John as though it did in fact lie on the background of something in the Synoptic Gospels, and especially in Mark (e.g., E. G. Hoskyns, *The Fourth Gospel*; J. Marsh, *St John*, Pelican Gospel Commentaries).

### 2. Judaism

The attitude to Judaism is ambivalent. On the one hand the Gospel is thoroughly Jewish in milieu and content. It is set within the scene of the Jewish festivals; it argues with reference to the main Jewish figures and types, Abraham, Moses, the prophets, the manna, the serpent in the wilderness; it treats of central Jewish matters, the temple, the law of Moses, the fathers, circumcision, purification, expectations of the Messiah and of the prophet. The author appears to be familiar with Rabbinic interpretations of Scripture, and with Rabbinic doctrines, formulae and legal procedure. On the other hand it is thoroughly anti-Jewish, and looks upon Judaism from a detached position as an episode in the past. 'The Jews' are constantly referred to as a single hostile people over against Jesus and his disciples, and the law of Moses can be referred to in a distant way as 'your law' (8.17). The Old Testament is quoted rarely and somewhat loosely. The Jewish doctrine of messiahship is mentioned only to be set aside, and the evangelist's 'doctrine of the Person of Christ is mainly worked out under other categories which are not those of Rabbinic Judaism' (C. H. Dodd). The manna in the desert serves to point to a pre-existent 'true' bread (6.32), which is not a Jewish conception. There are striking parallels between this Gospel and the heterodox Judaism of the Qumran scrolls. These are not sufficient to establish that 'John' was acquainted with the Qumran community or influenced directly by it, but such expressions as 'the children of light' and 'the children of darkness' found in the Qumran writings illustrate from Jewish sources a dualistic type of thinking found in this Gospel which has previously been put down to Hellenistic influences. The Qumran documents may also throw light on the sectarian character of the piety of this Gospel, in which the disciples are separated from the world, and are to be concerned with a love which is limited to the inner circle of the brethren.

### 3. Philo

Philo was a Jewish philosopher of Alexandria contemporary with the beginnings of Christianity (*c*.20 BC–AD 45), and he wrote a great deal.

His aim was to commend Judaism and the Old Testament to Gentiles, and in doing so he made use of popular Hellenistic (i.e., Platonist and Stoic) philosophy, and expounded the Old Testament in a symbolic and allegorical fashion. It is not suggested that 'John' had read any of the voluminous writings of Philo, but that the mixture of Jewish and Hellenistic thought in Philo may illustrate how certain conceptions and expressions could come to be used in this Gospel. Thus Philo refers frequently to 'the Logos', and does so in a bewildering variety of ways, as the model of the medium of the creation of the world, as the sum of the heavenly world, as the means of communication between God and men, etc. He still speaks, however, in a more Jewish manner of 'the Logos of God' or 'the divine Logos', whereas the evangelist refers to 'the Logos' simply without further definition. In Philo, as in this Gospel, 'light' plays a great part as a description of the divine, and so does the knowledge of God as man's true end and his eternal life. The adjective 'true' in the sense of 'heavenly' or 'divine', which is used in this Gospel of Jesus as the true bread and the true vine, is characteristic of Philo.

### 4. *Hellenistic religion*

Philo is himself a pointer to a wider hinterland of Hellenistic religious thought with which the evangelist could have had some contact. There is, for example, the Hermetic literature. This consists of a number of tracts dating from the second to the fourth century AD, which in places may contain teaching from the first century. This teaching takes the form of a message to be preached to mankind; it is couched in a kind of philosophical mysticism, in which salvation from the earthly element in man and the realization of the heavenly element in him are brought to the individual through his knowledge of God as light and life, and sometimes this knowledge is mediated by a heavenly or essential man sent by God to earth. Some have maintained that the Gospel of John is the least institutional and sacramental of the New Testament writings and the most concerned with the faith and knowledge of the individual.

Then there is *Gnosticism*. In its second century form it also exhibits in various shapes a scheme of salvation through knowledge. This is generally more cosmological and more pessimistically dualistic. The upper world of light and spirit is set over against a fallen world of matter and darkness. Men perish in this world because the light particles of mankind have been lost in the darkness until the redeemer gathers them together in a redeemed mankind which is his body. Did this second-century Gnosticism rest upon an earlier form of the same kind of belief in the first century with which the evangelist could have been in touch? Could this have been the source of this Gospel's dualism, where expressions like 'the above' and 'the below' (8.23) and 'the ruler of this world' (12.31; 14.30; 16.11) go beyond the ethical and eschatological dualism of Qumran? Does it throw light on the fresh use of the Jewish and Synoptic title 'the Son of man' to denote a pre-existent heavenly being who makes the double journey from heaven to earth and back? The evangelist would, however, have repudiated the Gnostic idea that matter was evil in itself.

### Purpose and thought

Along with Luke, but in contrast to Mark and

Matthew, John states the nature and purpose of his book (20.31). It is summarized as a narrative of selected signs, and it has been written in order that its readers, who are here addressed, might believe that Jesus is the Christ, the Son of God, and that in so believing they might have life in his name (through him). This could mean that the book was intended for publication and was written for the conversion of unbelievers. C. H. Dodd holds that it was written for non-Christians. On the other hand the recipients of I John, who were undoubtedly already Christians, are addressed in the same way (I John 3.23; 5.1–5, 12 f.). A notable feature of the presentation of the ministry of Jesus in this Gospel is that the hard saying about the necessity of eating the flesh and drinking the blood of the Son of man brings about an acute crisis, and from that moment a great many cease to be disciples of Jesus (6.52–71). This may echo the situation reflected in I John where there has been a defection from the community, and many false prophets have gone out into the world because they denied that Jesus was the Christ and that he had come in the flesh (I John 2.19–22; 4.1–6). The Gospel may thus have been written to strengthen Christians who were faced with such a disturbing crisis of faith.

The statement in 20.31 does indeed summarize a good deal of the contents of the book, though not all. Although the author uses the thoroughly Christian expression 'Jesus Christ' (1.17; 17.3), he remains near enough to the original tradition to use 'the Christ' in its proper sense of the Jewish Messiah, and debate over messiahship in general and over the messiahship of Jesus runs through the Gospel (1.20, 25; 3.28; 4.25, 29; 7.26, 42; 9.22; 12.34). It is still important to confess that Jesus is the Christ

(20.31; I John 2.22; 5.1), and in the Gospel this truth is revealed to the believer but concealed from the unbeliever. Nevertheless messiahship only touches the fringe of who Jesus is, and the deeper meaning of his work and person is indicated by other descriptions, and especially by 'the Son of God', 'the Son', 'the only-begotten' (i.e., unique), with their correlatives 'the Father' and 'my Father'. These terms provide the main thread of the Gospel, and the works and words of Jesus and his passion and resurrection are represented as the result of, and the unfolding of, an intimate relationship between the Father and the Son. While the term 'Son of God' has roots in the Old Testament as a description of Israel and of the king, and from there could have become a messianic term, it undoubtedly in this Gospel carries the Hellenistic sense of a supernatural being. As the Son of the Father and the Father's intimate Jesus is a pre-existent divine being whose day Abraham rejoiced to see (8.30–59), and who knows the divine secrets. He shares the divine glory (i.e., nature) and love from before creation (17.5, 24). He and the Father are a unity of purpose and action (10.30). He participates in the divine activities of conferring life and pronouncing judgment (5.17–29); belief in him is conjoined with belief in God (14.1); to have seen him is to have seen the Father (14.24). The opposition of the Jews in this Gospel arises from his claim to a unique sonship (5.18; 19.7). But while the term 'Son' in relation to the Father expresses the ego, even the egoism of Jesus, it also and at the same time underlines the contrary and complementary truth that Jesus is totally dependent on the Father, who is greater than he (14.28). The existence of Jesus is not a self-originated existence but derives from 'the Father who sent me' (a frequent term for God in this Gospel). He knows whence he comes and whither he is going (8.14). So also his words and actions do not originate in himself but proceed out of his knowledge of the Father (5.30–43; 6.37–40; 8.14–19, 26–29, 38–51; 10.17–38; 12.48–50; 14.10–24; 15.10–15). Hence the Jewish charge that he made himself 'independent of God' (this is the probable meaning of the words in 5.18) is the opposite of the truth. These complementary truths of the uniqueness of Jesus as the Son on the one hand and of his total dependence on the Father on the other hand are held in tension throughout the Gospel up to and including the prayer in ch. 17. Moreover, the passion and resurrection which follow are at one and the same time the result of the commandment and action of the Father and of the obedient will and action of the Son (10.17 f.; 14.30 f.; 17.4 f.).

The relation of Jesus to the world of men is expressed pre-eminently in the remarkable 'I am' sayings, which are without parallel in the Synoptics (6.35, 41, 48, 51, the heavenly, living bread; 8.12, the light of the world; 10.7, 9, 11, 14, the door of the sheep and the good shepherd; 11.25, the resurrection; 14.6, the way, the truth and the life; 15.1, the true vine). According to Rudolf Bultmann the majority of these are 'recognition' formulae, i.e., the 'I am' is to be taken as the predicate in the sentence, so that it should be rendered not by 'I am the true vine' but by the 'the true vine, it is I'. If this is so, it means that behind such a statement lies the idea that there are certain perfect or ideal entities or figures which men are awaiting, and Jesus is identified with these over against any false claimants. Behind this in turn is the thought that men as created beings have certain vital needs – food and sustenance, drink to

quench thirst, light to bring knowledge and to show the way to go, leadership along that way, community with one another and communion with the divine, and life itself. Only the 'true', living or divine form of these things is capable of satisfying human needs to the full, and that true form is Jesus, who both gives and is the true, living and heavenly bread, who gives the living water, who is the light of the world and the way to the Father, the good shepherd who leads and provides for his own, who is the true vine in whom believers abide and bear fruit, and who, as the resurrection itself, is the source of eternal life. In the prologue this is taken back to creation itself; the Word who, as Creator, is responsible for the world's existence, is the source of its true life, and this life throws light on all human life for good or ill.

Thus, whether in relation to God who is the Father or in relation to the world, Jesus is the unique and only revealer, and what he reveals and communicates in this Gospel is chiefly and almost exclusively himself and what he is. The function of everyone and everything else is to point to or bear witness to Jesus (an important theme; 1.7–3.33, John the Baptist; 4.39, the Samaritan woman; 5.39, the Old Testament; 10.25, the miracles; 15.26, the Paraclete; 19.35; 21.24, the beloved disciple). It follows that despite the evangelist's emphasis on the 'flesh' or humanity of Jesus (1.14; 6.51–63), no doubt in opposition to the spiritualizers or 'docetists' who were unable to accept that the divine and the material could ever be brought together (cf. I John 2.18–27; 4.1–6), he hardly escapes from some form of docetism himself. For the Johannine Christ is a heavenly man on earth; all his actions are highly symbolical; his discourses were never spoken in their present form; his feet barely touch the earth.

The most positive and inclusive term to describe what Jesus brings to men, according to this Gospel, is 'life' or 'eternal life'. In Judaism and the Synoptics, where it is to some extent a synonym for the kingdom of God, eternal life refers to what still lies in the future at the end of the ages; the phrase means 'the life of the age which is to come'. It is characteristic of the thought of this Gospel that it refers to what has become present here and now through the presence among men, first in the flesh and then through the Spirit, of the Son. It is almost a synonym for God. In I John 5.20 the true God, Jesus the Son and eternal life are conjoined. In the Gospel (17.3) a definition is given of eternal life as the knowledge of the one true God and of Jesus Christ as sent by him. It is not to be found in the knowledge of the Old Testament but only in Jesus to whom the Old Testament points (5.39); it is given now to him who hears (i.e., obeys) Jesus' word, becomes a believer, and therefore passes beyond the future judgment of the world (5.24 ff.; 6.47; cf. I John 5.11 ff.). This life is in the end life from the dead, and it is present through Jesus since he is himself already that which was believed to belong to the end of the world, namely the resurrection (11.25). This presence is made permanent by the Spirit. Here again the future is brought into the present. The 'second coming' or *parousia* of Christ is in this Gospel his return to his disciples to dwell within them by the Spirit. In four distinctive passages (14.15–17, 25 f.; 15.26; 16.7–15) the Spirit is called by a title, the Paraclete, which is unique in the New Testament (elsewhere only I John 2.1), and is difficult to translate. It is presumably meant to indicate the functions of the Spirit, which are described as glorifying and bearing witness to Jesus by teaching and bringing his words to mind, and so leading disciples into all truth, present and future, and as reproducing for them Jesus' own exposure of the sin and falsehood of the world. As the Son does not act independently of the Father, so the Spirit does not have a mission to men independent of that of the Son.

The passion of Christ is set in the context of his return to the Father after a completed work which is to be made available to men. It is hinted at several times in the Gospel as his (appointed) 'hour', and as soon as it begins the notes of time change, and the future 'not yet' gives place to 'now' (12.31; 13.31; 17.5). Jesus goes to his death in full knowledge of it (13.1 ff.), and is represented throughout as a royal figure who is in command of what is happening – there is no agony of doubt in Gethsemane in this Gospel, and the utterances from the cross are of fulfilment and triumph. On the negative side of 'salvation from', the death of Jesus is presented as that of the Passover Lamb, which was the memorial of Israel's deliverance from Egypt (19.14, 36). On the positive side, by a play on the double sense of the verb 'to lift up', the vertical hoisting up of Jesus by crucifixion is interpreted as being his exaltation to God and his glorification, i.e., his return to, and disclosing of, the being of God (18.32, referring back to 12.32 f.; cf. 3.14; 8.28; 12.23; 13.31, etc). It is this because Jesus lays down his own life as an act of his will (10.17), and this is the supreme act of love for his friends (15.13). But behind the love of the Son is the love of the Father; it is love which governs the relationship between them (3.35; 14.31; 15.9, 17, 24 ff.). It is from love of the world that the Son descends into the world at the bidding of the Father (3.16). The deepest point of this descent in obedience to the Father is his death, which is therefore the point where the love of God is most clearly shown. Into this love Jesus desires to draw his disciples through his exaltation, and for this reason the commandment to love, which dominates the discourse in chs. 13–16 and 17, is the only new ethical injunction in the teaching of Jesus in this Gospel, and even this is limited to love for fellow believers. This love is defined as keeping Jesus' commandments, but there is no indication of what these commandments are (13.34; 14.15–21; 15.10–14; 17.23–26).

Finally, the means by which the Christian truth is appropriated is faith and knowledge, or, since the nouns 'faith' and 'knowledge' are never used but only the verbs, personal acts of believing and knowing, which are sometimes synonymous (6.69). John's use of the 'to believe' is varied and profound. When the verb is used with the dative case of the thing or person it means to trust, as for example, Jesus, his words, the word of God or Scripture (2.22; 4.21; 5.38, 46 f.; 6.30; 8.45 f.; 10.37 f.). But involved in this is often believing in the sense of accepting as true some statement which Jesus makes about himself – that he has been sent by the Father, is in the Father, has come from the Father, is the Son of God (8.24; 11.27, 42; 13.19; 14.10; 16.27–30; 17.8, 21; 20.31). Here to believe is to perceive God acting towards men in the words and acts and person of Jesus. This in turn leads to 'believing upon . . .', a use which is the most characteristic of this Gospel and very rare outside it. It means a moral and personal allegiance to Jesus in virtue of what he is, and so to be involved in what he is. Behind all these uses and related to them is the absolute use of the verb, 'to believe'. This belief can be of an unsatisfactory kind (4.48), or transient (16.31 f.), but in itself it denotes a whole attitude in which the unseen is grasped hold of as lying behind the visible, and it leads to knowing God. It comes into being through Jesus, because he is the one who consistently acts and speaks with reference to the invisible Father. In adhering to him the believer adheres to the Father who is behind him, and so comes to know God. Not to believe is to refuse to do this, to insist on adhering to what is visible, and therefore to remain in darkness and to be shown up by the light.

C.F. EVANS

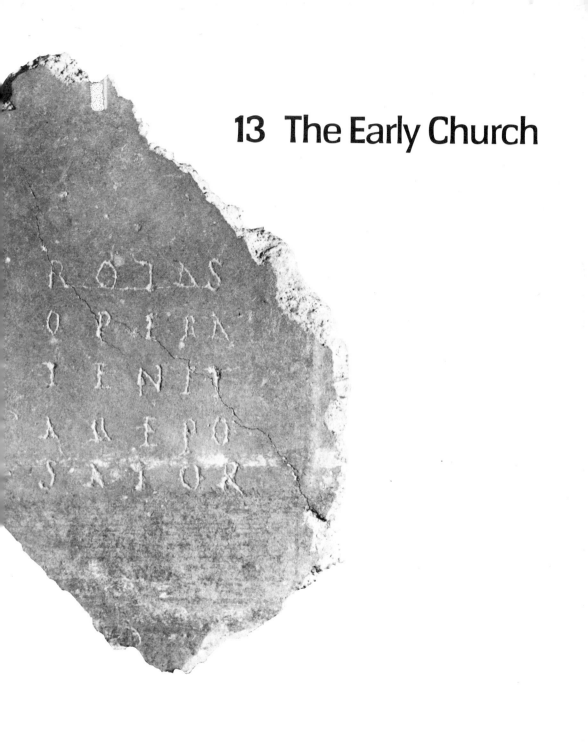

# 13  The Early Church

Much of the life and history of the church during the first century or so of its existence is veiled in obscurity. The archaeological evidence of buildings, inscriptions and papyri, the writings of Jews, Greeks and Romans, historians, poets and philosophers, which tell us so much about the world of the time, hardly spare a word for the Christians. There is no sinister reason for this: the simple fact is that the first Christians were not noteworthy in such a way. There were not very many of them, they formed essentially a working-class movement, their worship was private and unspectacular, and they had very good reasons for not wishing to draw too much public attention to themselves.

There are one or two references to Christianity in non-Christian literature and one or two archaeological discoveries which have some bearing on it. These will be mentioned where they are relevant. But the main source of our knowledge of the early church comes from Christian writings. There are quite a number of these, some of which received official sanction and some of which did not. On the one hand, we have the New Testament itself and other writings which date from about the same time, but which were not given the same status. The latter include: the *Didache* or *Teaching of the Twelve Apostles*, *I Clement* and *Barnabas* (all probably first-century works); seven letters of *Ignatius of Antioch* (written about 115); the *Shepherd of Hermas* (an allegorical work from early in the second century) and *II Clement* (a homily by a different author from *I Clement*). Works from rather after the New Testament period, like the writings of Justin Martyr in the East and Tertullian in the West, also offer some help. All these writers are included among the 'Fathers' of the church. On the other hand, there is now an increasing amount of material from the Christian underworld. Writings have survived, or have recently been discovered, from groups which were later regarded as heretical: discourses, poems, apocryphal 'Gospels' and 'Acts'. These writings, some of which are particularly important for our understanding of the development of gnosticism, seen alongside the more orthodox literature, indicate the great variety which Christian experience produced, almost from the very start.

## Names and dates

Most of the earliest Christian writing, especially the New Testament, raises two problems. First, it is difficult to know from what area a work comes and by whom it was written. Some New Testament documents were originally anonymous; it is more than likely that others were not written by the people whose names they bear; the Pastoral letters, the Johannine letters, the Petrine letters, James, Jude, all fall into this category. Reasons for this judgment will be given later, but since such 'pseudonymity', as it is called, is so frequent, it calls for a word of explanation here.

Under first-century conventions,

pseudonymity was by no means a dishonest practice. It might be intended as a way of gaining a wider public (no commercial factors were involved!); as a token of homage to a master or to continue his work for a new age; it might spring from a feeling that the words were more than just the author's. Whatever the reason, the result is that we often have to guess at the true origin and nature of a work simply from its contents, regardless of the name to which it is attached. The same is true of books to which early tradition assigned authors; authorship was a puzzle even to Christians of the second and third centuries, and many of them then seem to have been as much in the dark as we are.

A similar problem arises over the dating of books. None of the New Testament books, even the letters, bears a date of composition, and again we must work out the most likely background from the contents. It is easy to fix the first documents of the New Testament period, the letters of Paul, and the last, II Peter, but almost a century separates the two, and fitting the remaining books into this space of time is a complex business.

## Differences of opinion

Where there are so many imponderables and so many possibilities of different reconstructions, it is very difficult to reach anything like widespread agreement. Pictures of the New Testament church have to be impressionistic; so much must be left to the individual who attempts one that a certain amount of subjectivity is inevitable. Perhaps the most important thing to remember is how much we do not know; any picture should therefore be open-textured, leaving room for alteration by new

discoveries, without too much definition where definition is impossible. For with the kind of material that we have, the process of illustration is inevitably circular: the New Testament church has to be illustrated from the documents we possess and the documents have to be interpreted in the light of some picture of the New Testament church.

## The Acts of the Apostles

Of all the sources for the history of the early church, the Acts of the Apostles is the most important – and the most tantalizing. Did it all really happen like this? How much fact and how much fiction? A hard question, for Acts is the only document of its kind for just on three hundred years. The best way of finding an answer is to look carefully at what it has to say.

### 1. Date and authorship

Tradition has it that the Third Gospel and Acts (which beyond question belong together) were written by Luke the Physician, a companion of Paul (Col.4.14; II Tim.4.11). Recently, however, good reasons have been shown for questioning the tradition, which is not particularly strong. Fortunately, whichever side is taken in the debate, some conclusions are fairly clear. If Luke was the author of Acts, he was writing towards the end of his life, probably between 85 and 95, in different conditions from those in which the story he tells was played out. Furthermore, as will emerge, his knowledge of the earliest days of the Christian church was scanty: his account seems to be literary reconstruction based on a minimum of fact. His knowledge of the political and social conditions of the Roman world in the latter half of the first century AD may be excellent;

Palestine before AD 70 was a harder scene to bring faithfully to life.

### 2. *Luke as a writer*

Luke – as good a name as any for the author of Acts, whoever he was – was one of the great writers of the world, and Acts bears the stamp of his own particular brilliance. Unlike the Third Gospel, where fidelity to the sources is a dominant consideration, Acts is a work where the author has taken a free hand and has firmly shaped the material to his own design. The result is a unity in which the constituent ingredients are worked into shape with consummate skill. Luke must have used some sources, but where they leave off and his own work begins, or what relationship his own work bears to them, is extraordinarily difficult to see.

Legend has it that Luke was an artist: at the least, his word-pictures of the births of John the Baptist and Jesus, ascension and Pentecost, dominate the church's year. He is also a great story-teller, with a feeling for style and an ability to write so as not to weary his readers. For example, in the opening chapters of Acts, as at the beginning of the Third Gospel, his writing has a 'biblical', Old Testament flavour, in keeping with the solemnity of the first days of the church, so that at one time these chapters were even believed to be a translation of an Aramaic document; as he describes Paul's work in the Roman and Hellenistic world, his style changes in keeping with the subject-matter. Similarly, the beginning of the book is heavy with theological questions which have to be resolved; once these are settled the narrative becomes lighter, the pace quickens, and the story comes to its climax with a great shipwreck scene.

The many speeches with which the story is interspersed are constructed with similar care. Whatever their origin, in their present form they are designed for their place in the book and fit into an overall pattern. For example, the story of Israel and its failings, begun by Stephen in Jerusalem (7.2–53), is carried to its conclusion by Paul at Pisidian Antioch (13.16–43); where the same story has to be repeated, as in the case of Paul's conversion, which is narrated three times (9.1–19; 22.3–21; 26.2–23), details are varied so as not to produce tedium. Even the basic outline of the book is simple and straightforward, so as to avoid confusion in the reader's mind.

### 3. *Historicity*

Now actual events are seldom simple and tidy, and a first question which arises is: in achieving this brilliant piece of story-telling, how far did Luke succeed in representing accurately the events that happened and the motives that lay behind them? What do we have to allow for?

It is obvious that Acts is selective. It is not a history of all the apostles; on the contrary, some of its clarity is achieved by a concentration on two main figures, Peter in the first half and Paul in the second. If we simply follow Luke, all is well; but if we cross-question him historically, all sorts of awkward gaps appear. What happened to the 'twelve'? How did James come to be leader of the church? How did Christianity reach, e.g., Damascus and Rome, where the chief missionaries of Acts find it already established? Why do we hear nothing of Egypt, which must have been an early stronghold?

There are two possible reasons for selectivity of this kind: the author may omit some things either because he cannot tell us (he has inadequate information) or because he does not want to (for one reason or another his information does not fit in with the picture he has chosen to present). Selection inevitably means distortion – and both these motives seem to have been at work in Acts.

(a) If Luke was writing towards the end of the first century, his information on the earliest development of the church would be limited. There was some motive for the first Christians to preserve memories of Jesus' life; there was much less to do the same actively for their own history. They were more interested in their Lord and his coming than in their own affairs; the world was not expected to last long, and there was little reason for history writing. By the time Luke began his task, time had moved on. Jerusalem had fallen, and the first community there had been scattered. The days of Jewish Christianity were over; the future rested with the Gentile mission. Doubtless people at the important centres, Antioch, Caesarea, Ephesus, had traditions and memories, but little would have been written down. Luke would have had to travel about to glean information, and fitting the pieces of the jigsaw together can have been no easy task.

(b) Writing a history under these conditions, Luke would have had to make up his mind about the guiding principles by which to organize his material. His chief concerns emerge clearly from what he writes, and an understanding of them will help us to assess his historical reliability.

### 4. *The chief concerns of Acts*

For Luke, God is firmly in charge and has always indicated the way the church is to go. At each decisive step forward, events are taken out of the church's hands, whether by direct divine guidance or by the pressure of outward events, until Jesus' saying in Acts 1.8 has been achieved:

> You shall receive power when the Holy Spirit has come upon you; and you shall be my witnesses in Jerusalem and in all Judaea and Samaria and to the end of the earth.

Stage by stage the scene expands until it reaches its climax with the arrival of the gospel in Rome.

Acts opens with waiting, but then the Spirit is given at Pentecost to inaugurate the mission of the church (ch. 2). At first, activity is limited to Jerusalem (chs. 2–7), but as persecution drives the church further afield, so the Spirit indicates that its membership is to be extended, first to the fringe of Judaism (ch. 8), and then through Peter's dream and the conversion of Cornelius to the Gentile world (chs. 10; 11). This development, acknowledged by the Apostolic Council at Jerusalem (ch. 15), is the foundation on which Paul's mission is based: according to Luke, Paul works essentially untroubled by controversy within the church. He, too, is constantly guided by the Spirit, in dreams and visions, so that he is in no doubt about the way he is to go (e.g., 16.9; 18.9; 21.4; 27.23 f.).

In addition to this main theme, there are several important subsidiary themes:

(a) *The church*. Because the Spirit is in charge, the church is united and harmonious (2.44; 4.32; 9.31; 11.18; 15.28; 16.5). One main development carries its growth forward, and people outside this main development are unimportant. The church is never confused or at a loss what to do, and its teaching is clearly God-given.

(b) *Jerusalem* is the focal point of the church's unity. Jerusalem is the Holy City, the place of the resurrection, ascension and Pentecost, and the headquarters of the early church. In Acts, everything seems to revolve around Jerusalem, and the Jerusalem church exercises careful supervision of what goes on elsewhere. It is Jerusalem that sends down envoys to Samaria to approve the action of Philip (8.14), Jerusalem that sets the seal on the conversion of Cornelius (11.18), Jerusalem that is the scene of the Apostolic Council (15.4) and Jerusalem to which Paul has to return, to his peril, to give account of his missionary journeys (20.16; 21.11, 15 ff.).

(c) *Rome* is more than the destination of the gospel. It is the seat of government of the first-century world. An important theme of Acts is that Christianity is respectable and not subversive; it deserves to be left unmolested. Christianity is the proper development of Judaism; it is the true Israel, whereas the Jews have taken a fatally wrong turning. When Christians are involved in disturbances, Jewish mischief-makers are usually found to be the cause of the trouble (e.g., 14.2; 17.5; 18.12; 21.27), and to the credit of the Roman authorities, they usually see this (16.35; 18.17; 26.30 ff.). Even more, distinguished and senior Roman officials are attracted to Christianity and, indeed, are converted to it (10.48; 13.12; cf. 24.24).

### 5. A later picture ?

Now all this produces rather a different impression from that given by documents from an earlier period and from a consideration of a wider cross-section of the evidence for earliest Christianity. The Acts picture is too uniform, and does not leave scope for the development of the great diversity which we saw to be characteristic of the early church. It is too assured; the crises which the church undoubtedly had to surmount are minimized. There is no hint of concern about the delay in the Second Coming, no memory of the bitter controversy over circumcision and the Gentiles, no trace of the important debate about the place of the Jewish law in Christianity. In Acts, the central issue between Jews and Christians is rather the resurrection of Jesus.

The letters of Paul witness to a different atmosphere; there we find Paul fighting for his beliefs and by no means certain of winning (the state in which his letters are left suggests that for a while he fell into neglect). It is not just that there are discrepancies between the Acts account of Paul's career and Paul's own writing; the worlds of Paul and Acts are painted in different colours.

Yet when all this has been said, Acts is still vital evidence. It may offer less guidance to the early period than we should like, but if we put ourselves in Luke's place and try to understand him, we shall learn a great deal about the church of his day and the problems it faced, problems which needed for their solution above all the answer that God was still in charge and that the church was called to be one, and to press on confidently.

### The ascension

### Acts 1.1–11

Acts opens with a picture which is usually thought of as 'the ascension' of Jesus. It raises many problems, not just for our modern view of the world. But to ask directly on the basis of Acts what 'the ascension' was can lead to trouble, for only Luke, in the whole of the New Testament, presents it in this way. It is safer to approach indirectly, and above all to try to understand Luke against the background of the New Testament.

Other New Testament writers describe what happened to Jesus after his death and led to the birth of the church in two different ways, as resurrection and as exaltation. Resurrection and exaltation, and indeed the giving of the Spirit, are seen first as aspects of one complex event (cf., e.g., Rom.8.34; Phil.2.8 f.; Col.3.1; Heb.1.3; 10.13; Matt.28.16 ff.; John 20.22). Luke, however, splits the complex into three distinct parts and, following his practice of portraying divine action in the world in the form of vivid, objective pictures, has given each aspect (resurrection, ascension, Pentecost) a life of its own.

There is some doubt about the exact place of the ascension in Luke's sequence. According to the majority of ancient manuscripts, one ascension, on the day of the resurrection, is recorded at Luke 24.51, which clashes with the ascension after forty days in Acts 1.9. As the text between Luke 24.51 and Acts 1.6 has a number of peculiar features, it has been suggested that the passage between these two verses was supplied later, when the New Testament was given its present order and what was originally a single volume, Luke-Acts, was split. This removes some, but not all, the difficulties.

It would be wrong, however, to emphasize these difficulties too much or, indeed, to lay too much stress on the physical feature of 'ascension' here. After all, the description of the two ascensions together occupies less than two verses. It is the message that accompanies them that is more important. For Luke, the ascension is a means to an end. It marks his recognition that the period of the church is not like the period of the earthly ministry of Jesus and that Jesus must take on a new status if he is to give the Spirit to the church. Luke depicts this transition in a way which was meaningful to the audience of his day and which had the stamp of 'biblical' authority.

Thus the way to think of the ascension is to concentrate on Luke's use both of first-century imagery to express what he wanted to say (e.g., in the three-storeyed universe, heaven, the home of God, was 'above'): and of Old Testament models (see especially Gen.5.24; II Kings 2.1–12).

### The twelve

#### Acts 1.12–26

Luke fills the interval between the ascension and Pentecost with an account of the election of Matthias to fill the vacant place in the twelve left by Judas' death. The Spirit is not yet given, so the time-honoured method of choice by lot is used (1.26). As often in these early chapters, there is much about this episode which is vague and puzzling if it is studied in depth. We have the impression that Luke has discovered it in isolation and is not quite certain how it fits in or what all its details mean. He therefore uses it primarily as a vehicle for his own purposes, to tell us what an apostle is (vv. 21 f.: in his view, not in Paul's, cf. I Cor.9.1).

Matthias does not appear again, and the twelve as a group fade out of the subsequent narrative, except for a passing mention in 6.2. The list given in Acts differs from those in Matt.10.2 ff.; Mark 3.16 ff.; which suggests that some of the twelve were soon forgotten. We have only legendary details about the later career of most of them. It is probable that they were chosen not so much as potential leaders of a future church, but rather as partners in the coming kingdom proclaimed by Jesus, where they were to sit on twelve thrones judging the twelve tribes of Israel (Matt.19.28; Luke 22.30: see further below, on 'Church Order').

## Pentecost

### Acts 2

The story of the giving of the Holy Spirit is another of Luke's pictures and is evidently the end-product of a process which has mixed reminiscence, symbol and legend. Whatever happened, the basis can hardly have been a conjuring trick with languages; that goes against both our theological and our scientific understanding. We know from Paul that 'speaking with tongues' was a phenomenon in the early church (I Cor.12.10, 28, 30; 14.2 ff.), but it does not seem to have been like this. It probably died out later and Luke, while knowing of it, is somewhat confused about its nature (cf. Acts 10.46; 19.6).

It is possible that Luke intends the picture to suggest that Pentecost reversed the confusion of tongues at the tower of Babel (Gen.11); this is a hope for the last days held by some Jews ('Ye shall be the people of the Lord and have one tongue', *Testament of Judah*, 25.3). In the first century, too, Jews observed Pentecost above all as a commemoration of the law-giving on Sinai. Perhaps the wind and tongues of fire here derive from that.

If we may be doubtful about the accuracy of the picture, we may be sure that its symbolism reflects the experience of the first community. The church began with something which outstripped the expectations of the first followers of Jesus, dispelled their doubt, created a community of love, began to forge a unity which could eventually overcome barriers of race and endowed Christians with a strong sense of mission. This Jerusalem crowd is still Jewish, but there could hardly be a more vivid illustration of Paul's memorable words:

There can be neither Jew nor Greek, there can be neither bond nor free, there can be no male and female: for you are all one in Christ Jesus (Gal.3.28).

## The early church

### Acts 3–5

Luke's picture of the life of the Jerusalem church is made up of two main ingredients, supplemented with speeches: particular incidents and more general comments in summary form. All the signs point to this being a way of carrying forward the story with a minimum of available material rather than summarizing an embarrassingly large amount of information. Luke may well be right in much of the general drift of his interpretation, but there is probably also exaggeration and the kind of uncertainty we noticed in the story of the choice of Matthias.

Public preaching and mass conversion may well have had less prominence in the early mission than Acts suggests. Luke's figures in Acts 2.41 (5000) and 4.4 (3000) must be exaggerated; at the time the total population of Jerusalem was less than 30,000, and to suppose such a high proportion of Christians already goes against all the rest of our evidence. Other features of the summaries seem to derive from the incidents involving individuals. The 'many wonders and signs' (2.43) is illustrated only by Peter's healing of the lame man. The theme of communism seems to grow out of the episode of Joseph Barnabas (4.36), who sold a field and gave the proceeds to the church.

How far did the first members of the church have possessions to sell (2.44 f.; 4.32 ff.) ? Might Barnabas be remembered because he was a welcome exception to the rule ? Some explanation like this would help to elucidate the difficult story of Ananias and Sapphira, which, as it stands, is almost inexplicable (5.1–11). It makes slightly better sense if we suppose that their fault was not so much being dishonest in a situation where everyone else was relinquishing their property as seeking special status by a striking gift which was not completely honest. Some scholars believe that, as at Qumran, so in the early church there was a group of *perfecti*, an inner circle of whom special sacrifices were demanded. To these Ananias and Sapphira would have aspired to belong.

In addition, these chapters show the church surviving its first persecution; the theme of resurrection is brought out for the first time in the apostolic preaching to the peril of the preachers (this pattern occurs often later: 4.2, 33; cf. 17.18, 32; 23.6 ff.; 24.15, 21; 26.23).

### The seven

#### Acts 6

Most strain between Luke's picture and the material he uses is evident in the story of the appointment of the seven. On the surface, there is tension between Hellenists and Hebrews over the daily distribution (6.1). To obviate this, seven men are chosen as administrators, 'to serve tables', headed by Stephen (6.2 f.). But some questions are unanswered. Who are these Hellenists, and where do they come from ? Why should *Hellenist* widows be neglected ? If the seven are chosen to look after poor relief, why do they all come from the same group (they all have Greek names) ? Would we not expect half of each ? Furthermore, when the seven are chosen, Stephen, who holds the centre of the stage immediately afterwards, seems more a preacher than an administrator.

One interesting suggestion is that what we

have here is a trace of the first serious division in the church, between the (more conservative) original Jerusalem church and a (more liberal) Hellenistic wing, which was causing increased tension with the Jewish authorities over its views and practices. The seven would be the leaders of this wing of the church. Certainly, according to Acts, when persecution breaks out over Stephen's death, only part of the church is affected (8.1; 11.19); we next find the Hellenistic group as the basis of the church at Antioch (11.19; 13.1).

### Philip

#### Acts 8

Acts 8 is a kind of half-way house; a step forward in the Christian mission, but by no means a clear one. The activity connected with Philip takes place in a kind of twilight zone. First, he works among the Samaritans, who are not fully Jews, nor yet fully Gentiles either. Then he is directed to meet an Ethiopian official. Is this man a Gentile ? He could be, but he is reading the Old Testament; that might make him a proselyte. After all, he has come to Jerusalem to worship. Luke does not bother to inform us further, but he conveys that things are moving, short of the decisive step of the Gentile mission.

The way in which Jerusalem is involved in this further step is in keeping with Luke's approach: Peter and John are sent to ensure that Philip has done everything in due order. The story of Simon, like that of Ananias and Sapphira, is obscure. In later tradition Simon became an arch-enemy of the church and was associated with gnosticism

### The conversion of Cornelius

#### Acts 10; 11

The turning point in the Christian mission is the conversion of Cornelius, which is directly associated with Peter. Paul has been brought on the scene by the vivid account of his conversion (ch. 9), but the Gentile question is essentially settled without him. Does Luke mean to suggest that the Jerusalem church was directly responsible for the development of the Gentile mission without the requirement of circumcision? Paul's later struggle (particularly Gal.2.7 f.: 'I had been entrusted with the gospel to the uncircumcised, just as Peter had been entrusted with the gospel to the circumcised') points in a very different direction.

A second problem is that during the reign of Herod Agrippa, no Roman troops were stationed in his territory. How, then, does Cornelius come to be there? Luke's predilection for prominent Roman figures and his particular approach to the Gentile mission may have led him to develop his story along the lines of the incident of the Roman centurion in Luke 7.1–10.

In any case, the length at which the story is treated shows how important Luke felt this development to be, and suggests that the final version is very much his own work. The approval given to Peter by the church as a whole indicates that any further danger to the church will meet with a united response.

### Life in the early church

Following the narrative of Acts is one way of looking at the life of the early church; an alternative one is to ask specific questions of all the sources at our disposal and to see what answers they provide.

#### 1. The spread of the church

As we have seen, the picture of the expansion of Christianity in Acts is a simplified one, and in any case it only covers a short period. Other sources offer a wider view.

Jerusalem, at first the centre of the church, held its position only for a limited period. According to a report in the fourth-century historian Eusebius, Jewish Christians withdrew from Jerusalem in AD 66, before its fall, and settled at Pella, a city of the Decapolis. Jerusalem did not regain its importance until the fourth century, when it became a place of pilgrimage. Jewish Christianity lived on, but became increasingly a backwater, of little more than historical significance.

Although the New Testament is silent about it, Christianity must have spread south to Egypt at an early date. Our earliest scrap of New Testament text, a papyrus fragment of the Fourth Gospel dated about 100, comes from Egypt, and the strength of the church, particularly in Alexandria, in the second century points to an early mission.

To the north-east, the boundary of the Roman empire and a difficult language barrier proved an early obstacle, so that the main thrust of Christianity was northwards and westwards. The mission consolidated itself through Syria and Asia Minor, with sizeable churches in Antioch, Smyrna, Miletus, Ephesus and Sardis, and from there moved north to Thrace, northern Greece and Bulgaria. It had little influence in the south of Greece, where only Salonika and Corinth had noticeable Christian communities.

Rome, of course, was soon a powerful church, despite persecution, and rapidly became the most important Christian city. The church there seems to have had some rich and influential members. Settlements were also made early in southern Italy and Provence. Finally, while Paul himself did not succeed in his plan to visit Spain, the signs are that Christianity was not long in arriving there. If we allow, as again is probable, for early missions on the north African coast, during the second century Christian influence will in some way have circled the entire Mediterranean sea.

Evidence for precise dating of these movements is diffuse and sometimes difficult to assess: some of the archaeological remains are particularly ambiguous. For example, a cross-shaped sign has been found on a wall at Herculaneum, in southern Italy – but is the cross to be associated with Christians at this time, and is the sign any more than a mark of a shelf-bracket ? A famous word-square turns up twice at Pompeii, at Cirencester and at Dura Europos on the Euphrates:

R O T A S

O P E R A

T E N E T

A R E P O

S A T O R

As they stand, the words make insignificant sense, but rearranged they can be formed into A PATERNOSTER O (the first two words of the Latin Lord's Prayer, framed by Alpha and Omega), both vertically and horizontally, the two lines forming a cross over the central N. Pompeii was destroyed by an eruption of Vesuvius in AD 79; could there have been Christians there using Latin in this sophisticated way so early ? Might the square have another significance ?

With its rapid spread, and with many crucial questions still unsolved, Christianity must have adopted many different forms. Its kaleidoscopic panorama has been vividly illustrated by Professor Moule:

A traveller soon after the middle of the first century – say about AD 60 – going from Jerusalem to Ephesus, would encounter a wide range of doctrine and practice among communities who all, nevertheless, claimed some attachment to Jesus of Nazareth. Somewhere in Judaea he might have found the circle of James the Lord's brother still worshipping in a Christian synagogue consisting of practising Jews who also believed in Jesus as God's Messiah, but who may have gone only a very little way towards formulating a doctrine of Jesus as divine ... In Samaria, who knows that kind of Christian colony there might be ? One, possibly, which highly honoured the name of John the Baptist (whose mission had been vigorous in those parts and whose tomb, perhaps, they boasted), and which treasured traditions many of which are now embodied in the Fourth Gospel ... Cosmopolitan Antioch (even to judge from no more than the references to it in the New Testament, let alone its later history) would present a strange amalgam of oriental astrology, Jewish legalism and Christian beliefs. By journey's end he would be prepared for the seething diversity of Ephesus, where the Pauline churches were to be quickly invaded by antinomianism, Judaizing Christianity and influences of a Johannine type. If he then took ship from Melitus to Alexandria, he might there find himself confronted with yet other types of Christian colony, or, if he had already met them at Ephesus or elsewhere, they would be even more concentrated and more clearly defined. Finally, in Rome, all sorts and kinds

213

would jostle one another – Judaizing Christian synagogues, the most liberal of liberal gnosticizing sects, looking more like a mystery cult than the Israel of God, Petrine congregations, Pauline congregations and the rest.

Extend that picture across the Mediterranean northwards and westwards, over a century in time, and the true characteristics of early Christianity begin to emerge. It has to be extended, too, in terms of social class and literacy. Our knowledge of the church comes predominantly from written records, the thoughts and expressions of those who could put across their faith coherently, orthodox or not. But these would be only a small part of the Christian communities, which then, as now, would consist of many different kinds of people. In these circumstances, a first necessity was a gradual striving towards discipline and clarification of belief, particularly against the onset of the creeping menace of gnosticism, that amalgam of religions which misled so many early Christian congregations, taking them along paths that it would have been better for them not to tread.

## 2. *Gnosticism*

Christian thinkers borrowed many ideas, symbols and concepts from the intellectual world of their time to explain the significance of Jesus and what had been done through him. Their approach to worship and to practical questions was also influenced by their environment. But how much outside matter can Christianity absorb before it ceases to be Christianity and turns into something else? This was the problem of the first two centuries, and the answer had to be discovered almost by trial and error. For quite some time, satisfactory and unsatisfactory ideas existed side by side,

and it was only when their consequences were taken past a certain point that it was clear what would do and what would not do. Gnosticism is a convenient term for describing much of what eventually would not do.

Gnosticism took many forms, so a short definition of it is far from easy. Perhaps the easiest way to describe it is to begin at the end of the second century, when it had developed fully enough to reveal its inadequacies (this form of Gnosticism is usually given a capital G), and to trace its growth backwards from there.

For a long time, much of our knowledge of it was derived from attacks made by the church fathers, particularly Irenaeus of Lyons (*c*. 180). From these attacks we see that Gnostic writers differed from one another in their views, but held several points in common in their explanation of the world and their offer of redemption:

(a) The world is not the creation of the true God, but was made by a subordinate being (Demiurge), often identified with the God of the Old Testament. Matter is therefore less than good.

(b) Man is essentially akin to the divine; he is a spark of light imprisoned in a material body because of some kind of 'fall', and yearns for release.

(c) Salvation is brought by saving knowledge (*gnosis*) which gives Gnosticism its name. Man is to be awakened and freed – by a saviour who descends from the true realm of light. But his deliverance will bring chaos to the present world and is therefore strenuously opposed by its powers.

Here is a blend of Christianity with elements of many different philosophies, elaborated to such an incredible degree that some scholars wondered whether the polemic of the church fathers did their opponents justice. However, the discovery of an extensive Gnostic library at Nag Hammadi in Egypt, with more than a thousand pages of Coptic texts, has so far shown that while Irenaeus and others disagreed, they did not seriously distort.

At its best, Gnosticism had much that was attractive, but it was fatally flawed. It was too dualistic, separating the Redeemer God from the Creator God. Its negative attitude to matter (and to what actually happened in the past) diminished the significance of Jesus. Above all, it had disastrous ethical consequences. If matter was evil, then the only alternatives were extreme asceticism or extreme libertinism: paying too much or too little attention to the physical element.

These comments, of course, relate to the end of the second century, after the New Testament period. But this approach hardly sprang up overnight. A less developed form of gnosticism (without the capital G) may therefore have existed in the New Testament period and before. Whether gnosticism is pre-Christian is debated; but the problems which Christians faced in explaining the world also troubled Jews, and later Gnosticism certainly contained Jewish elements.

Because gnosticism is not developed in the New Testament period, it is not at all easy to see what was gnosticism and what was not. Paul was troubled with a problem of this kind (e.g., I Corinthians, Galatians, Colossians; see also Ephesians). He had a constant fight against what seem to be gnostic tendencies, some of them arising from misunderstandings of his own teaching. He lost the battle in the short term; by the end of the first century most of Asia Minor seems to have gone gnostic. The Johannine writings face a similar difficulty: I John and the Fourth Gospel both attack a form

of gnosticism, while themselves having a close affinity with it. In the Pastoral letters we see an appeal to tradition and sound doctrine in the face of 'gnostic' ideas. The approach typified in the Pastorals was continued; it is out of this kind of response to gnosticism that the later fixed form of church order and the canon of the New Testament came about.

### 3. Places of worship

It was only in the third century that churches began to purchase property for their own use, and 'churches' proper date from towards its end. Before that, worship took place in private houses (Acts 2.46; I Cor.16.19; Philemon 2). Because of the relative poverty of the first Christians, most of these houses would have been of the kind lived in by the lower and middle classes.

In Palestine and Asia Minor these were one-family buildings, anything up to four storeys high. The only large room, the dining room (upper room), was at the top of the building, and as the central element in Christian worship was a meal, meetings will have taken place there. The room usually contained a simple table and three couches (the *triclinium*); where there was a particularly large crowd, other seating had to be pressed into use (Acts 20.8 !).

In Rome, on the other hand, the tenement was the norm. Tenements had apartments horizontally across them, and would not necessarily have boasted a dining room. Churches still standing mark the sites of tenements which in the fourth century were remembered as having been house-churches.

A Christian house-church has conveniently been preserved at Dura Europos on the Euphrates. It is later than the New Testament period, dating from the early third century, but gives a good indication of what a house-church will have been like. A dividing wall was demolished to make a room large enough for a congregation of about fifty; earlier congregations may well have been smaller.

### 4. *Baptism and eucharist*

Baptism was the universal form of initiation into the church. By the time of the earliest literature that we have, the letters of Paul, it is firmly established, though there is much about its origin that is obscure. Christian baptism was doubtless connected with Jewish proselyte baptism and more specifically with the baptism of John, with which a strong tradition associates Jesus. There is a remark in the Fourth Gospel that Jesus himself did not baptize, and the command to baptize in the threefold name at the end of the Gospel of Matthew is agreed to have been read back on the lips of Jesus. Whether the twelve were baptized (presumably not) and under what precise circumstances baptism was introduced remains a mystery. Candidates were, of course, primarily adults. When infant baptism was introduced is again disputed, but it may well have been early. Much depends on the interpretation of the phrase 'the house of' (e.g., I Cor.1.16).

The house-church at Dura Europos has been modified by the addition of a baptistery, but this provision would have been rare in the early period. Baptism seems to have been administered, by immersion, wherever there was water; in the desert between Jerusalem and Gaza (Acts 8.38), in a river at Philippi (Acts 16.15); later accounts show it to have been performed in public baths, in fountains, and in the sea.

The earliest celebration of the eucharist probably followed the pattern of the Last Supper. First would come the blessing, breaking and distribution of bread; then followed a meal, probably of bread, salt and fish; at its conclusion wine was taken, blessed and distributed. The pattern closely resembles Jewish table-custom.

A development has taken place by the time Paul writes I Corinthians. In I Cor.11, the two acts of the sacrament seem to have found a place together at the end of the meal. Abuses of the celebration have begun: the rich stuff themselves, while the poor, who were customarily invited as an expression of charity, starve. This disruption of common life led to a complete separation of meal and sacrament by the time of Justin (*c.* 150). The meal continued for a while as a separate observance and was given a title of its own, *agape*, or love feast (see Jude 12). Eventually it fell into disuse. Later, more detailed descriptions of the eucharist show that portions of the consecrated elements were sent to those unable to be present.

The eucharist was probably celebrated weekly, on Sunday evening. In addition, from an early period Christians also seem to have had a morning gathering. In a famous letter to the emperor Trajan in 112, Pliny, governor of Bithynia, writes:

> They maintained that it was their habit on a fixed day to assemble before daylight and recite by turns a form of words to Christ as a god.

Jewish prayers were held at this hour, as a reinterpretation of and counter to sun-worship, and this pattern may have influenced Christians. Early in the second century the eucharist itself seems to have been transferred to the morning. The suspicion which fell on meetings of 'clubs' within the Roman empire made it impossible for Christians to assemble in the evening as they had done, and so the eucharist and this 'ministry of the word' were united.

How the two were related at an earlier time is not always clear. The analogy of synagogue worship suggests that there may long have been a service apart from the eucharist, to which, of course, only baptized members of the church were admitted. From the letters of Paul we hear of varied activities in worship. Paul knows that his letters will be read out there; worship will also have included prayers, sermons, singing, extempore prophesying and praying. By the time of Justin we hear of the reading of Scriptures, and of course one of the presuppositions of form criticism is the regular use of parts of the Gospels in worship.

### 5. *Sabbath and Sunday*

Pliny's letter also has an undoubted reference to the observance of Sunday, a Christian innovation. Jewish Christian churches in Palestine will have observed the sabbath, following custom here as in the practice of fasting, circumcision, food laws, temple tax and temple worship. But from the start there will have been some tension in the observance. Jesus was remembered to have broken the sabbath on a number of occasions; and the increasing Gentile influence on the church will have helped to lessen its significance.

At the same time, Sunday begins to take on a special meaning. Paul singles it out in I Cor. 16.1 ff. As he does not explain it in any way, it may well have been established for some time by then. The title 'the Lord's day' is first mentioned in Rev.1.10, and can be found in the writings of some of the Apostolic Fathers. The passages in which it occurs all come from Asia Minor and Syria, so the expression may have originated there.

'Lord's day' suggests a connection with the Lord's supper. Sunday was in fact primarily a day of worship. It seems to have a direct connection with the resurrection of Jesus; an added factor will have been the practical need of a regular day for meeting. Christians did not observe Sunday as a holiday. First, most of them will not have been able to afford the luxury of not working on that day. Secondly, to have called attention to themselves by not working then could well have invited persecution. Only in 321, when Constantine had officially sanctioned Christianity as a state religion, was Sunday rest introduced.

### 6. *Church order*

Jesus' preaching was concerned with the kingdom of God and the Son of man; he left no instructions and made no arrangements for a church to follow him. As we saw, the twelve were not chosen as potential leaders of a future church; the very few passages in the Gospels which point to a detailed church order are almost certainly the work of the early church and do not come from Jesus himself.

Organization and ministry in the church was therefore something that the first Christians had to work out as they went along, in the light of changing circumstances. Answers seem to have differed according to time and place; the one thing that is clear is that for the New Testament period there is no settled church order. The threefold hierarchical pattern of bishop, priest and deacon was adopted throughout the church at a later time.

As the twelve (or most of them) disappear from view, the increasing prominence of James, the brother of Jesus, comes as something of a surprise. Some scholars believe that the resurrection appearance reported in I Cor.15.7 was a special commissioning, others that the 'caliphate' principle of dynastic succession was at work. But there is insufficient evidence to tell.

Jesus' own following was more than twelve. Both the Gospels and Acts mention others, including Jesus' mother and brothers. But again, what happens to them is impossible to trace.

Although the phrase 'the twelve apostles' is so familiar, in the New Testament the *apostles* and the twelve are not always identical. The origin and meaning of the word apostle are hard to establish; 'apostle' means different things to different New Testament writers. For Luke, an apostle is one who 'accompanied us during all the time that the Lord Jesus went in and out among us' (Peter: Acts 1.21), thus excluding Paul. But for Paul himself, apostleship is something to be proud of; he is very anxious to defend his own (I Cor.9.1). For him, the apostles are those who have been commissioned by an appearance of the risen Lord, larger than himself and the twelve. Later, in the Pastoral letters, Paul is '*the* Apostle', the guardian of the faith. The one point of agreement is that apostleship is not something that can be passed on.

A famous passage, I Cor.12.28, mentions in succession apostles, prophets and teachers, and Eph.4.11 has a similar list. It is doubtful, however, whether these can be regarded as different classes of ministry. Rather, they are different activities, more than one of which might be practised by a single individual.

*Deacon* is usually a general term, describing any form of ministry or service ('deaconess', which occurs in Rom.16.1, is probably to be understood in this general way). In two passages, however, the deacon seems to be a particular minister, subordinate to the bishop (Phil.1.1; I Tim.3.8–13). If the two terms are used technically in Phil.1.1, this is the only evidence we have of such a formal ministry from the Pauline letters, so the terms may be general even there. In I Tim.3, the more formal use is certain.

*Elders* are not mentioned at all by Paul, but they are to be found as ministers throughout Acts, appointed by Paul and Barnabas 'in every church' (Acts 14.23; cf. 15.2 ff.; 16.4; 20.17; 21.18). Here Jewish practice is followed. Villages and towns had their groups of Jewish elders, seven in a village, twenty-three in a town and seventy in Jerusalem. When a place fell vacant, it was filled by the laying on of hands. This is the pattern to be found in Acts.

It may be that the word *bishop* occurs in a technical sense at Acts 20.28, but as in Phil.1.1 the word may be used generally ('overseer'). Bishop is a definite office in I Tim.3.1–7; Titus 1.7–9. The relationship between elders and bishops is a classic problem, as at times the two terms seem to be synonyms. The difficulty is to find an explanation accounting for the situation at the end of the second century when each particular area was in the charge of a single bishop ('monarchical episcopacy'). The most likely answer is that all bishops were elders, but not all elders were bishops.

We have even less evidence about the ministry at this time than about other important matters, and what is said in the Apostolic Fathers does little to help. Clearly the pattern varied from place to place, and development was by no means uniform.

### 7. Persecution

To become a Christian was to join a group

with a different attitude to society and government from that of others. In a world which had many different religions, membership of this group was probably not too dangerous as long as Christians were not forced into the limelight. Nevertheless, a flashpoint was never far away, particularly in relationships with Judaism and Rome.

Jesus had been a Jew, and many of his followers were Jews. But while they borrowed much from Judaism, Christians were reacting against it, too: the result was a love-hate relationship. On the one hand, Christians claimed to be the true Israel; on the other, they made light of the distinctive features of the chosen people – the law, circumcision, the temple, the sabbath.

Rome was the world power, and was tolerant provided that religion did not interfere with public order; it had even exempted the Jews from taking part in official religion. But Jesus had been crucified on at least a semi-political charge, and his followers took to meeting together and adopting what were regarded as anti-social attitudes. A word of complaint to the local governor from an offended neighbour, and even the most benevolent regime would have to take action.

(a) *Jewish persecution.* During the first century, relations between Jews and Christians seem to have got steadily worse. One reason will undoubtedly have been the great pressure under which Judaism suffered as a result of the first Jewish war and the fall of Jerusalem. Christians, as hybrid Jews, cannot have been looked on with much favour in that difficult period.

Before AD 70, as far as we can tell from the evidence, which is largely that of silence, the Jews showed remarkable restraint. Acts pictures them stirring up trouble for Paul wherever he goes, but it will be the active missionary, like Paul, who will have been most open to danger. In any case, we do not know how much Luke's mention of constant Jewish troublemaking is one of the stereotypes he uses to further his own purposes. At least, Paul escaped with his life. Only three martyrdoms are recorded at Jewish hands for this period: Stephen, James, the son of Zebedee, and James, the brother of Jesus. There would have had to be particular reasons for extreme measures.

By the end of the first century, on the other hand, there are signs of a clear break between church and synagogue. The remarks in the Fourth Gospel about 'putting out of the synagogue' (John 9.22; 12.42; 16.2) are puzzling in the light of other contemporary evidence, but it was certainly at this period that the *Birkat ham-minim*, the 'Heretic Benediction', was added to the other petitions of the Jewish Eighteen Benedictions. It read (in part):

May the Nazarenes (Christians) and the *minim* (heretics) perish as in a moment and be blotted out from the book of life.

The Gospel of Matthew, with its particularly harsh sayings against Judaism, seems to have been hammered out in this kind of situation.

(b) *Roman persecution.* Not only Jewish – Christian but also Roman – Christian relationships were affected by the position of Jews in the Roman Empire. This was inevitable, because of the close connection between the two and the Christian attempt to win the same favoured position as Judaism. It is interesting to note that the charge made against Christians by Tacitus, among others, is exactly that levelled by the populace against Jews: they are guilty of *odium generis humani*, hatred of the human race. They are anti-social, unpatriotic. And, of course, because of their attitude towards the state religion and their lack of outward ceremonial, Christians were soon regarded as 'atheists'.

To begin with, Christians did not even have a special name to distinguish them. For Paul, the phrase 'in Christ' does duty instead. The word 'Christian' appears only three times in the New Testament: in Acts 11.26 we are told that it was first used in Antioch. 'Christian' is a Latin form, not a Greek one, and a plausible suggestion is that it arose almost as a joke. Nero had a following of youths, so to speak a permanent fan club, who were known as the *Augustiniani*, followers of Augustus. He visited Antioch with this group in AD 60, and, Antioch being a sophisticated place, it may just have been that the followers of Christ were dubbed *Christiani*, to mock both them and Nero's claque. Certainly, to begin with the word is used far more by outsiders than by Christians themselves.

Be this as it may, the first Roman persecution of which we have any reliable details was launched by Nero after a fire had destroyed two entire quarters of Rome. Nero himself was thought to be responsible for the fire as a savage piece of slum clearance, but, as Tacitus records:

Nero fastened the guilt and inflicted the most exquisite tortures on a class hated for their abominations, called Christians by the populace. Christus, from whom the name had its origin, suffered the extreme penalty during the reign of Tiberius at the hands of one of our procurators, Pontius Pilate, and a deadly superstition, thus checked for the moment, again broke out, not only in Judea, the first source of the evil, but also in the City.

The savagery of Nero's measures, also reported by Tacitus, is well known.

This may not be the first time that Christians were in trouble in Rome. In his life of Claudius, the historian Suetonius writes:

He expelled the Jews from Rome for continuously rioting, *impulsore Chresto*.

The last two words are to be translated 'at the instigation of Chrestus'. Is this a reference to Christians ? It is impossible to be sure. 'Chrestus' is certainly a frequent spelling of Christ in the West, but it is also a common Greek personal name.

If Tacitus' account is fuller, there is still much that is obscure. In particular, it is hard to discover what subsequent consequences Nero's persecution had. It does not seem to have given rise to any general proscription of Christians (at any rate, we know nothing of such a move); apparently it was a temporary police measure carried out personally by Nero. Unfortunately, however, it did bring the church into prominence in an unwelcome way and put it on the wrong side in any troubles that might arise later.

There is little to illuminate more general Roman – Christian relations in the first century. Acts and the Pauline tradition are concerned to be on as good terms as possible with Rome; I Peter and Revelation show signs of persecution. Revelation, especially, is full of a bitter hatred.

Revelation is thought to have been written in the reign of Domitian and to bear witness to persecution then. But although the author is exiled on Patmos, he has not suffered a particularly harsh penalty. There is nothing to support the common view that Patmos was a penal colony; John's punishment was probably *relegatio in insulam*, a form of banishment which did not even involve the loss of property or rights. His one reference to past martyrdom, the mention of Antipas (2.13), gives no indication of how Antipas met his end. Recent persecution seems to have been limited and local; John's fears are for the future.

Other available evidence hardly adds up to the fourth-century picture of Domitian as the second great persecutor of the church. Admittedly, Domitian was despotic and megalomaniac, but his only specific action which may have been anti-Christian was his arrest of a prominent Roman, Flavius Clemens, his wife Flavia Domitilla, and Acilius Glabrio, consul for 95. The charge was 'atheism', in that they had slipped into Jewish customs'. The men were executed and Flavia Domitilla exiled. The charge may indicate Christianity, and Flavia Domitilla was regarded as a Christian in the fourth century, but early accounts do not actually use the word.

The last detailed piece of evidence from the New Testament period shows just how fluid and uncertain the situation was even in the early second century. Pliny's letter to Trajan was written because Pliny was uncertain how to deal with Christians:

In investigations of Christians I have never taken part; hence I do not know what is the crime usually punished or investigated, or what allowances are made . . . whether pardon is given to those who repent or whether a man who has once been a Christian gains nothing by having ceased to be such; whether punishment attaches to the mere name apart from secret crimes, or to the secret crimes connected with the name.

He goes on to describe his method of questioning and comments how, once it became known that Christians were being prosecuted, the charge became commoner. He proudly notes that his firm action has increased attendance in the 'almost deserted temples'.

Trajan approves Pliny's approach and replies:

Nothing can be laid down as a general ruling involving something like a set form of procedure. They are not to be sought out; but if they are accused and convicted, they must be punished – yet on this condition, that who so denies himself to be a Christian, and makes the fact plain by his action, that is, by worshipping our gods, shall obtain pardon on his repentance, however suspicious his past conduct may be.

He adds that too much notice is not to be taken of anonymous denunciations.

It emerges from all this that Christianity is for some reason an offence, but that the official policy is to 'let sleeping dogs lie'. If Christianity is brought to the notice of the authorities, they have to act, but they are not actively hostile.

In short, the main threat to Christianity in the New Testament period, before the later, classic persecutions, came from the possible hostility or malice of the people among whom they lived. Tertullian put the position in his usual witty way: 'If the Tiber rises too high or the Nile too low, the cry is: "The Christians to the lion".'

### 8. *The appeal of Christianity*

Why did anyone think of becoming a Christian at this time ? Much tends to be said about early Christianity without consideration of this vital question.

The Christian mission was far from being a saturation programme of mass evangelization, though vague memories of a few general statements in Acts sometimes produce such a misconception. Of course, at certain times and in certain places there was public preaching of a missionary kind, but it was probably less widespread than we imagine.

Usually, most Christian activity was semi-private, and this led to prejudice and misinformation. The Christian vocabulary gave rise to suspicions of incest, human sacrifice and other forms of immorality. The books written to contradict such ideas in the first two centuries or so probably had few readers outside the church; then as now, it seems unlikely that religious publishing reached many uninvolved laymen.

Causes for further inquiry might be the sight of (or news of) a martyrdom, curiosity, friendship. Above all, the care taken by Christians of the needy was a strong point. Tertullian's 'See how these Christians love one another !' is not ironical. On proof of his faith, any Christian was guaranteed up to three nights' hospitality with no questions asked; there was, too, an elaborate system of care for the poor. Again, with its claims of equality, Christianity obviously had an appeal to women, even if the full consequences (as with slavery) were not drawn for centuries.

Above all, Christianity answered the vague, helpless, speculative interest, so widespread in the first century, that had been fostered by the shallow talk of philosophers: the desire to feel at home in the world, resentment of Fate, the need for security. It was probably in these terms, rather than in presenting the character of the human figure of Jesus, that it made its mark, for outside the Gospels (and only to a limited degree even in them), little attention is paid to the personal traits of Jesus of Nazareth, except to affirm that he *was* human. In a fine study of conversion, A. D. Nock gives an attractive summary of the appeal of Christianity:

> The success of Christianity is the success of an institution which united the sacramental-

ism and the philosophy of the time. It satisfied the inquiring turn of mind, the desire for escape from fate, the desire for security in the hereafter; like Stoicism, it gave a way of life and made man at home in the universe, but unlike Stoicism it did this for the ignorant as well as for the lettered. It satisfied also social needs and it secured men against loneliness. Its way was not easy; it made uncompromising demands on those who would enter and would continue to live in the brotherhood, but to those who did not fail it offered an equally uncompromising assurance.

### Literature from the growing church

#### 1. *The pastoral letters:*
#### *I and II Timothy, Titus*

This is the name given to two letters to Timothy and one to Titus written in the name of Paul. Modern scholars, however, agree almost unanamously that Paul is not their author. Reasons are: the style and vocabulary of the letters differs widely from the authentic letters of Paul; it is very difficult to fit them into what we know of Paul's life; in several ways they indicate a different situation, later than that of Paul's day. The letters may possibly have genuine fragments of Paul's work in them, but even if they do, the fact has little bearing on their general content.

The three letters belong in a group, though their subject-matter differs slightly: *I Timothy* and *Titus* have a good deal about the ordering of the church; in *II Timothy* false teaching is vigorously attacked. They are not a very exciting part of the New Testament; it is often claimed that they are hortatory, monotonous and unmemorable. There is no argument, and the thought is all too often kept within the bounds of a paragraph. One scholar has remarked that they seem to be the work of someone with no real thoughts of his own. But this should not blind us to their positive significance.

The Pastorals come from a church which has to cope with the problems of living an everyday life in the world; they present a Christianity for the ordinary man when the first excitement has worn off. Part of the trouble is that there are far too many misleading excitements about (II Tim.2.14 ff.; 23; 3.6). Some form of early gnosticism lies in the background. Against this, the characteristic phrases of the Pastorals stress 'the faith' (I Tim.4.6), 'sound words' (I Tim.6.3), 'the truth' (II Tim.1.14), though this faith is presupposed rather than outlined. The practical virtues enjoined are those widely approved in the Hellenistic world: 'godliness with contentment' (I Tim.6.6); 'self-discipline' (Titus 2.6); 'good conscience' (I Tim.1.18). A more formal ministry is developing in the church (see above). All this suggests a date right at the beginning of the second century.

### 2. Hebrews

Unlike the Pastorals, the Letter to the Hebrews was not thought to be Pauline even in the early church; its place in the New Testament was disputed up to the fifth century. Pauline authorship is, in fact, impossible; style, language and argument are quite different.

Not only is Hebrews not by Paul; it is doubtful whether we should really call it a letter. Comparison with the letters of Paul shows that it lacks the characteristic opening greetings; the final ch. 13, which contains closing greetings, may not be part of the original. It is better understood as an unusually long sermon, with a coherent argument making a series of theological points followed by related exhortations.

This argument is: God has spoken through a Son, in a superior revelation to that to the prophets (chs. 1; 2). The Son is Jesus, who is superior to Moses and his own namesake Joshua (3.1–4.13: Jesus is Greek for Joshua, hence AV). Jesus is the great high priest who has passed through the heavens, but at the same time he is completely human (4.14–7.28). He is no shadow, but true, and offered his own blood; so Christians may have boldness to enter the holy place (chs. 8–10). The work concludes with a long account of the power of faith (ch. 11), its consequences and implications (chs. 12; 13).

Hebrews sometimes looks Platonic, but is not directly so; the pattern of Jewish sacrificial worship is the strongest influence, and the work of Jesus is described in these terms. His career is presented more in the form of exaltation than of resurrection.

A subsidiary theme is that of the people to whom Hebrews is addressed, and may even account for its name. They are the wandering people of God, on pilgrimage through the world with no lasting rest or city, but seeking one that is to come.

Place and date of authorship are uncertain. Alexandria has often been suggested; as the allusions to the temple are literary, it cannot be placed definitely before AD 70.

### 3. The catholic letters:
### I, II and III John, I and II Peter, James, Jude

'Catholic' means 'intended for the whole church', but this later title for the group comprising I–III John, I and II Peter, James and Jude is hardly apt. It does not really fit at least I Peter and II and III John, which in their present form have specific destinations; nor are all the group properly letters.

The *Johannine letters* come from the same circle as the Fourth Gospel; some slight differences may mean that their author is not exactly the same, but his approach is remarkably similar. Thus the section on the Fourth Gospel should be read in close conjunction with this paragraph.

*I John* points to a defection from the community: false prophets have gone out, denying that Jesus was the Christ and that he had come in the flesh (2.19). They say they have no sin (1.8) and claim to know God. Here, again, is a form of gnosticism. In countering these opponents John comes near to gnosticism himself. But the dominant feature of his letter is his stress on the claim of love within the community, in imitation of the act of God in Jesus Christ.

*II and III John* are slighter. Whether they are addressed to one community is unclear, but the situation is much the same. Again there is a form of gnosticism, coupled in III John with a power struggle.

If the Johannine letters belong together, the *Petrine* ones do not. They come from very different periods: II Peter is probably the latest book in the New Testament and has affinities, rather, with Jude.

It is doubtful whether *I Peter* was written by the apostle Peter. Its form alone raises suspicion. At present it is a letter, but it is obviously made of other elements. There is a clear break at 4.11. Before this the letter was written in general terms; because of the many references to baptism, this part has been thought to consist of an exhortation or exhortations connected with baptism: to take it as an actual liturgy, as

some scholars do, seems to be going too far. 4.12–5.11 is much more specific, and seems to be directed to Christians undergoing persecution. The thought often seems post-Pauline, and the instruction on the nature of Christian life and the use of the word 'Christian' indicates a period nearer to that of the Pastorals.

*II Peter* styles itself a second letter of Peter and therefore presumably knows of I Peter; but the two have nothing in common. Chapter 2 is a revised edition of the brief Letter of Jude. *Jude* is a brief exhortation contending for 'the faith once for all delivered to the saints' (v. 3) against false teachers who 'defile the flesh' (v. 8). It treats the apocryphal *I Enoch* (vv. 14 f.) and the *Assumption of Moses* (v. 9) as Scripture. These references are changed by II Peter, which has strict views and is very concerned about the interpretation of Scripture (1.20; 3.14; cf. II Tim.3.16 – an important anti-gnostic point). II Peter 1 is a farewell discourse by 'Peter' and ch. 3 is an explanation of the delay in the Second Coming. There are other features here which recall the Pastorals, especially the concentration on one authoritative figure.

*James* is more a homily or series of homilies, though it has the form of a letter. Its date and background are much disputed. At first sight it is so Jewish as to appear hardly Christian. But it can be seen to presuppose Paul's theology, misunderstood (2.14–26). Closer study shows other remarks more characteristic of Christianity than Judaism (1.18; 1.21; 1.25; 5.8, 12). The argumentative presentation of its thought recalls the Hellenistic form known as the diatribe. All this makes it doubtful whether the author was the brother of the Lord.

### 4. Revelation

This book, to many the most enigmatic in the

New Testament, was written by a certain John on Patmos, possibly during the time of Domitian (see above on 'Persecutions'). We know no more about its authorship. It consists of a brief preface (ch. 1), letters to seven churches (chs. 2; 3), the revelation or 'apocalypse' proper (4.1–22.5) and an epilogue (22.6–20). It is thus Christian apocalyptic literature.

Despite many resemblances to Jewish apocalyptic, it has distinct characteristics of its own. It is not attributed to a figure of the distant past (Enoch, Daniel, Ezra), nor does it survey past ages in the guise of prediction. It is prophetic in the best sense of the word and Jewish apocalyptic is transfigured by the influence of Christianity.

Imminent persecution by Rome is expected; Revelation is written to strengthen and advise those who face it. The message is given symbolically. Pages are filled with symbols and numbers: swords, eyes, trumpets, horns, seals, crowns, white robes; 7, 12, 1260 days, 42 months, 666: the number of the beast. As a result it has been searched down the centuries for hidden knowledge of the future. But there are no secrets of this kind in Revelation. It is poetry, a continuous meditation on the Old Testament, with reading and vision inextricably combined. It may seem strange, savage and barbarous to us, but understood in its own terms, as a picture of the situation of the Christian church in a hostile world in which the power of Christ was still at work, it has as much to tell us about what it was like to be a first-century Christian as many other books of the New Testament.

JOHN BOWDEN

# FOR FURTHER READING

## A The authority of the Bible

Barr, James, *The Bible in the Modern World*, SCM Press 1973
Dodd, C.H., *The Authority of the Bible*, Fontana Books 1960
Grollenberg, Lucas, *A Bible for our Time*, SCM Press 1979
Nineham, D.E., *The Use and Abuse of the Bible*, SPCK 1978

## B Some reference books

Black, M., and Rowley, H.H., eds, *Peake's Commentary on the Bible*, Nelson 1962
Brown, Raymond, Fitzmyer, Joseph and Murphy, Roland E., eds., *The Jerome Biblical Commentary*, Geoffrey Chapman 1969
Hastings, J., ed., *Dictionary of the Bible*, revised by F.C. Grant and H.H. Rowley, T & T. Clark 1963
*The Interpreter's Dictionary of the Bible*, four volumes, Abingdon Press 1962
Laymon, Charles M., ed., *The Interpreter's One-Volume Commentary on the Bible*, Collins 1973
May, H.G., *Oxford Bible Atlas*, Oxford University Press 1974
Richardson, Alan, ed., *A Theological Wordbook of the Bible*, SCM Press 1950

## C On the Bible as a whole

Grollenberg, Lucas, *Rediscovering the Bible*, SCM Press 1978
Hayes, John H., *Introduction to the Bible*, SPCK 1971

Sandmel, Samuel, *The Enjoyment of Scripture*, Oxford University Press 1972

## D The New Testament: general

Baker, T.G.A., *What is the New Testament ?*, SCM Press 1969
Dale, Alan T., *New World*, Oxford University Press 1966
Davies, W.D., *Invitation to the New Testament*, SPCK 1979
Filson, F.V., *A New Testament History*, SCM Press 1965
Grant, R.M., *A Historical Introduction to the New Testament*, Fontana Books 1971
Hooker, M.D., and Hickling, C.J.A., *What about the New Testament ?*, SCM Press 1975
Hunter, A.M., *Introducing the New Testament*, SCM Press 1972
Moule, C.F.D., *The Birth of the New Testament*, A.C. Black 1966
Neill, S., *The Interpretation of the New Testament 1861-1961*, Oxford University Press 1964

## E Background information

Barrett, C.K., ed., *The New Testament Background: Selected Documents*, SPCK 1957
Jeremias, J., *Jerusalem in the Time of Jesus*, SCM Press 1969
Josephus, *The Jewish War*, Penguin Books 1959
Lohse, Eduard, *The New Testament Environment*, SCM Press 1976
Reicke, Bo, *The New Testament Era*, A.& C. Black 1955

Sandmel, Samuel, *The First Century in Judaism and Christianity*, Oxford University Press 1969

Sandmel, Samuel, *Judaism and Christian Beginnings*, Oxford University Press 1978

Vermès, Geza, *The Dead Sea Scrolls*, Collins 1977

Vermès, Geza, *The Dead Sea Scrolls in English*, Penguin Books 1962

#### F **The Gospels**

Audrey, Sister, *Jesus Christ in the Synoptic Gospels*, SCM Press 1972

Barclay, William, *The Gospels and Acts*, two volumes, SCM Press 1976

Beare, F.W., *The Earliest Records of Jesus*, Blackwell 1962

Davies, W.D., *The Sermon on the Mount*, Cambridge University Press 1966

Dodd, C.H., *The Interpretation of the Fourth Gospel*, Cambridge University Press 1953

Evans, C.F., *The Beginning of the Gospel*, SPCK 1968

Jeremias, J., *New Testament Theology Vol.1: The Proclamation of Jesus*, SCM Press 1971

Manson, T.W., *The Sayings of Jesus*, SCM Press 1949

Nineham, D.E., *Saint Mark*, Penguin Books 1967

Reumann, John, *Jesus in the Church's Gospels*, SPCK 1970

#### G **Jesus**

Barrett, C.K., *Jesus and the Gospel Tradition*, SPCK 1967

Barclay, William, *Jesus as they Saw Him*, SCM Press 1962

Bornkamm, Günther, *Jesus of Nazareth*, Hodder & Stoughton 1960

Cupitt, Don and Armstrong, Peter, *Who was Jesus ?*, BBC 1977

Dodd, C.H., *The Founder of Christianity*, Fontana Books 1973

Fenton, J.C., *What was Jesus' Message ?*, SPCK 1971

Grollenberg, Lucas, *Jesus*, SCM Press 1978

Vermès, Geza, *Jesus the Jew*, Fontana Books 1976

#### H **The parables**

Dodd, C.H., *The Parables of the Kingdom*, Fontana Books 1961

Hunter, A.M., *Interpreting the Parables*, SCM Press 1960

Jeremias, J., *Rediscovering the Parables*, SCM Press 1966

#### I **Miracles**

Fuller, R.H., *Interpreting the Miracles*, SCM Press 1963

Keller, Ernst and Marie-Luise, *Miracles in Dispute*, SCM Press 1969

Richardson, Alan, *The Miracle Stories of the Gospels*, SCM Press 1960

#### J **Paul**

Barclay, William, *The Mind of St Paul*, Fontana Books 1965

Bornkamm, Günther, *Paul*, Hodder & Stoughton 1971

Bruce, F.F., *Paul: Apostle of the Free Spirit*, Paternoster 1977

Davies, W.D., *Paul and Rabbinic Judaism*, SPCK 1955

Grollenberg, Lucas, *Paul*, SCM Press 1978

Hunter, A.M., *The Gospel according to St Paul*, SCM Press 1966

Jewett, Robert, *Dating Paul's Life*, SCM Press 1979

Robinson, J.A.T., *Wrestling with Romans*, SCM Press 1979

Sanders, E.P., *Paul and Palestinian Judaism*, SCM Press 1977

Stendahl, K., *Paul among Jews and Gentiles*, SCM Press 1977

Whiteley, D.E.H., *The Theology of St Paul*, Blackwell 1974

## K  The early church

Dunn, James D.G., *Unity and Diversity in the New Testament*, SCM Press 1977

Haenchen, E., *The Acts of the Apostles*, Blackwell 1971

Hengel, Martin, *Acts and the History of Earliest Christianity*, SCM Press 1979

Theissen, Gerd, *The First Followers of Jesus*, SCM Press 1978

Wilken, Robert L., *The Myth of Christian Beginnings*, SCM Press 1979

# INDEX OF BIBLICAL REFERENCES

## OLD TESTAMENT

## APOCRYPHA

## NEW TESTAMENT